Arab Comic Strips

Arab

To D. P.-T., ^cA. P.-T. and the memory of S. P.-T.

Cntents

Acknowledgments

To write acknowledgments for a book such as this is to write years of one's life. We were both nourished on comics from early childhood. Pogo and Tintin have been haunting our imaginations (and our bedtime reading) for decades. A trip to the Middle East in 1975 turned into a voyage into the world of Arab comic strips. We walked the streets and *souk*s of Beirut, Cairo, and Damascus collecting them. It was then that Arabic versions of Mickey Mouse and other Arabic comic strip heroes began to share the bookshelves in our house that had been for so long inhabited by their Western relatives. Later trips to the Middle East only added to the collection. Iraq's turn came in 1983. The minister of culture, Latîf Jâsim, and ʿAbd al-Razzâq ʿAbd al-Wâhid, then director of the Dâr Thaqâfat al-Atfâl, were generous with both their time and their material.

In 1986, Jean-Claude Vatin, Alain Roussillon, and the C.E.D.E.J. at Cairo urged us to publish a monograph on French and Egyptian comics in their prestigious Dossiers series. This incited us to begin turning an intellectual hobby into a domain for scholarly activity. Subsequent invitations to present papers at C.E.D.E.J. conferences were so many opportunities to continue our work in this area.

In 1988, we took the plunge. Without the encouragement of friends and colleagues, then, this book would likely have remained a figment of our imagination. The Council for the International Exchange of Scholars generously provided us with a joint grant (supplemented by funds from the University of Texas University Research Institute) to travel the Middle East, North Africa, and France in search of comic strips. Gary Garrison deserves special thanks for his help and confidence on that front. Once in Cairo, Ann Radwan and her wonderful office staff greatly facilitated our research. The American Research Center in Egypt was, as always, a haven where one could run in and ingest some quick coffee or tea and exchange ideas with whomever happened to be there. We were fortunate in having long-time Egyptian friends and colleagues whose mere presence in Cairo was an inspiration: Shukrî ʿAyyâd, Jamâl al-Ghîtânî, Sherif Hetata, ʿIzz al-Dîn Ismâʿîl, Salâh Marʿî, Muhyî Mahmûd, Muhammad Mustajâb, Yûsuf al-Qaʿîd, Nawâl al-Saʿdâwî, Mayy Trad. In Tunisia, Robert Krill, Keith Peterson, and their staffs went beyond the call of duty, helping us with a wide variety of things, ranging from accommodations to research permits. Abdelwahab Bouhdiba, Muhammad Roz, and other members of the C.E.R.E.S. made us feel welcome. Jeanne Mrad, with her customary hospitality provided us with comfortable research facilities. Edward Thomas and his staff welcomed us to Morocco. In Paris, we had the good fortune to be associated with the Commission Franco-Américaine and its director, Geneviève Acker.

An astounding variety of governments (those of Egypt, France, Iraq, Morocco, Syria, Tunisia, the United Arab Emirates, and the United States), cooperated in aiding our research, though these states were often at odds (even tragically so) with one another during these years. We were also helped by political and religious organizations with widely differing viewpoints and agendas. Yet none ever sought to censor us or influence our point of view except through the competition of their generosity.

But it is the artists, cartoonists, and scenarists from all corners of the Arab world whose help has been most crucial. When we say that without them our book would not have been possible, we mean it. They have all been extraordinarily generous, showering us with their hospitality. They have provided us with copies of their work, sometimes otherwise inaccessible. (In one case, a relative was prevailed upon by the artist to release a childhood copy of an album!) They have provided us with their time, during which we could ask any questions that came to mind. They have provided us with intellectual and physical sustenance. And, most important, they have provided us with their friendship, for which we are truly honored and grateful.

Everywhere we traveled in our search for comic strips and children's magazines we were met with open arms. From the official religious organizations like the High Council for Islamic Affairs in Cairo through the government party headquarters in Syria and Tunisia and the Ministries of Culture of Syria and Iraq, to the cultural offices of the Palestinian Munazzama, editors of children's magazines transmitted their infectious enthusiasm and commitment to the education of Arab children. We might be ashamed to reveal how often they provided us with complete runs of their magazines. Kamâl al-ʿAskarî, Najâh al-ʿAttâr, Dr. Bahâ' al-Dîn, Dalâl Hâtim, Hannâ Mîna, ʿAbd al-Hamîd al-Qusantînî, Bilkhâmisa al-Shâdhilî, Farîd al-Shamlî, al-Tayyib al-Tirîkî, Yahyâ Yakhlif, Yâsîn Zuhdî: no matter what the city or the organism, all marshaled their office staff in an attempt to help us gather materials. We could not have worked our way through Dâr al-Hilâl without Yûsuf al-Qaʿîd. Al-Hâjj Marzûq Hilâl afforded us a close look at the workings of an Islamic children's magazine.

The time we spent traveling the Middle East, from Abu Dhabi to North Africa, was sheer pleasure. We were always overwhelmed with excitement, ours and that of the people we were writing about. Looking back, we feel that we were living in a magical time and space in which one door would open on to another and yet another, each leading us to rooms full of riches. What an unparalleled opportunity it was to have our long-time friend Georges Bahgory arrive in Cairo at approximately the same time we did! His contacts and his friends became ours. How numerous were the afternoons and evenings we spent with the prize-winning cartoonist and scenarist, Ahmad Hijâzî! Moments of pure delight during which Hijâzî, with his extraordinary generosity, shared with us his own friendships and years of experience as one of the Arab world's leading cartoonists. Only he knows how indebted we are to him.

Like a magician, Hijâzî opened for us doors that seemed at the time impenetrable. Thanks to Hijâzî, we were able to chase down ʿAlî Farzât, Shalabiyya Ibrâhîm, and Nadhîr Nabʿa in Damascus. There, these new friendships sealed our already existing affection for the Syrian capital. Thanks to Hijâzî, we were able to travel to Abu Dhabi and the wonderful kingdom of *Mâjid*. There, Ahmad ʿUmar took us under his wing and treated us like royalty. We became honored members of the *Mâjid* family and participated in all their activities, from printing and color mixing to illustration and writing.

How fortunate we have been, indeed, to have friends who were always there, ready to help us at the drop of a hat! In Morocco, Driss Ouaouicha shared his apartment and his numerous contacts. Muhammad Bennani introduced us to the world of Moroccan art and artists. Morocco would not be the same without the hospitality of Malika and Muhammad Dahbi, and the generosity of Zoubida Chahi. In Tunisia, Amel Ben Aba made her house ours and Ibrahim and Jane Muhawi took us into the fold and introduced us to Palestinian artists and writers. Al-Bâqî Hirmâsî, Thurayyâ al-Mutawallî and Muhammad al-Qinâwî, Kristina Nelson and Humphrey Davies: all opened their houses and their hearts on trips to Tunisia. In Cairo, Jean-Claude Vatin sustained us with years of friendship. When we arrived in Paris, loaded with books and overflowing with excitement, it was Philippe Cardinal, Jacqueline Cohen, Assia Djebar, Jean-François Fourcade, Roselyne Gaude, Burhân Ghalyûn, and Jérôme Lentin who welcomed us. Evelyne Accad and Paul Vieille made it possible for us to spend an absolutely idyllic time in a picture-perfect French village, Vern-sur-Seiche, outside Rennes. There, the generosity of Marc and Claudine Gontard permitted us to begin drafting chapters of the book. And, as always, Bahgory was there. He was as effective in Paris as he had been in Cairo in helping us attach faces to names and in sealing friendships, in particular with Kaci, Muhyî al-Dîn al-Labbâd, and Bahjat ʿUthmân. Wisâl Khâlid deserves special thanks. Without her, we would not have been able to benefit from Zakariyyâ Tâmir's knowledge of *Usâma*. The same can be said of Susan Slyomovics and Nadjib Berber, who helped put us in touch with Farid Boudjellal and Slim.

To say that we have also been fortunate in having friends with whom we could discuss the book as it was taking shape would be an understatement. It is difficult to remember how late into the night we stayed up discussing various issues with artists, writers, and critics on both sides of the Atlantic: Etel Adnan, Simone Fattal, Lee Fontanella, Helena de la Fontaine, Zulfikar Ghose, Susan Napier, Ron Napier, James Piscatori, Jaroslav Stetkevych, Suzanne Pinckney Stetkevych, Jay Wright. Their encouragement and faith have been invaluable.

The biggest sacrifice was that of all those friends who gave of themselves to read the typescript: Roger Allen, Michael Beard, John Esposito, Sherman Jackson, James Piscatori, Denise Spellberg, Jaroslav Stetkevych, Renate Wise. The combination of short notice and a long manuscript did not keep them from shunting their own work aside and giving us the benefit of their intellectual experience. Antonio Loprieno and Jan Johnson used their Egyptological expertise to help us chase down a migrating mummy.

In the last stages, it was Dean Morton Lowengrub's generosity (and that of the College of Arts and Sciences at Indiana University) that came to the rescue. The all-too-familiar madness that sets in as a book is nearing completion was made considerably easier by nothing less than two state-of-the-art notebook computers, running simultaneously for what seemed like twenty-four hours a day.

How much we would like to say that S. P.-T. was also there all along! But no. Her untimely death will not permit her to witness the birth of the book. The sadness over her loss serves to remind us daily of the fragility of life. This we now happily share with D. P.-T. and ʿA. P.-T. May they be able to witness more than this book!

Note on Translation, Transcription, Abbreviation,
Citation, and Illustrations

All translations in the text are our own unless otherwise indicated, and all references are to the Arabic or French originals.

Proper names common in English are left in their most usual form (e.g., Nasser). When individuals already have standard Romanizations of their names (e.g., in bilingual environments), these have been retained. Otherwise we have used a simplified transcription system in which the lengtheners on lower-case vowels are indicated with the French circumflex accent. The ʿayn and the *hamza* are represented by the conventional symbols. Specialists should be able to easily identify the Arabic words.

EI² refers to *The Encyclopaedia of Islam*, 2d ed. (Leiden: E. J. Brill, 1960–).

References to comic strips and albums discussed extensively are placed in brackets in the text. Full bibliographical information is given in the notes and sources.

Figures are numbered consecutively within each chapter, except for figures 3.2–3.5, 4.2–4.5, and 9.1, which appear in color following page 48.

Arab Comic Strips

1

Introduction: The World of Arab Comic Strips

Arab comic strips: to most in the West, the reality is so unsuspected that the phrase itself almost rings like an oxymoron. Yet Arab comic strips are a flourishing genre with an enormous readership and a political and ideological range extending from leftist and other secular modernist to Islamic religious perspectives.

All comics are political. The American artist Walt Kelly, who himself has been criticized for introducing political material into the funny page, tells an amusing story. In the 1950s an American illustrator was attacked by a member of the United States Congress. Why, the distinguished lawmaker wanted to know, had he drawn the three little pigs one black, one white, and one spotted? Worse still, why was the black one apparently the smartest?[1]

But what about "innocent" productions, strips that deal exclusively with children's concerns, apparently eschewing the adult world of politics? In a set of polemical yet devastating studies, Dorfman and Mattelart have argued the political, indeed the imperialist, implications of both Disney comics and other children's literature.[2] It is generally accepted today that media productions for children, whether traditional or contemporary in origin, play a vital normative role and that the values expressed in such works themselves have major political and ideological implications. This understanding of the cultural and ideological role of comic strips has already spawned a large critical literature, largely (though no longer exclusively) on the eastern side of the Atlantic.[3]

In sharp contrast, the considerable comic-strip production of the Arab world has remained almost virgin territory. Indeed, if one excepts a handful of specialized works in French, Arab comics have yet to receive major critical attention.[4] More general studies, such as Mohamed Aziza's wide-ranging and thoughtful *L'Image et l'Islam*, do not even mention these imaged narratives. This is all the more interesting considering that so influential a figure as Frantz Fanon, in *Peau noire masques blancs*, identified them over twenty years ago as prime agents of cultural imperialism and alienation.[5] Of course, the entire area of Middle Eastern mass-media and cultural studies is still quite young.[6]

Arab Strips in East–West Context

The situation of Arabic comic-strip production is distinctive in several ways. In the West, comic strips, a medium mixing pictures with written text, have a considerable prehistory, linked to longstanding iconographic modes of communication, of which church decoration ("the book of the illiterate") is but one example.

In the world of Islam, iconographic representation, while certainly not absent, played a far more modest role. Though the popular notion that Islam eschews the image is an exaggeration, in general in Arabo-Islamic civilization it was the word that was sacred and the image suspect. The more conservative religious experts even considered any visual representation, whether two- or three-dimensional, to be an improper aping of the divine power to create forms.[7] This is not to say that there were no elements in classical Islamic civilization that bore similarities to comic strips or could have served as a kind of foundation for them. One such element is the popular shadow play, performed with puppets and viewed through a two-dimensional screen. Shadow plays were generally comic and based on stock characters, of whom the Turkish Karagöz is by far the most famous, though Arabic examples existed as well.[8] Of course, these plays were designed to be performed, not read, but one could easily imagine them turned into comic strips with balloons for the speech of the characters. On a more exalted literary plane, medieval Arabs also produced heavily illustrated (and not merely illuminated) texts, such as those of the *Maqâmât* and *Kalîla wa-Dimna*, the Arabic version of the fables of Bidpai.[9] The highly narrative, even episodic, nature of these texts and the high density of illustrations make them almost imaged narratives.

The true comic strip is a narrative, consisting of several frames at least, in which verbal and visual elements combine, most commonly through the device of attaching speech balloons to the pictures of characters.[10] Some scholars like to distinguish between comic strips (like those in newspapers) and comic books. Though there are some formal differences between the two, notably the possibility of organization by whole pages in the latter case,[11] the distinction rests on the existence of these two genres as they have developed in the United States with often differing contents and tendencies. These genres of comic production are not well reproduced in Western Europe, still less in the Middle East. The majority of comics in the Arab world appear neither as newspaper strips nor in American-style comic books. Their most common loci are illustrated children's periodicals, a form that has been extremely important in the "comic" history of France, among other countries. And their tendencies are correspondingly different from those of American comic books. Hence, following the logic of continental European practice, we are using the term *comic strips* to refer to all examples of the medium, whatever their publication format.[12]

As such, comics have come to the Arab world from the West. But strips, like other cultural forms, do not come empty-handed. They bear alien images, values at once threatening and seductive. Western comic strips are part—indeed, for economic reasons one of the largest parts—of the invasion of Western mass media into the Arab world. Since the time of Frantz Fanon, leftist intellectuals have recognized the threat of cultural and personal alienation associated with the absorption, especially by children, of frequently ethnocentric Western cultural products. A recent sophisticated examination of Western-Islamic cultural relations, Akbar S. Ahmed's *Postmodernism and Islam* underlines the power of this cultural invasion by speaking of the "demon" media.[13] In the past two decades, increasing numbers of Arab intellectuals and artists have become concerned with this phenomenon. Mickey Mouse and Donald Duck are two of the most ubiquitous images in Arab countries today. The response of Arab artists and writers to this challenge has been to create their own mass culture in which comic strips (much cheaper to produce, for example, than animated cartoons) play a leading role.[14]

Tracing the first Arab comic strip is a bit like choosing the earliest example of any art form; it depends on where in the line of preceding forms one wishes to start. As Bertrand Millet has shown, cartoonlike visual narratives can be found from before the turn of the century. But the Arab comic strip has really only come into its own in the second half of this century. The biggest expansion has been since the late 1970s, after the oil boom pumped money into the economies of virtually all Arab countries. For a time, Arab comic-strip production looked as if it might be swamped by translation of materials imported from the West, principally from the United States and France. But the production is now largely indigenous and original. It forms part of an emerging regional mass culture whose forms may appear Western but whose content has long since ceased to be so.[15]

Compared with their Western equivalents and even given the smaller populations of the countries in question, the publication runs of Arab comic-strip periodicals seem modest. Probably the most successful, the United Arab Emirates' *Mâjid*, sells over 150,000 copies.[16] The Egyptian *Samîr* claims a circulation of eighty thousand.[17] Others sell considerably fewer copies. Yet these figures understate the impact of the periodicals in question. Comics, like other popular magazines, are often passed from one reader to another, and this process is especially important in poorer countries (most of those in the Arab world). But the recycling of Arab comics goes further. Most of the publishers of such illustrated children's periodicals publish reprints of their issues in annual bound volumes, sold at the same newsstands where the originals are sold. In a more artisanal way, "used" issues of the more popular Arab comic-strip magazines are also collected, irregularly and cheaply bound together, and sold at still other newsstands, in the large outdoor used-book markets, and in the bazaars. In this way the same strips are circulated downward from upper- and middle-class children to those of the lower-middle and sometimes even the lower classes.

Language

The term *Arab* in "Arab strips" refers to a national or ethnic group, the Arabs. *Arabic* refers to the language. But not all Arab strips are written in the Arabic tongue. For historical reasons, some of the most creative Arab strips are produced in French, in Algeria. But even writing in Arabic opens linguistic choices. In the West, comics are normally written in a fairly popular, often conversational, form of the standard national language. In Arabic, the formal standard form of the language, called *fushâ*, is considerably divorced from the spoken dialects. Thus the dialects are closest to the forms used in the West. But Arab dialects are not usually written; moreover, they are reasonably mutually incomprehensible to ordinary speakers, especially when the countries in question are geographically distant. To choose dialect, therefore, is to sacrifice a broader pan-Arab distribution for a potentially greater local popularity. Only one dialect is sufficiently well known in the region to have any pretensions to wider accessibility, and that is the dialect of Cairo, Egypt. Thus it is chiefly, though not exclusively, Egyptian magazines that have adopted this form. The overwhelming majority of other strips and many Egyptian ones as well are written in the formal language.

But even using *fushâ* does not settle the matter. Except for special texts such as the Qur'ân and poetry, Arabic is normally printed without short vowels. Some people in the region advocate the use of fully vocalized forms, especially as a pedagogical tool for beginning readers. Vocalizing the texts does teach the correct pronunciation; but by increasing the gap between the written and spoken varieties of the language (in the latter the short vowels often vary from dialect to dialect), it can make the printed text more scholastic and perhaps more difficult to comprehend. The majority of comic-strip texts are printed without short vowels but often in an otherwise simplified style. It is largely in the countries of the Arab West, the Maghrib, where Arabic is less well known than farther east, that fully vocalized Arabic is a common occurrence.[18] This usage reflects the more pedagogical role that Arabic-language comics are expected to play in these countries.

Politicization

Arab comic-strip production is especially political from several points of view. Comics, as a form of children's mass literature, have long been the subject of morally inspired censorship and regulation, whether it be the moral strictures of the American Comics Code or the French postwar ban on American superheroes.[19] In the political environment of the Arab world, where formal censorship is ubiquitous, concern about the political and ideological content of comics is all the greater.

Relations between Arab comic-strip magazines and their governments are varied. Many of the most successful are government publications, directly paid for and run by the ministries of culture or the official parties or youth groups. Such is the case, for example, with the Tunisian *ʿIrfân*, the Syrian *Usâma*, the Iraqi *al-Mizmâr*, and the Kuwaiti *al-ʿArabî al-Saghîr*. One would-be government, the Palestinian Liberation Organization, has its own children's magazine, *al-Ashbâl*. The Egyptian *Samîr* is technically independent, but it is a product of Dâr al-Hilâl, a nationalized publishing house. *Sandûq al-Dunyâ* is published in Cairo by the Egyptian Association for the Publication of Knowledge and World Culture. But this nonprofit organization took the periodical over from a U.S. philanthropic and political program, the Franklin Books project, which was dedicated to spreading knowledge of the United States throughout the Third World.[20] This outside support has not kept *Sandûq al-Dunyâ* from appropriately celebrating the Egyptian government. Most Arab comic-strip magazines (which are also children's magazines) receive some kind of subsidy from a governmental or paragovernmental source. Capitalism is growing in the Middle East, and in recent years a few private companies have created their own strip periodicals, such as the Egyptian *Bâsim* and the Tunisian *Qaws Quzah*. Yet even private magazines can be influenced economically. Most states in the region control the importation and distribution of publication-quality paper, often disbursing it in limited amounts at subsidized prices. And of course there are both official censorship and an ever-present threat of the banning of any publication which the government of the moment deems to have stepped outside the bounds of permissible discussion.

One result of the quasi-official character of so many Arab strips is a far greater and more open treatment of civic, political, and ideological themes than readers are accustomed to in the West. This difference, at first sight considerable, is reduced somewhat if one remembers that the ostensible apoliticism of most U.S. and European comics was sharply reduced during wartime[21] and that the majority of Arab countries have been frequently in and out of a technical state of war during the past forty-five years.

One may see this politicization as an invasion of the innocent joys of childhood, an insidious manipulation of entertainment and education for propaganda purposes. Indeed, that is sometimes the case in the comic strips of the Arabs. Yet there is another perspective. If one agrees that all normative material has implied political content, then the frank expression of political options can often be more liberating than their occultation.

This last point is particularly important given the general climate of political discussion in the region. Political debate undergoes varying degrees of censorship in most Arab countries. Even where considerable freedom of discussion prevails, as in contemporary Jordan and Egypt, the memory of earlier restriction lives on in the popular consciousness. The most notable result has been to push politics and political implications into other areas, such as literature and poetry. Comic strips have been no exception to this trend. Furthermore, as historians have long recognized, censorship breeds sharp readers, and Arab readers have more than matched their writers and artists in the search for hidden political and ideological messages. The politicization of

Arab comics, generally designed to serve the interests of the regimes, can be a double-edged sword. In the Arab states, as in most of the Third World, culture is seen by virtually everyone as an essentially political domain. This consensus of artist and public can produce effects both conformist and subversive.

Reinforcing this tendency is the fact that Arab comic-strip production is modeled on both European and U.S. practices. In the United States, comics have rarely earned the respectability among adults that they have long possessed in Europe; comics have generally been treated by the guardians of high culture as irremediably childish or dangerously antisocial, when not both. In France and Italy, figures such as Comès, Crépax, and Hugo Pratt have long written for sophisticated adult audiences, and comics often attain, and are credited with, a high level of aesthetic seriousness. Only recently have more European attitudes appeared in the United States with the reception of Art Spiegelman's *Maus*, a reception linked as much to the consensus nature of its theme (the Holocaust) as it is to the artist's powerful and sophisticated stripology.[22]

While most Arab strips are barred by the greater moral strictness of their societies from imitating the frequently pornographic forms of European adult strips (let alone the deliberate provocation of U.S. underground comics),[23] the seriousness and aesthetic sophistication of European production has clearly influenced a number of Arab political strips aimed at adolescent and adult audiences. In Algeria and among the Arabs of France, a hybrid form has developed, blending French and Arab comic-strip traditions and often aimed at adult audiences.

But even when Arab comics are destined for children (the majority of cases), their authors take them quite seriously as political and cultural products. The individuals who create Arab comics are among the best that their societies have produced in literature and the arts. Often they have already made a name for themselves as serious writers, painters, or political cartoonists. They are motivated by the need for self-expression and by professional ambition, certainly, but they are also, as a group, genuinely concerned about the future of contemporary culture and particularly that of the children of their society.

Visual vs. Verbal

By their nature, comic strips combine two languages, the visual and the verbal. This double coding leaves greater space for ambiguity and contradiction, making strips an ideal location for the examination of unconscious messages. The comic sign can be read in three ways: in isolation, in its visual or textual series, and in the intersection of these two series.

An example of the kinds of cultural meaning produced by the combination of text with visual form can be seen in Saddâm Husayn's victory monument in Baghdad. Kanan Makiya, writing under the name of Samir al-Khalil, devoted a small book to this sculpture, but he remained stymied on the explanation of the Iraqi leader's decision to use precise casts of his own arms, instead of more-or-less idealized forms, for the triumphal arch. Why must these be Saddâm Husayn's arms? A text by the Iraqi president selected for the arch's inauguration gives part of the answer: "The worst condition is for a person to pass under a sword not his own . . . " But this is what the Iraqi army does when it passes under Husayn's sword-bearing limbs. The monument signifies, among other things, the Iraqi dictator's control over his army, a message that would not be so clear if the arms were not precisely his own.[24] That a work has overt political meaning does not mean there are not other, more hidden, levels of political and ideological content. It is part of the potential of art forms, be they mass or elite, to represent more than their creators intend for them.

With their transmission of socially defined norms for children, their frequent politicization, and their geographical extension, from Algeria to Arabia, Arab comic strips are an invaluable window into the mentalities and politics of the Arab world and a growing part of a developing international mass culture.

Like other art forms, Arab comic strips are not the placid representation of a static consensus. They are buffeted by three major social forces: (1) state propaganda combined with state-supported ideologies, generally secularist Arab nationalism with more or less attention to Islam as identity and as private morality; (2) the encroachment of world-capitalist mass media, of which Disney is the clearest example; and (3) the Islamic revival movement, which serves as opposition to the first two.

Chapter 2 deals directly with the problem of Disney imperialism, while chapters 3 and 4 analyze the secular nationalism embodied in the treatment of political leaders as comic-strip superheroes. The subversive strips of Ahmad Hijâzî, discussed in chapter 5, show the limits of Western consumerism and state propaganda in Arab comics and the space often open for leftist critiques of both. Islamic comics have become increasingly visible in several Arab states, and chapter 6 explores the forces but also the limits and contradictions of the contemporary Islamic current in comic-strip production. Chapters 7 through 11 show how specific countries have evolved different blends of these forces, adapting them to local circumstances, with Syria as the most secular and state-controlled, Tunisia as a laboratory for the rewriting of the Arab tradition, or *turâth*, and the United Arab Emirates' *Mâjid* as a case study in the successful blending of political and religious elements accompanied by a negotiation of local and regional identities that supports its pan-Arab circulation. Finally, if Algeria's heavily French strip production is knee-deep in the world of Western images (verbal as well as visual), the comic strips of the Arabo-French Beurs are up to their hips in that same cultural universe.

Ever the corporalized manifestation of civilizational values, women have served as a major battlefield for the contending forces in Arab strips. The struggle is not between Western liberation and Eastern oppression but between three visions of women, each tied to its own model of society: the leftist secular one, the Islamic one, and the Western one with all its contradictions between forces for liberation and the media exploitation of woman as sex object. These issues come to the fore in the chapters that deal with the strips of Syria, Tunisia, and the United Arab Emirates, as they do in the discussion of Algerian strips, where exploitative Western genres collide with traditional Islamic attitudes. Nor is it surprising that the problematic status of women is a leading issue in the strips of the French Beurs. Indeed, despite some shared Mediterranean values, it is difficult to think of an area of greater cultural dissonance in the conflict between the Beurs' Arab and Islamic traditions and the French society into which they are partly assimilated.

From Europe to Arabia, Arab strips reflect their societies' cultural and political tensions while the societies and their strips participate in some of the debates that echo through virtually every corner of the planet. In this way as well, they bridge regional and international culture.

2

Mickey in Cairo, Ramsîs in Paris

Comic strips are an inescapably Western product. Their creation in an Arab context necessarily puts their makers on the front lines of a battle over Western culture. Should it be imported, shunned, or replaced with local imitations? Thus comics, in the Middle East, automatically take a position in an ideologically significant division between the foreign and the indigenous—in concrete historical terms, between East and West.[1]

A variety of possibilities exist for the adaptation of comics to the Arab cultural environment. On one hand, we have the translation into Arabic of European adventure comics in book form, such as *Tintin, Astérix le Gaulois*, and *Lucky Luke*, all published by Dâr al-Ma'ârif. On the other hand, we have completely indigenous comics, such as the Tunisian *'Irfân*, published monthly.[2] There is a yet a third possibility for Middle Eastern comics, and that is a mixture of the two: translation of foreign comics published along with indigenous forms in the same magazine. It is this third case which most clearly exposes the strategies of cultural naturalization.

The Egyptianization of Mickey Mouse

It should come as no surprise that Mickey Mouse, who has conquered much of the Western world, should also have invaded the Middle East. Translations of the adventures of Mickey Mouse, Donald Duck, and other Walt Disney characters have been undertaken in Egypt by Dâr al-Hilâl and distributed in other parts of the Arab world. These Walt Disney comics, sold under the title *Mîkî*, are an excellent example

of the mixed form: foreign-translated and indigenous. Walt Disney characters probably vie with Coca-Cola as international symbols of Americanism. In their polemical
but penetrating *How to Read Donald Duck: Imperialist Ideology in the Disney Comic*, Dorfman and Mattelart characterize "disnification" as a cultural invasion of capitalist and
imperialist ideas that help to justify the exploitation of the Third World.[3]

The interjection of indigenous elements into this quintessentially U.S. product
can be seen, therefore, as a means of conjuring its cultural-imperialist threat. And this
conjuring is done, first of all, by the introduction of what are clearly designed to be
characteristically Egyptian elements. For this reason, the adaptation of the Mickey
Mouse comic to a native public represents more than another stage in the constant
process of borrowing and modifying Western cultural products. It also provides a relatively unguarded and therefore extremely valuable expression of at least one Egyptian self-image. A high point of the Disney invasion of Arab comics came in the early
1970s, and we can see this process of adaptation most clearly in the corpus of the fifty-
two weekly editions of *Mîkî* for 1972.

The Egyptianization of Mickey Mouse takes place on several levels. First, there is
the embedding of the indigenous comic strips within the foreign-translated ones.
Most often the Egyptian strips are the first comic item one encounters in *Mîkî*, preceded only by two pages of noncomic material, including crossword puzzles, letters
from readers, games, and the like. Second, there is the Egyptianization of the noncomic material. Here the reader is treated to a variety of elements, which can be classified as either Egyptian or Pharaonic. Though Pharaonic elements can be subsumed
under the Egyptian label, it is more profitable to isolate the strictly Pharaonic from the
Egyptian, the former involving clear references to or associations with the ancient civilization of the Nile.

In the majority of cases, the Pharaonic elements appear in the crosswords. Thus
we have a crossword puzzle in the form of a sphinx (issue no. 573); one in the form of
Tût ʿAnkh Amûn's head, clearly labeled with his name; one with two Egyptian girls
holding up a lotus leaf (see fig. 2.1); and one showing Uncle Scrooge in the costume of
a Pharaoh (fig. 2.2) (nos. 580, 584, and 592).[4]

General Egyptian elements can also be found in crossword puzzles. There is a
puzzle in the form of the Egyptian eagle (fig. 2.3), one with Mickey dressed as an
Egyptian and carrying worry beads (fig. 2.4), and another in the form of a map of
Egypt (nos. 594, 599, and 607). But by far the most common location for the Egyptian
elements is the cover of the magazine. One, for example, portrays Mickey Mouse
wearing a galabia while fishing (no. 577). In another instance (no. 599), Mickey, clad
in a galabia, is standing between two recognizably Cairene mosques, shooting off a
rocket while wishing everyone a "Ramadân Karîm" (fig. 2.5). A third cover portrays
Mickey celebrating the 1972 Olympics in Munich while running in front of an Egyptian flag (no. 592).

Aside from these strictly Egyptian or Pharaonic elements, there are a few purely
Islamic images: a drawing of the formula "Allâhu Akbar" in the form of a city skyline
(fig. 2.6), a crossword puzzle with the word Allâh on top of a triangle (nos. 573 and
597). These are by far the least numerous.

2.1. *Crossword puzzle in shape of lotus.*

2.2. *Crossword puzzle with Scrooge as Pharaoh.*

This Egyptianization thus is essentially secular, one might even say non-Islamic. In effect, the relatively few Islamic elements present are so much a part of the normal fabric of Egyptian life that their specifically religious content is relatively meager. Mickey wishing his readers a "Ramadân Karîm" is almost (but not quite) as nonreligious a gesture as would be an equivalent Western Merry Christmas. Egyptianization through Pharaonism is even more non-Islamic. Not only did ancient Egypt precede Islam but Pharaoh is as negative a figure in strict orthodoxy as he is in the Old Testament.[5] This de-emphasis of the specifically Islamic combined with the valorization of Pharaonic themes is true for all aspects of the Egyptianization of Mickey Mouse.

2.3. *Crossword puzzle in an Egyptian eagle.*

2.4. *Crossword puzzle with Mickey in Egyptian garb.*

في هذا العدد :
☐ ثلاث قصص كاملة
☐ ألف ليلة وليلة

العدد ٥٩٩ — ١٢ أكتوبر ١٩٧٢   الثمن ٣٠ وليما

2.5. *Mickey Mouse celebrates Ramadân.*

2.6. *Skyline as Allâhu Akbar.*

The Indigenous Strips

Though all of these elements (the Pharaonic and the Egyptian as well as the Islamic) represent forms of Egyptianization, they do so in isolation and are always secondary to the object being Egyptianized (e.g., Mickey or a crossword puzzle). As such, they remain on the surface of the comic as literary text and Western cultural product. There is, however, one component in these comics that transcends the isolated Egyptianized elements in its significance—the indigenous comic strips. For 1972 there are three such narratives, appearing in weekly installments. The first of them, serialized from January 13 to April 13, is "The Adventures of Ramsîs in Paris" (Mughâmarât Ramsîs fî Bârîs). The second, "Mickey and Red Cat, Adventure on Mars" (Mîkî wal-Qitt al-Ahmar, Mughâmara fî al-Mirrîkh), begins on May 4 and ends on August 3. The third is "Ahmos and the Green Sands" (Ahmos wal-Rimâl al-Khadrâ') and runs from August 31 to October 19. Each weekly installment consists of two pages, and the dates tell us that there is an indigenous episode for most of the year. Thus the interculturality inherent in the project of the Egyptianization of Mickey manifests itself here as a literary intertextuality.

The third strip (nos. 593 to 600) was written by Sayyid Hijâb and illustrated by Ayman. It deals with a young Pharaonic hero, Ahmos, who is entrusted with the rule of Egypt. During a period of relative prosperity, a wise old man delivers a Macbethlike prophecy: women will conquer the land of Egypt and will occupy it until the sand turns green and the trees walk. Despite Ahmos's initial surprise, the prophecy is gradually fulfilled. Hotep, the leader of the "desert bedouin," seeking to profit from the land of Egypt, leads his men to war. To succeed in this, he dresses them as women. In the process, Ahmos's sister, Tî, is abducted, and the condition for her release is that the land become green. Though Tî is prepared to sacrifice herself for Egypt, Ahmos orders his subjects to disguise themselves as trees and go to her rescue. With these events, the prophecy has come to fruition. The bedouin are driven back to their land, and Tî's closing words are "Egypt is a paradise for us and a hell for the usurper."

The second adventure, that of Mickey and Red Cat (nos. 576 to 589), was written by Majdî Najîb and illustrated by Muhammad al-Tuhâmî. Mickey is heading a team of scientists who, along with him and two children, are to go to Mars. Red Cat and his cohorts, disguised as scientists, secretly board the spaceship. On Mars, the entire group is discovered by the Martians and taken prisoner. The Martians possess a weapon resembling radar that can tell what someone is thinking. They discover that Red Cat and his group are after the gold on Mars and consequently decide to punish them with an "animal machine" capable of turning someone into an animal.[6] Before Red Cat can be transformed, he seizes a gun and escapes with his fellows. With Mickey's help, the Martians capture Red Cat and his group and decide to turn them into cats (sic). Mickey is outraged; he considers this process a crime against "humanity" and concludes that he must save Red Cat. Accordingly, he asks a Martian to take him to the King of Mars. Along the way they discover a pyramid with two Egyptian Pharaohs next to it. It turns out that the Pharaohs were brought from earth by the King of Mars to build him pyramids like the ones at Giza. But these Pharaohs want to escape from Mars and Mickey promises to help them. One of the Pharaohs has taken a radio from the Martians that can communicate with other periods of time, and with it, the group sends a message to the Pharaohs on Earth. The latter address Ramsîs, who in turn consults the statue of Military Genius. The statue advises him that there is no alternative but to attack Mars with rockets. The Egyptian military engineer then makes the rockets (which resemble mummies). The Egyptian soldiers, led by Ramsîs, ride on the rockets to Mars and rescue the earth visitors. Upon their return, the guilty are punished and all returns to order.

Of the third strip, "The Adventures of Ramsîs in Paris," we need only note at this juncture that it takes place in the present-day world.

Thus we have three indigenous strips, that of Ahmos, that of Mickey and Red Cat, and that of Ramsîs. Each takes place in a different historical period: Ahmos in the Pharaonic period or the past, Ramsîs in the present, and Mickey in the future (though with connections to the past). Not only are we presented with an enormous temporal span, but all three periods are evoked within one year's worth of comics. And despite the chronological variety, all three strips exploit a clear Pharaonic element. In Ahmos, the characters and the setting are Pharaonic. In Ramsîs, as we shall see shortly, although the setting is contemporary, the protagonist is Pharaonic. In Mickey's adventures on Mars, the Pharaohs appear on Mars to build pyramids. Even more dramatic, they construct rockets which, though they resemble mummies, reach Mars nonetheless. "Red Cat" thus involves a temporal telescoping as it moves back and forth between ancient Egypt and the future. As we shall see, this temporal telescoping also exists in "Ramsîs."

All three stories foreground Pharaonic components. In Ahmos, one can argue, the Pharaonic presence is natural, since the story is set in ancient Egypt. But in the remaining two strips these elements do not fit as naturally into their settings. Instead, they function as chronological intrusions—properly speaking, as anachronisms. Ramsîs, in the strip devoted to his adventures, is a Pharaonic hero consciously placed in the modern world. Similarly, in "Mickey and Red Cat," the Pharaohs are intruders (when not prisoners) from another time. Not only are the Pharaonic elements most discordant with the setting of the story, but they are also the least necessary to the unfolding of the plot. The presence of the Pharaohs on Mars is not essential, and the rescue sequence involving the Pharaohs from Earth could also have been eliminated. In that case, Mickey would have ingeniously solved the problem, as he is wont to do in other strips. In other words, where the Pharaonic elements are not present in the story's setting or essential to its construction, they are worked into the plot.

What is the significance of this constant Pharaonic presence? The most outstanding factor is clearly nationalism. It is perhaps easiest to locate in the two strips that radiate chronologically outward from "Ramsîs," that of Ahmos and that of Mickey and Red Cat. The edifying adventures of Ahmos and Tî, who successfully rid their country of invaders, evoke the good qualities of Egypt and the superiority of the Egyptians. Tî's closing words express the nationalism of the strip in its totality when she proclaims that Egypt is a paradise for them and hell for the usurper. And this nationalism, because it is Pharaonic, is essentially secular. In fact, Ahmos is a name already familiar to Egyptian children and, in this case, almost certainly alludes to the first Pharaoh of the New Kingdom, who is credited with driving out the Hyksos invaders.[7] Not only secular, this nationalism is also exclusively Nilotic. Describing the invaders as desert bedouin, while it might accurately transcribe one of the realities of Egyptian history, hardly suggests pan-Arabism.

In "Mickey and Red Cat," the nationalistic elements, because they are more extrinsic, are in a certain sense more significant. First, we have the kidnapped Pharaohs who are abducted by the Martians to build pyramids like those of Giza. Second, we have the rescue sequence involving Pharaohs from earth with their mummiform rockets. Since these Pharaonic components are superfluous, they are doing more than advancing the plot. In fact, they represent the same type of nationalism present in the Ahmos adventure. They glorify the same Egypt which Ahmos glorifies, Pharaonic Egypt. Yet the nationalistic aspects are infinitely more dramatic in "Mickey and Red Cat." Egyptian pride is validated by reference to the most advanced Western technological development, space travel. Not only are rockets built for the Egyptian army to travel to Mars, but Egyptian Pharaohs have already been "imported" there to build pyramids. Egyptian cultural artifacts transcend their origin and reach out into space.

The Adventures of Ramsîs in Paris

"The Adventures of Ramsîs in Paris" takes place in contemporary Egypt. The strip opens with the famous statue of the Pharaoh Ramsîs II, standing in the square in front of the railway station in Cairo. The crowd bustles around him. A woman is calling out for a taxi. Someone is selling cigarettes, while someone else is yelling out the names of various newspapers. Ramsîs declares that life has become quite unpleasant and that he wants to return to Luxor to live with his family. In the next few frames, we see little children annoying the statue. Ramsîs states that though he is a statue of stone, he does have feelings. Then, discovering that he is capable of movement, he begins to move, as people watch him in surprise.

One evening Ramsîs decides to flee. People stare in amazement as the statue moves. During this episode, Ramsîs discovers that if he presses on his left foot, his size decreases and he becomes life-size. Then he realizes that he needs clothing to disguise himself. He seizes some from a street vendor, promising to repay him in time. The garments include a galabia, a turban, boots, and an overcoat. Meanwhile, people discover that the statue is missing as Ramsîs goes to the train station in order to visit his relatives in the Saʿîd (Upper Egypt).

At this point, the search for Ramsîs begins. The police consult a computer, who tells them to look for him in the museum. While the police are surrounding this building, Ramsîs makes his way onto the train. In the museum, the police search for Ramsîs. Two Pharaonic statues wonder what is going on. One tells the other that Ramsîs has fled. Unable to find Ramsîs in the museum, the police conclude that the computer has made fun of them.

They return to the computer, who replies that they had not given it sufficient information. It then informs them that if Ramsîs is his normal self, they should search for him near the Pyramids of Giza. The police naturally proceed to Giza, where they of course do not find Ramsîs and conclude that the computer has erred a second time.

When they return to the computer, however, the machine explains that their information is wrong and proceeds to tell them that Ramsîs is disguised in clothing, that he has changed his size by pressing on his left foot, and that he is on a train heading for Luxor. On the train, Ramsîs, trying to avoid being recognized, enters a first-class car. Suddenly his size increases, and he asks the people in the compartment to close their eyes for a moment while he presses on his foot and becomes normal again. Meanwhile the conductor comes by to collect tickets. Ramsîs, helpless without a ticket and in an attempt to convince the conductor not to surrender him to the police, changes his size, first to the statuesque, then back to the human.

The conductor is not impressed. On arrival at Asyût, Ramsîs is thrown in jail. But he escapes by increasing his size. Then he discards his clothing and rides on the back of a train to Luxor. Arriving in Luxor, he awakens his relatives, who express amazement at his small size. The statues then inform Ramsîs that Tût ʿAnkh Amûn has been taken to the land of the Khawâgât (the West) and that Ramsîs was supposed to be taken as well.[8] Ramsîs replies that he loves Egypt and hates travel. But when he discovers that Tût ʿAnkh Amûn has been taken to represent Egyptian culture in France, Ramsîs demands a war chariot.

The other Pharaonic statues inform Ramsîs that a chariot will not get him to France; he should take a plane from the Luxor airport. When he departs, they give him automatic crushed-rock arrows. Subsequently Ramsîs steals a helicopter, mistaking it for a plane, and the airport officials become aware of the theft and of the identity of the thief.

The Egyptian army in helicopters then pursues Ramsîs, who heads for Paris and shoots his arrows, saving one to announce his arrival in that city. Once there, he shoots his last arrow and, when asked who he is, identifies himself as Ramsîs, the famous king.

When Ramsîs disembarks from the helicopter, the police surround him. Although people laugh at him, he is convinced that the President of France will welcome him and declares that he himself will look for the President. Meanwhile, the Egyptian police contact their French colleagues and ask them to seize the runaway statue.

In the final episode, Ramsîs searches for the person in charge of Paris. Television cameras photograph him, while he wonders where Tût ʿAnkh Amûn is. He discovers an obelisk and announces to the French that his great, solemn history is inscribed on it. Then he sees an announcement about the Tût ʿAnkh Amûn exhibit. He is upset that the French are honoring Tût ʿAnkh Amûn and not him. "Where is justice?" he exclaims. Our hero finally arrives at the Louvre, convinced that his "rival" is hiding there. But the French police seize him and handcuff him. He says to himself that had the person in charge met *him*, he would surely have put him in the exhibit and would have honored him more than Tût ʿAnkh Amûn. He wonders what he will tell people in Egypt when he returns in handcuffs.

After a few hours, Ramsîs arrives in Cairo. The police tell him that what he has done deserves punishment, but since he represents culture, they will content themselves with returning him to his place. In the last frame we see Ramsîs standing as a statue in his original place at the train station, surrounded by children. He says: "*Yâ salâm* . . . There is nothing better than Egypt . . . despite the naughtiness of children!!"

Narratology

"The Adventures of Ramsîs in Paris" can be analyzed on several levels. The first, and perhaps the clearest, is the narratological: the significance of the events in the tale seen as a pattern—the narrative structure of the strip. On the simplest plane, "Ramsîs" is a clear example of a cautionary children's tale designed to show the dissatisfied individual that though the grass may seem greener on the other side, the world is fraught with difficulties and one is better off at home. In the English-speaking world, Beatrix Potter's Peter Rabbit is perhaps the best-known example of such a moral tale. It should come as no surprise, of course, that "The Adventures of Ramsîs in Paris," written for Egyptian children, should conform to this well-established pattern.[9]

What is more original is the agency of Ramsîs's return. It is not so much the objective difficulties or disappointments that Ramsîs encounters which force him to return home, though these are quite real. It is the police who, from the very beginning, hunt him down, capture him, return him to his pedestal, and even consider punishing him for his misdeeds. An ideological message has been added to the purely moral one: he who steps out of his appropriate place in Egyptian society will be forced back by the police, if need be in handcuffs. Of course, while the moral part of this message was almost certainly consciously intended by the authors of this story, the ideological message probably was not. This distinction between the consciously delivered messages, the overt propaganda, and the unconscious though ideologically significant elements operates in other places in the strip.

But the archetypal children's pattern and the ideological implications of the Egyptian children's strip interact in yet another way. In a typical cautionary tale such as Peter Rabbit, the chastened hero returns to a fundamentally loving and natural home environment. That is not the case with Ramsîs. He returns (and under guard) to a condition which is essentially that of imprisonment, since he is forced into immobility, though he now considers his "place" (at once social and topographical) more tolerable. And yet this place, this spot in the square, is not Ramsîs's home. His home is in Upper Egypt among his relatives. From a certain point of view, therefore, Ramsîs escapes not *from* his home but *to* his home. Since this home is in the country, Ramsîs's nostalgia for it also represents a romantic longing for the simpler life of the country and dissatisfaction with the hustle and bustle of the city—a theme which Dorfman and Mattelart have identified in Donald Duck comics.[10] In a rapidly urbanizing country like Egypt, whose cities teem with recent rural migrants, such nostalgia would find ready echoes. Of course Ramsîs arrives to find that his home is not the paradise he had imagined. It has been disrupted by Egyptology, by the Europeans' longing to see Tût. In essence the young Egyptian readers are being told that they must live in modern urban crowded Egypt, that they cannot go back to their idyllic origins because of the reality of European intervention. If we historicize this statement, it becomes: Western imperialism destroyed traditional Egyptian society and is, as a result, responsible for the negative aspects of its modern replacement. What is more, these same Europeans will aid in the apprehension of anyone who challenges the contemporary social status quo.

Self-Criticism

The narrative element does not, of course, exhaust the practical ideological significance of this tale. Ramsîs's dissatisfaction is based upon a specific aspect of contemporary Egyptian society: overcrowding and noise. The overcrowding is what initially moves Ramsîs to leave his position in Cairo and seek the calm of Upper Egypt. In the third frame of the first episode (issue no. 560), Ramsîs declares that he wishes to return to live with his family in Luxor (fig. 2.7). The importance of this frame and the ideas it represents are reflected in a highly unusual stripological procedure. It is, in fact, one of only three examples in this text of a type of narrative overcoding. The frame consists entirely of Ramsîs's face and two balloons. On the bottom is a standard speech balloon through which Ramsîs expresses his desire to return to Luxor. The upper balloon is a thought balloon linked to Ramsîs by bubbles. In it, instead of verbal signs, we find pictographic ones: two Pharaonic statues sitting in calm repose, with a few hieroglyphs on the wall behind them. Pictographic representation is not a uniform characteristic of thought balloons in "The Adventures of Ramsîs." Characters, including Ramsîs himself, often express their thoughts through purely verbal thought balloons. Pictographic representation is used exclusively to duplicate verbal messages, as in this case. This doubling of the verbal mes-

2.7. *Ramsîs with pictographic thought balloon.*

sage with a pictographic one is a distinctive device of "Ramsîs," and it is always linked to the central preoccupations of the strip.

The calm of Upper Egypt is transmitted not only on its own merits but also in opposition to the bustle of Cairo. The crowding in the opening frames is repeated in later ones as well. Crowds fill the streets and the areas around the train. Overcrowding is emphasized by showing both people and animals (nos. 560 and 561). Concomitant with this is the problem of noise. When Ramsîs arrives at the train station, we are told in the supplementary information at the top of the frame that he wants to get away from the noise (no. 562). When he finally boards the train, he bids good-bye to the noise and the square (no. 563).

"The Adventures of Ramsîs" incorporates this critique of Egyptian life into a strategy of ideological recuperation which Roland Barthes refers to as "L'opération Astra."[11] In this operation, one starts by highlighting the well-known negative aspects of an accepted institution, only to conclude that it is lovable. Dorfman and Mattelart have shown the role of similar devices in Disney comics.[12] In the strip under discussion, the operation is complete when Ramsîs can declare that Egypt is wonderful despite the naughtiness of its children.

East vs. West

The issues already discussed relate to the structures and strategies of "Ramsîs" taken as a whole. An approach based more closely on the rhetorical (which, in this context, means stripological) level of the text will permit the isolation of other thematic elements. Perhaps the best place to begin is the title of the strip itself: "The Adventures of Ramsîs in Paris." According to the title, we are dealing with an Egyptian, indeed a Pharaonic, protagonist in a European city.

This title and subject are similar to those of a series of commercial Arabic films starring Samîra Tawfîq as a country girl lost in a modern city, with titles such as *Badawiyya fî Rômâ* and *Badawiyya fî Bârîs* (A Bedouin Girl in Rome, A Bedouin Girl in

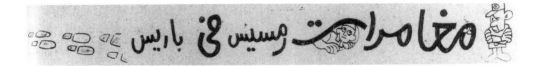

2.8. *Title with Ramsîs hiding from French policeman.*

Paris).[13] Unlike the characters in the Samîra Tawfîq films, however, Ramsîs spends relatively little time in Paris. In fact, the episodes in the French capital represent only two of the fourteen installments, or one-seventh of the strip. The rest of the story takes place entirely in Egypt, be it in Cairo, Upper Egypt, or en route between the two. Hence the title does not accord with the story it is meant to label.

This Gallic emphasis in the title (and thus its discordance) is further stressed by the graphism of the title and the pictographic elements coordinated with it. In the title (fig. 2.8), Ramsîs, the statue, hides under the *tâ'* of the word "Mughâmarât" while a policeman, clearly decked out as a French officer of the law with the characteristic *képi*, stands to the side watching the hiding Ramsîs. This piece of creative stripology reinforces the message of the title. And the importance of the title should not be underestimated; it appears weekly at the top of every installment.

Thus, though only two episodes of Ramsîs's adventures transpire in Paris, this location is stressed in the title of the strip on both the semantic and the visual levels. The strip clearly seeks to highlight the European angle. The opposition of a Pharaonic protagonist and a European capital accentuates the difference between East and West, a difference already present in the strip. For example, the Egyptian police are initially unable to locate Ramsîs and thus are obliged to resort to a computer to discover his whereabouts. The computer, a Western technological product, misleads them twice. The third time they consult it, it turns out that the computer possessed the knowledge all along but did not correctly inform the police, because they did not communicate with it properly. This suggests an unease with advanced Western technology.

These episodes with the officers of the law are significant from another perspective. Although our protagonist is captured by the Egyptian police, he manages to escape. It is the French authorities who apprehend him without mishap and send him back to Egypt with dispatch. Here again is the contrast between East and West: the French police deal more efficiently with the Egyptian fugitive.

Egypt in the West

The contrast between the Egyptian and the French police is not stressed on its own merits in the narrative but must be isolated by a comparative analysis. On a conscious level, however, what is clearly intended to impress the young reader is the importance of Egyptian culture, and hence of Egypt, in the West. This is manifest in several instances. The first reference to this phenomenon is in the episode in which

2.9. *Pictographic balloon: French and Egyptian cultural symbols.*

Ramsîs is talking to his "relatives" in Upper Egypt (no. 569). One of the Pharaonic statues explains to him that Tût ʿAnkh Amûn has been taken to the country of the Khawâgât. On the same page, Ramsîs hears that Tût ʿAnkh Amûn was taken to represent the culture of Egypt in France. In this frame, we find the same narrative over-coding discussed above, signaling ideological significance (fig. 2.9). The statue, ad-dressing Ramsîs, has two balloons. The bottom one is a speech balloon explaining that Tût ʿAnkh Amûn was taken to represent the culture of Egypt in France. At the top of the frame we find the same statue's thought balloon. This thought balloon is once again pictographic, containing two drawings, one of a mummy case, obviously representing Tût ʿAnkh Amûn, and the other, of equal size, of the Eiffel Tower. On one level the pictographic message echoes the semantic one: the representation of Egyptian culture in France. But the pictographic message does more. By making the mummy case and the Eiffel Tower the same size, these images suggest the cultural equality of Egypt and France.

There are other examples in "The Adventures of Ramsîs" of the importance of Egyptian culture in the West. Significantly, these remaining cases take place in Paris. First, we can cite the frame in which Ramsîs finds himself "in front of one of the Phar-aonic obelisks in Paris." He thereupon exclaims: "O Frenchmen . . . My great solemn history is recorded on this obelisk" (no. 573). This is a clear reference to the obelisk of Luxor now in the Place de la Concorde, a monument erected by the historical Ramsîs II. Second, we have the reference to the Tût ʿAnkh Amûn exhibit, also in Paris. In fact, we never see the exhibit itself but only the announcement for it (no. 573). The last case of the presence of Egyptian culture in the West is, of course, Ramsîs himself. Al-though the French people are frightened when they see "the giant" in the streets, Ramsîs is very aware of his own regal status. He therefore inquires of the French peo-ple where their President is, firmly believing that the person responsible in Paris will recognize him and give him his proper due (nos. 572 and 573). The possible recogni-

2.10. *Archaeology as theft in a
pictographic balloon.*

tion and honoring of Ramsîs by political leaders testifies to the importance of the
Egyptian presence.

Archaeology or Theft

The representation of Egyptian culture in France in "The Adventures of Ramsîs"
brings with it a very significant issue: the despoliation of Egyptian national treasures.
The problem appears in the episode with Ramsîs in Upper Egypt among his relatives
(no. 569). His reaction at being there is that of relief and joy, as he comments on the
sun and the calm existence in Upper Egypt. To this, however, one of the statues asks
him what calm he is searching for there, to which yet another statue replies that he
obviously is not aware of the latest news. When Ramsîs inquires about this, the statues argue back and forth about which of them will give him the incredible news. The
next frame (fig. 2.10) shows the head of a statue explaining to Ramsîs that "they took
the statue of 'Tût 'Ankh Amûn' to the West [literally, to the lands of the Khawâgât]."
Here again we find the same telltale doubling of balloons: a verbal speech balloon below and a pictographic thought balloon above.

The verbal message is clear: Tût 'Ankh Amûn has been taken to the West. But
what is the pictographic message? The pictographic balloon is at least twice the size of
the verbal one, whereas in the earlier examples, both balloons were of the same size.
But more interesting are the balloons' contents. The pictographic message consists of
a large mummy case being carried by three men wearing Western clothing and Western hats, therefore obviously Europeans. The positions of the men's feet and the

clouds of dust and speed lines drawn around them show that they are running. In addition, all three are glowering as they look over their shoulders, as though evading someone. The man in front is smoking a cigar. Clearly the image of these characters is that of "heavies." To say the least, the Europeans are not "good guys," and their body language, if we may call it that, turns the act of carrying the mummy case into a clandestine one. If the verbal balloon tells of a mission of cultural diplomacy, the pictographic one says theft.

This pictographic narrative overcoding adds new implications to the general message of pride in the international importance of Egyptian culture. First, it suggests a perfectly understandable concern with the theft of Egyptian national treasures, which is, of course, a continuing problem. But second, by associating this representation of theft with the Tût ʿAnkh Amûn exhibit, the pictographic balloon suggests a fundamental anxiety and ambivalence about even the temporary export of such valued cultural artifacts. Nor is it a coincidence in this context that when Ramsîs was told that he was also considered for the trip, he declared that he hated traveling. In this highly charged frame, then, the gap between the pictographic and the verbal balloons dramatically manifests the latent conflict between pride in the Western appreciation of ancient Egyptian culture and misgivings over such foreign interest.

The reference to the obelisk of Luxor in Paris evokes similar resentments. In Luxor today, Egyptian government tour guides make a point of explaining that the famous exchange between Louis Philippe and Muhammad ʿAlî which brought the obelisk to Paris was unfair because the clock which the French monarch gave in exchange stopped functioning a few months after its arrival in Egypt.

Finally, it is these cultural conflicts and resentments which help to explain Ramsîs's trip to Paris. After all, Mickey Mouse is an American cultural product and it is the threat of U.S. cultural imperialism (the dominant form in Egypt during the years when the strip was written) which the Egyptianization of Mickey Mouse seeks to conjure. Yet Ramsîs does not go to New York, Washington, or another Western capital— but to Paris. That is because, in terms of the larger cultural (and political) issue of Western Egyptology and Orientalism, it is France which, since the activities of scholar administrators such as Mariette Bey and Maspero, has loomed largest in the Egyptian consciousness. If the threat of political hegemony has come from the United States or the Soviet Union, that of cultural despoliation is associated with France. Ramsîs's fictional trip to the French capital was premonitory in a way that confirmed the geographic choice of the Egyptian scenarist. A few years after the publication of the strip, the mummy (not the statue) of Ramsîs II was taken to Paris to be treated for an infection in its desiccated flesh.[14]

Ambivalences about cultural expeditions and exploration also surfaced in the story of Mickey and Red Cat. There, as we saw, a group of disinterested scientists is secretly joined by criminals who, disguised as scientists, are only after the gold on Mars. This can easily be seen as a parallel to Western expeditions to Egypt (or the New World), with their combinations of disinterested scientists and simple thieves.

But in addition to concern for Egyptian cultural artifacts, "The Adventures of Ramsîs in Paris" also displays the standard superstitions propagated about Pharaonic

Egypt. It is interesting that these attitudes are shown as current in present-day Cairo. When Ramsîs's escape is discovered, the reader is treated to a frame which consists entirely of sets of newspapers. The one on the top, with the logo of *al-Ahrâm*, is clearly meant to represent the Cairo daily. The headlines read: "The disappearance of Ramsîs under obscure circumstances? Was he stolen by thieves . . . or is there a new and grave Pharaonic secret?" (no. 562).

The other references to this phenomenon occur in the museum, when the police are searching for Ramsîs. People in the museum, upon seeing the police, wonder what is going on. One person declares that they are searching for Ramsîs, to which a woman rejoins that she has indeed heard about the curse of the Pharaohs when they are angry. In the same episode, in a later frame, the lights go out. All that we see are eyes in the darkness, and a balloon emanating from one pair of them, in which we read: "The curse of the Pharaohs!" (no. 564).

Ramsîs as Symbol

These evocations of common superstitions about ancient Egypt do not play an important role in "The Adventures of Ramsîs." The most potent purveyor of information on Egypt is Ramsîs himself. Ramsîs is, of course, first and foremost a Pharaonic protagonist. As such, the Pharaonic elements in the strip are natural. They are not added to enhance the Egyptian consciousness, as in "Mickey and Red Cat." Yet, since our protagonist is Pharaonic, his existence in contemporary Egypt is that much more telling. When he ventures out into present-day Egypt, he decides that he must wear some clothing to disguise himself. He dons a galabia, a turban, an overcoat, and boots. This disguise is extremely significant. We are dealing with a multilayered vestmental phenomenon consisting of three distinct components: (1) the Pharaonic core, that is, Ramsîs himself with his ancient Egyptian garments and beard; (2) the Egyptian component, that is, the turban and the galabia; and (3) the European overcoat and boots. In the episode in which Ramsîs acquires his disguise, we are treated to a magnificent frame occupied by the full figure of Ramsîs, in which all the sartorial components are clearly present (no. 562). The total effect represents different phases of Egyptian history or consciousness: a Pharaonic core, a Western exterior, and, sandwiched in between, modern Egypt.

What better visual representation could one imagine of the idea of eternal Egypt? Nor is it coincidental that clothing is used here to represent the historical epochs. In the contemporary Middle East, clothing is a potent symbol and focus of the battle between tradition and Westernization. This importance has been both exploited by artists such as Najîb Mahfûz[15] and noted by commentators from Bernard Lewis to Kate Millett.[16]

Furthermore, the three layers of Ramsîs appear at one and the same time. This phenomenon contributes to a telescoping of time: the three Egypts coexist in the same chronological span. This telescoping was also evident in "Mickey and Red Cat." Its principal effect, besides the nationalist one of associating ancient and contemporary Egypt, is to suggest the coexistence within contemporary Egypt of structures (social or mental) associated with different historico-cultural epochs.

Yet the whole conception of the strip is founded on a sense of anachronism. Ramsîs is a Pharaonic figure wandering unhappily and amid myriad frustrations in the contemporary world. The emphasis on France in the title, despite its lesser importance in the text, when combined with the consistent and ambivalent focusing on East-West relations, indicates that the modern world with which Ramsîs is in conflict is a Western-dominated one. In a manner which is much more essential than is, for example, the case with "Mickey and Red Cat," "The Adventures of Ramsîs in Paris" is a story about a society digesting the relationship between its past and its alternative presents.

Ramsîs as Hero

But Ramsîs is not simply a symbol of eternal Egypt; he is also a hero—the hero of the strip. What kind of hero is he? On one hand, he is able to change his size when it is useful for him to do so. On the other hand, he is successfully captured by the French police and returned to Egypt. In other words, Ramsîs displays the characteristics of both a superhero and a mere mortal. He stands between the superhero and what du Fontbaré and Sohet have called an "héros déchiré," whose existence is characterized by his being in the throes of an identity crisis.[17] At the same time, Ramsîs is a childish hero. This is shown frequently throughout the strip with his naive egotism, his jealousy of Tût ʿAnkh Amûn, and his exaggeration, as in Paris, of his own importance. In a way it is this childishness which forms the characterological link between his superhero and *héros déchiré* statuses.[18]

This ambivalence in the heroic status of Ramsîs is related to another, even more fundamental, one: is Ramsîs a statue or a person? In the first episode of the strip, the question of Ramsîs's humanity is debated in several frames. While the people and the children in the street claim that Ramsîs has no feelings, he himself insists on the opposite. And, of course, throughout the story this ambiguity is emphasized as Ramsîs is at times a statue and others a real person. By extension the ambiguity is also related to whether Ramsîs is living or dead.

Ramsîs also plays a number of symbolic roles. He represents Egypt, and his adventures in the modern world can almost be read as an allegory. He can also be seen as a symbol of power and aloofness, as in a song from the popular contemporary film musical *Khallî Bâlak min Zouzou* (Watch Out for Zouzou).[19] Nasser was often compared to the Pharaoh Ramsîs II, and Sadat himself was to exploit this association after the Camp David agreements.[20] Finally, in "Red Cat," it was the Pharaoh Ramsîs who led the Egyptians to Mars to rescue their compatriots.

In the last episode, Ramsîs is told that he would normally have been punished for his acts but that since he represented culture, he would be allowed to return to his post. The ambiguity of his role reflects an ambiguous relationship to culture. Should culture, specifically ancient Egyptian culture, be considered something alive or something dead and relegated to a purely symbolic role?

And this ambiguity creates its own anxiety. We saw the fears associated with European interest in Egyptian culture. When Ramsîs begins to move, he frightens the onlookers, as he does when he changes size while on the train. In fact, it is Ramsîs's changes of state which generate fear. Ramsîs may be a cultural symbol, but he becomes a potentially dangerous one if he develops his own dynamism.

"The Adventures of Ramsîs in Paris" can be taken as an unconscious comment on the entire project of which all three indigenous strips are part, that is, the Egyptianization of Mickey. As we have seen, the most important instrument in this Egyptianization was the repeated insertion and foregrounding of Pharaonic material. The Egyptianizers of Mickey Mouse, by making Pharaonic culture the focal point of an Egyptian identity, are trying, in their way, to make the ancient Egyptian heritage something live, even politically significant, in contemporary Egypt. "The Adventures of Ramsîs in Paris" casts an unconscious doubt on the efficacy of such a project. Perhaps, it suggests, Pharaonic culture cannot be made to live in contemporary Egypt but must remain merely a symbol, honored and placed on a pedestal, to be sure, but lifeless and immobile.

3

Nasser, or the Hero in Strips

It is evident that comics have a political dimension, and Arab comics are far from being an exception. This political-ideological dimension is related not only to the content of a strip but also to its formal properties. That is even more the case when the strip is overtly political in its aim. Equally clearly, some political subjects lend themselves better to stripological exploitation than others.

In a medium long associated with superheroes, it should come as no surprise that one of the most important political manifestations should be biographies of "great men," those superheroes of the political world.[1] Such comic strips, of course, carry an explicit political and ideological content. But to do so, they are obliged to work within the parameters of the strip medium. A comic-strip biography of a national hero presents a series of challenges at once stripological and political.

These challenges are taken up in a biography in comic-strip form of the Egyptian leader Gamal Abdel Nasser. Entitled *Jamâl ʿAbd al-Nâsir*, it was composed by J. M. Ruffieux and Muhammad Nuʿmân al-Dhâkirî, with the assistance of Salmâ al-Dhâkirî and others, for the African Journalists' Collective and published in 1973, three years after the death of the great man. Written in Arabic, it is largely in the literary language but has passages in Cairo Egyptian dialect.[2]

Comics and History

Nasser is a world historical figure. His life is important chiefly because of the role he played in major historical events. Hence the story of his life cannot be told, even on the most simplistic level, without also writing history.

Yet writing history in comic-strip form is not as straightforward a process as it might appear. The etymology (and indeed, the literary origin) of history is, in this case, quite misleading. Since the word *history* in English includes the word *story*, there is always a temptation to view Clio's products as simply another species of narrative.[3] In *Metahistory*, Hayden White probably gave this interpretation its fullest development when he classified historical narratives by essentially fictional, narrative categories such as tragedy, comedy, and irony.[4]

And yet nothing shows more clearly both the limitations of the history-cum-narrative approach and the fundamental differences between historical narratives and most fictional ones than the adaptation of historical materials to the comic-strip format. An ordinary comic-book narrative involves the actions of a limited number of characters, all of whom are represented visually in the strip itself. As a general rule, little or no other information is necessary to understand the significance of the actions themselves. In "The Adventures of Ramsîs in Paris," for example, we need no information other than the description of what Ramsîs did, what the police did, etc. to appreciate the story.[5] The explanatory matter sometimes presented at the tops of frames is kept to a minimum. Finally, since we are dealing with fiction, the actions of an institution, such as the police, can be represented through the acts of a few individual policemen.

To a considerable degree this schema holds true for all traditional fictional narratives. Even a sociological novel carries its description largely through the actions of characters. And much of the setting can be made equivalent to background illustration in a comic. The use of historical or other material in an essentially nonnarrative way can only be occasional in the novel and must remain subordinate to the evocation of conditions through the actions (or thoughts) of characters. As much can be seen in the novels of Dickens, Zola, and Jules Romains, despite the sociological and historical sophistication which informs them.

History, no matter how dramatic the incident recounted, depends on the inclusion of narrative and description on a level of generalization higher than that normal to fictional narratives and, more important for our purposes, higher than that easily transmitted in traditional comic-strip form. That can be seen most easily in attempts to recast traditional history into comic-strip form. Such attempts have been made most extensively, and overall probably most effectively, in France, especially in the *Histoire de France en bandes dessinées* series published by Larousse.[6]

In the volume of the *Histoire* on the Third Republic, for example, we find a text which begins at the bottom of the first frame and says of the French colonizers, "To achieve their dream, they are ready to brave the incomprehension of their fellow citizens . . ."; continues under the next frame, "the greatest difficulties, diseases . . ."; and ends in the third frame, ". . . death." In these frames the scenes correspond only analogically with the text (see fig. 3.1). In the first frame, a French citizen, through his speech balloon, expresses his dislike of the French colonizers. In the second, a native guide warns his European master: "Lieutenant! The landing is blocked!"[7]

Clearly, the dominant discourse, the one which makes sense of the entire text

3.1. *Parallel discourses in a
French historical strip.*

and ties it together, is the explanatory material at the bottom of the frames recounting
the types of difficulties the French colonizers had to overcome, from political hostility
at home to danger abroad. This discourse is, also equally evidently, a historical discourse. The material illustrated in the frames and provided with speech balloons consists only of examples of the types of phenomena described in the explanatory material. As such, it is, properly speaking, fictional. We have no reason to believe that a
native guide on precisely such a river emitted the exact words "Lieutenant! The landing is blocked!"

More important, the frame makes no sense at all if it is deprived of the explanatory material. The only connection between this frame and the previous one lies in

the material that is not illustrated, because it cannot be. Hence that part of the total text which carries the historical discourse and which, as a result, represents the principle of continuity across the text is precisely that part on the margin of, when not completely outside, the strip qua strip.

This coexistence of two parallel discourses, one of which (the explanatory, historical) is continuous and potentially independent of the other, permeates the entire *Histoire* series. The result is not so much the presentation of the history of France in comic-strip format as it is the illustration, with comic-strip frames, of a history presented, in effect, in normal written discourse.

This phenomenon is not accidental to the Larousse series and is, indeed, closely bound up with the entire problem of the presentation of overtly historical (or more generally ideological) material in comic-strip format. As such, it shows up in similar attempts to transmit ideological messages through imaged narratives. Gino Nebiolo, for example, has characterized certain Chinese political texts as comic strips when they are really illustrated narratives. There are no balloons, and the story is really carried forward by the text, which sits below each picture.[8] By choosing this system, the Chinese authors avoided much of the problem of dual discourse which exists in the Larousse series, and in which one must read first the text in the balloon and then the explanatory text (or vice versa), keeping the two distinct. A similar situation obtains in more traditional materials such as saints' lives, in which the same solution of an illustrated text is adopted.[9]

That this problem and the accompanying "solution" of merely illustrating an essentially explanatory text are directly linked to the nature of historical narrative is shown by the adoption of the same solution in comics that could be defined as historical fiction or partially fictionalized history. This is the case, for example, with *Aymeric et les Cathares*, the story of a youth from Occitania (southern France) who, though himself a Catholic, becomes involved with the struggle of his fellow southerners (Cathar and Catholic alike) for religious liberty and regional autonomy.[10] Those parts of the comic which describe the personal adventures of the hero, Aymeric, follow traditional strip format. The story is conveyed through the normal combination of pictures and speech balloons, with a minimum of explanatory material. When it is a matter of recounting the crusade of Simon de Montfort, however, the text adopts the familiar device of a narrator who provides explanatory material with illustration, often without any speech balloons at all.[11]

There are, of course, ways of getting around these problems. One is the selection (or foregrounding) of that aspect of the historical narrative which is most like a fictional narrative. Such a narrative, of course, is more easily represented in traditional stripological discourse. This tendency is epitomized by a comic album in a series devoted to "les Grands Capitaines" entitled *La Longue marche*.[12] Here, though the subject of the strip is nominally Mao Zedong, the narrative concentrates on the events of the Long March itself and treats them essentially as parts of one great adventure, as a series of acts of heroism. As a result, the story as a whole functions virtually as a standard (and fictional) adventure story and is easily portrayed with normal stripological procedures and little additional explanatory material or illustration. A similar situation pertains with an Iraqi comic strip based on aspects of the life of Saddâm Husayn.[13]

The authors of *Jamâl ʿAbd al-Nâsir* did not accept such limitations. The text seeks to present its hero in full historical context and to describe all the major aspects of his action, in war and in peace, in domestic and in foreign affairs. Thus it has had to develop strategies for the integration of this complex historical material into the format of the comic strip.

But instead of simplifying the historical field, one can introduce fictional narratives into the historical one. The fictional insert provides greater immediacy for the reader and breaks the pattern of explanatory or didactic material. This is done in the Larousse *Histoire de France en bandes dessinées* for the twentieth century by the device of creating a father-and-son team, but this fiction does not relieve the text of turning to explanatory material and illustration (just as the fictional *Aymeric* did) when it becomes necessary to transmit the historical material which forms the true content of the story.[14] The introduction of a father and his two sons (with the attendant masculinization of the world of history and politics) plays a larger role in a comic-strip biography of Charles de Gaulle.[15] Here the father, like a modern-day Shahrazâd, narrates the story of de Gaulle to his sons, and his narration plays the role usually assigned to explanatory material.[16]

The comic biography of Nasser contains no frame story and no specific valorization of the family, either that of Nasser himself or that of an Egyptian audience. But it would be a mistake to see in this a lower value placed on the family in Egyptian than in French society. The contrary is probably the case. Nasser's wife never appears in the strip, but that is realistic given that she rarely appeared in public in Egypt.

Women, however, do play an auxiliary political role in the Egyptian text. They are the quintessential victims. On the page (31) that recounts Israel's capture of Jerusalem, the leading refugee, foregrounded in the lower-left frame (and much larger than any of the others) is a young woman (fig. 3.2). Similarly, the tragedy of the first Arab-Israeli war is personified in a full-frame image of a sobbing widow figure (p. 2). The appeal is, of course, a traditional one. The female must be protected from the foreigner, and her victimization is both the greatest indignity and the greatest pathos. Such pathos is an important element in *Jamâl ʿAbd al-Nâsir*.

Women are occasionally present in political situations in the Nasser biography, as part of the popular crowds that support the Egyptian leader. On a page (38) devoted to the Aswan Dam, for example, we see a woman foregrounded among a crowd of Upper Egyptian peasants. In a more famous scene, when the Egyptian crowd takes to the streets to protest Nasser's decision to resign after the 1967 debacle, a woman cries out in the front row (p. 34). This is apparently a well-established iconography, since in his film version of the same events, *al-ʿUsfûr*, Yûsuf Shâhîn made the first person in the street a woman.[17] When the evocation of the people is particularly dramatic, then, women do appear, but generally in *Jamâl ʿAbd al-Nâsir* they are removed from political activity. Yet the fact that women appear in politicized, as opposed to domestic, situations is concordant with a leftist ideology which, rather than stressing the importance of intermediate groups like the family, sees the people as a political unit. This representation of the Egyptian people has implications across the strip biography.

The comic-strip text is preceded and followed by noncomic, written materials. *Nâsir* begins with a prose survey of the life of its hero and ends with a selection from the writings and speeches of the Egyptian leader. The transition between prose text and strip text is mediated; the minibiography is accompanied by a series of disarticulated comic-strip frames selected from the comic text itself. These are not presented in the mode of direct illustration of an explanatory text but as a parallel tracing of Nasser's life in pictures. The concluding section of quotes (organized both chronologically and thematically) is also accompanied by a selection of frames from the strip. The political messages of these sections are all-the-better integrated into the comic strip itself.

Nasserite Stripology

Jamâl ʿAbd al-Nâsir uses no frame story to introduce an outside narrator; nor does it fictionalize its text by inclusion or exclusion. Instead, the comic-strip biography makes extensive use of creative stripological procedures to transmit essentially historical concepts. In fact, the techniques employed are among the most original and sophisticated of any existing historical strip.

The shapes of the frames often play significant narrative-historical roles. The most distinctive frame shape is the medallion. Though small medallions are used on several occasions to give emphasis or as forms of stripological elegant variation, there are three cases in which this shape dominates the entire page, along with a similar visual arrangement employed in a fourth example. These medallion pages are the most dramatically composed sheets in the comic-strip biography. They also mark the most important events in the text.

The first of these pages (10) evokes Nasser's famous speech in Alexandria announcing the nationalization of the Suez Canal (fig. 3.3). The second and third both concern the 1967 War, one (p. 29) representing Egypt's defeat in the Sinai (fig. 3.4) and the other (p. 31), Israel's capture of East Jerusalem (fig. 3.2). The last medallion page is also the last page (40) of the comic-strip text, and it describes Nasser's funeral procession through the streets of Cairo (fig. 3.5).

The significance of these choices is evident. All the events are turning points in Nasser's career. Even the funeral procession was essentially a political event, the last, in Nasser's "life," since what we are shown on this page is the political fact of the reaction of the Egyptian people and not the personal, more purely biographical fact of their leader's death. All these pages also evoke Nasser as leader of Egypt, not as a young man preparing or an officer accomplishing the military coup that brought the Free Officers to power. The chief of state eclipses both the man and the conspirator.

But the precise forms of these pages carry signification. Of these four cases, two foreground the face of Nasser in closeup (figs. 3.3 and 3.4).[18] The other two do not put the hero of the story in the center of the visual field; both present large medallions in the center of the page. Each circle consists in a crowded scene visualized as a long shot, which differentiates it from the images which surround it.[19] The effect produced reminds one of a view from a telescope. The first is an overview of the old city of Jerusalem, easily recognizable by the Dome of the Rock (fig. 3.2). Arrows pointing around the cityscape mark the maneuvers of the victorious Israeli army. The other pictures Nasser's flag-draped coffin being pulled by horses through the streets of the Egyptian capital, surrounded by a crowd of soldiers and onlookers (fig. 3.5). These two scenes are the only such geometric arrangements in the text. The page shown in fig. 3.3 bisects its central medallion with a horizontal line, while the page shown in fig. 3.4 does not really present a medallion at all but is based on a complex type of star pattern.

The striking formal similarities between the funeral page, on one hand, and the conquest-of-Jerusalem page, on the other, create an equivalence in the events themselves. The capture of Jerusalem becomes a type of death, just as Nasser's death echoes the loss of the holy city. This assimilation stresses the common elements in the two events, the religious theme of the holy city along with the religious character of the funeral procession, and the political significance of the defeat in Palestine.

This equivalence also elevates the importance of the loss of Arab Jerusalem. The death and funeral of the Egyptian leader is a central biographical fact; its place and treatment at the end of the story are altogether normal, biographically speaking. The capture of East Jerusalem is a less obviously biographical or significant event. It could, for example, have been completely subsumed under the general Arab defeat in the Six-Day War. This treatment magnifies its importance in the life of the Egyptian president and, in effect, makes it a commentary on Nasser's entire life and career. The final result of this equivalence (and the fact that three of the four medallion pages deal with spectacular losses or failures, while only one recounts a success) is to bathe the entire comic strip in an atmosphere of tragedy and mourning. The life of Nasser becomes colored by the sweet sorrow that is such a prominent mood in so much of contemporary Egyptian popular culture, as can be seen, for example, in many of the songs of the popular Egyptian vocalist Farîd al-Atrash.

The Jerusalem Page: Narrative Synchrony

The page devoted to the capture of Jerusalem is important for another reason. It displays a kind of stripological synchronicity. The center of the page, its oversized middle register comprising a large bisected rectangle in the center of which lies the medallion, links synchrony with diachrony. The left side shows street fighting in an Arab city as an Arab soldier (complete with kûfiyya) fires down on Western-garbed Israeli soldiers. On the right, we see a well-equipped army of Israelis invading the city. The frame on the right slightly precedes chronologically the one on the left (in the normal Arabic reading order of right to left), since it represents an invasion of the city while the left frame pictures street fighting. The medallion in the center communicates with both of these pictures and, in a sense, links them, since it covers part of each of the two side panels, as if it were placed over them. The placement is appropriate, of course, because the medallion presents the summary and significance, in a word the generalization, of what is in the two side panels: Israel's capture of East Jerusalem. The central explanatory text, which tops the medallion, merely describes this relationship, pointing out that the Israelis invaded the city and that the Palestinians fought them from house to house. The stripological procedure is so sophisticated here that the relationship between the events in the three frames is clearly indicated by their arrangement. The explanatory text is almost superfluous.

The relationship between these three frames, the medallion and the two side panels, is not a traditional narrative one. The frames do not exhibit a true chronological order, since the medallion in no sense stands chronologically between the two side panels. Its relationship to the side panels is purely synchronic. It represents a narrative which unfolds at the same time as that in the side panels, but on a different level of reality. Such synchronicity is a departure from the normal rules of stripological discourse in which spatial relationships (top to bottom and left to right for the Roman script, right to left for the Arabic) indicate narrative sequence. The use of frame arrangements to indicate synchronicity and parallel narratives is a highly creative solution to the problems of stripifying historical discourse. A distinguishing quality of historical discourse (including historical narrative) is the presence of simultaneous narrative sequences, sequences which often operate on different levels of generalization. After all, it was the need for two levels of generalization which led to the double discourse in the *Histoire de France en bandes dessinées*.

While synchronous frame arrangements are not unknown in other historical strips,[20] *Jamâl 'Abd al-Nâsir* makes the greatest and most sophisticated use of this technique of any comic we have seen. The Egyptian comic uses page arrangement to create the balance of synchrony and diachrony essential to historical narrative.[21] The Jerusalem page, for example, is really divided into three registers. The top register, moving from right to left, begins with a profile of King Hussein in front of an image of his country being traversed by Israeli jets. The text explains that the Israelis offered the Jordanian king the opportunity to stay out of the war, an offer he rejected. The second frame shows the advance of Israeli soldiers through Arab territory, while its text states that the Israelis invaded Jordan backed by their air force, which had already destroyed its Egyptian counterpart. Hence the top register sets up the circumstances of the war between Israel and Jordan. The middle one is concerned with the loss of East Jerusalem. The bottom register contains two frames. The right one shows the defeated Jordanian army blending into a picture of a pensive and preoccupied Nasser. Its text explains that the Jordanians were obliged to accept an armistice, while Nasser expresses his hope for an eventual victory. On the left, we see refugees crossing a river, a theme echoed by the explanatory text.

The registers taken together form a familiar historical triad. They show the causes of the event, the event itself, then its consequences. And the hierarchy of importance in this sequence is reflected visually: the central register is as large as the top and bottom ones combined.

Nor is it either accidental or devoid of significance that this segment of historical narrative occupies a single page. The arrangement of these frames on one page focuses attention directly on the medallion in the center. Thus the medallion, with its image of the holy city, communicates not only with the two contiguous frames but with all the events on the page, defining them all as aspects of one great tragedy.

Such a technique is also a departure from traditional stripology. As the term *strip* indicates, the traditional comic strip consists of a number of frames whose relations one with another are essentially syntagmatic. In its most basic form, the comic strip is organized like a scroll, not like a painting. Hence also, the strips can be cut into pieces and published serially in a newspaper. However, as Fresnault-Deruelle points out, the recent tendency to publish comics in one-page units has tended to promote a certain degree of composition by page. This has led to the creation of pages (or two-page spreads) as "great syntagms," which represent relatively significant groupings of events.[22] In this case, however, the frame is not the only unit of signification, that is, a unit which carries meaning, like a morpheme. On another level of signification, the frame becomes a mere unit of distinction within the page, which is then the new unit of signification.[23] If the frames on the Jerusalem page were distributed on other pages (but kept in the same sequence), this final level of signification would be lost.

This semiotic technique is particularly well adapted to historical discourse. Its essence, of course, is to divide the narrative chain, isolating one sequence of events, which then becomes an episode. While all sophisticated narratives (fictional or historical) rely on such divisions, the analysis which logically precedes any historical narrative demands a greater and more sophisticated division of the narrative chain into episodes and subepisodes, which are in turn complicated by the existence of parallel narratives on different levels of generalization. Organization by page, therefore, is an important carrier of historical signification, and the organized pages in *Jamâl 'Abd al-Nâsir* become major historical (and biographical) foci in the text.

The result is a creative symbiosis between two avenues of stripological innovation. The a priori antagonism indicated by Fresnault-Deruelle—"on the one hand create a visual piece, construct a two-dimensional ensemble . . . on the other hand, tell a story"[24]—is not simply eliminated, it is replaced by its opposite, the adaptation of the generic limits of the strip to the distinctive discourse of a special kind of story. The stripological freedom and synchronicity suggested by the organization by page answers one of the major methodological challenges of adapting the comic strip to historical discourse.

Nasser in History: Defeat in the Sinai

A more sophisticated example of this type of organization is shown in fig. 3.4; it also recounts an episode of the Six-Day War. Though this page does not contain a medallion, we grouped it with the other three because it possesses a unified visual organization around a central, dominating form. The formal arrangement of this page is more complicated than that of the Jerusalem page, both in its geometric patterning and in the relationship between its forms and its frames.

The visual divisions of the page are themselves complex. The frames are grouped into three horizontal registers. But superimposed over this division, in a complex geometry reminiscent of the compound geometric patterns of Islamic art, are converging diagonal lines which form the pattern either of an hourglass or of a star, depending on whether or not one visualizes the horizontal lines separating the registers as part of the design.

But the patterns themselves are not defined solely by the boundaries of the frames. In the middle of the central frame and dominating the page as a whole is the bust of Nasser. Though no frame line separates it from the rest of the material in the central register (a point whose significance we will discuss shortly), its size and color make Nasser appear as a separate form whose lines interact with the boundaries of the frames on the page. This formal separation of Nasser is also accomplished through color. The background of the central frame and those on the right and left wings of the top and bottom registers are dominated by the color of desert sand and other light pastels, making these scenes form a kind of pattern around Nasser. In addition, Nasser is in closeup, which distinguishes him from the battle scenes on the sides of the page and links him to the central images above and below him, which are in closeup.

These formal, visual complexities are not merely decorative. They organize the historical relationships between the event-images displayed on the page. Setting aside for the moment the central frames, enclosed within the diagonal lines, the three registers divide the historical event into its three basic elements. In the top register, we see the preparations. On the right, Israeli jets streak over an unprepared territory, pointing toward the center of the register. On the left, an enemy tank advances, its gun pointing downward and to the right. The text explains that the Israeli air force was free to attack Egyptian military targets and that no force was available to check the actions of the Israeli military. In the central register, an Egyptian army is being routed by enemy aircraft, an image confirmed by the text. This image becomes the central fact of the page. The bottom register shows the battlefield strewn with dead Egyptian soldiers and destroyed equipment in the right frame, while in the small left frame the Israeli army pushes onward without resistance, the clear result of the destruction of the Egyptian army.

The frames enclosed within the diagonals have a different function: they add the international dimension. On the top, we see the Soviet leader whom we are told has condemned the Israeli aggression, though tanks would have been better than words. Below him are enframed President Lyndon Johnson with his foreign and defense secretaries along with the explanation that the United States, after having tricked the Egyptians, will prevent the Soviet Union from taking any action. Below the central register is the French spokesman explaining that his government will embargo arms to both sides.

In effect, the central frames can be read according to two different schemata.

They can be read as part of their registers, in which case the Soviet and U.S. reactions are part of the conditions which leave the Israeli armed forces free to destroy their Egyptian counterparts. Similarly, the French declaration becomes part of the reaction to the Egyptian defeat. But these central frames can also be read as part of their own narrative, one chronicling the international developments that coincide with the strictly military ones.

The double potential elegantly expresses the duality of the historical narrative in visual terms. On one hand, like all narratives, it moves forward in time. On the other hand, it demands for its proper comprehension the understanding of parallel narratives and their mutual relationships. These relationships are clearly shown in the top register, where the international reactions explain the lack of constraints on the Israelis pictured and expressed in the left frame. Pictures and arguments reinforce each other.

But images often go further than arguments, and there are visual elements in this page which transmit information not available in (or in contradiction with) the verbal text. The most noteworthy of these is the bust of Nasser superimposed upon the central frame. The most obvious effect of this juxtaposition is to suggest narrative synchronicity. Though not physically present at the rout of the Egyptian army, the leader is spiritually there. His narrative (that is, the biography) continues while the military story advances. In fact, this synchronicity of biography and extrabiographical historical developments is set up on the very first page of the strip, in which the image of the earlier Egyptian nationalist Saʿd Zaghlûl, is superimposed upon the frame recounting Nasser's early life.

Nasser's superimposition upon the Egyptian defeat in the Sinai suggests more than mere synchronicity. Though Nasser stands in the middle of the frame (and his image covers a space from its top to its bottom), he does not bisect it. The action continues around and behind him. He does not divide the frame so much as he is within it. This is also why the figure of the Egyptian president is not enclosed in a medallion or any other type of frame. In a disregard for comic-strip "realism," there is no linear boundary separating him from a scene in which he, after all, cannot really be physically present. Had Nasser been enclosed in a medallion, he would in some sense have been isolated from the scene, outside it. As it stands, he could not be more involved. An Israeli jet seems about to fly over his shoulder; and it almost looks as if he could be hit by the flying bullets.

But Nasser is not only in the scene; he also seems to be bursting out of it. In a technique also frequently employed by the brilliant Egyptian filmmaker Shâdî ʿAbd al-Salâm, Nasser's head has been cut off by the top of the frame.[25] The effect is dramatic; not only does it permit the face to be larger (both absolutely and relative to the rest of the frame), but it also focuses attention on the eyes.

Along with his furrowed brow and slightly downturned lips, Nasser's eyes communicate a message of deeply pensive sadness, of quiet and dignified anguish. Here the visual message departs from the verbal, textual one. The explanatory material immediately below the central frame indicates that Nasser remained ignorant of the disaster which had befallen the Egyptian forces (indeed, for many hours this was true).[26] The picture, however, says otherwise. The anguished Nasser in the center of the page clearly "knows" and "feels" his country's defeat. The events on the page are refracted through his consciousness. And this transmutation redefines them for the reader. The tragedy appears somewhat cold, clinical, in a sense historic, when seen through the relatively small images of the Egyptian soldiers being routed in the central frame or lying dead on the bottom right and center. But the scene takes on an element of pathos when reflected through Nasser's eyes, which give emotional content to the entire page.

Cutting the Egyptian leader's head with the frame border projects his form out of its frame. The central frames of the top register seem to flow directly from Nasser's head. Their form fits over his head almost like a hat, and the communication between the bust of Nasser and the central frames is reinforced by the similarity in appearance. In this way Nasser is linked to the international event-images and to the military defeat, both vertically and horizontally. The organization of the page brings together the separate historical strands through the common effect they have on the (visually and thematically) central character. This history, it reminds us, is a biography.

Nasser and the People: The Suez Canal

The synchronicity of narrative elements which we saw in both the Jerusalem page and the page just discussed (the Egyptian defeat in the Sinai) is carried further by the page shown in fig. 3.3. This page recounts Nasser's famous 1956 Alexandria speech announcing the nationalization of the Suez Canal, and it represents a complete synchronicity signified by a sophisticated visual organization and the creative application of stripological techniques.

This speech was an important one, not only because in it Nasser defied the Western powers and seized control over one of his country's more important military and economic assets but also because it represented a milestone in his political relations with his people. The speech received an enthusiastic reception from its Egyptian audience, partly because Nasser adopted an informal style and made jokes at the expense of the agents of those Western diplomatic and financial powers which had recently humiliated Egypt.[27] This aspect of the speech is only communicated visually. It is not indicated either in the explanatory material or in the speech balloons attributed to Nasser.

The visual organization of the page functions as a combination of the medallion of the Jerusalem page and the star pattern of the Sinai defeat page. This produces a considerable division into separate frames combined with a page organization directing all the frames toward the center. In fact, instead of the triad of registers which we found in the other two pages, the Suez Canal page is divided in two horizontally. The absence of the triune division reflects the absence of the three-part sequence of preparation, main event, and consequences. All the events on the Suez Canal page take place in perfect synchrony, during Nasser's speech itself.

The text of the speech, presented largely in Nasser's speech balloons, does have a diachronic, narrative tendency. To follow its text, one has to read it in the usual Arabic strip order, from right to left and from top to bottom. It is not a coincidence, however, that the verbal text tends to border the visual one, occupying the top row of the page and a space at the bottom. This arrangement allows the visual material to escape the diachrony implicit in verbal language and to create, instead, an absolute synchrony.

The images on the Suez Canal page are effectively simultaneous. All exist in the undifferentiated time of the delivery of Nasser's speech; all reflect the speech and its reception. For example, on the top we first see Nasser speaking in front of microphones, and on the left, a group of men listening to this same speech on the radio. It is obvious that they must be listening at the same time Nasser is speaking. On the far right is a picture of Muhammad ʿAlî square in Alexandria—the place where Nasser is speaking—while on the far left one sees an audience of urban-looking Egyptians. Finally, immediately above the central medallion, crowning it, is a group of photographers posed to memorialize the occasion.

All these frames represent different (but chronologically synchronic) aspects of the same event: Nasser's speech announcing the nationalization of the Suez Canal. The same is true of the frames on the bottom half of the page. We see a predominantly middle- and upper-class audience on the far right; the outstretched arms of an apparently more popular one in Port Said, by the banks of the canal, on the far left; and in the bottom center two mirrored frames of Nasser talking. The effect of the mirror is to suggest synchronicity at the very moment that the speech moves forward diachronically. What could be more simultaneous than an image and its reflection?

There is yet another important element in the composition of this page, one which is properly speaking neither purely textual nor completely visual. This is the laughter. The laughter on this page is indicated by the groups of Arabic characters that signify "hâ hâ," "qâh qâh," etc. These "words" are not transmitted in the normal stripological procedure for presenting oral text. They are not neatly printed on the white backgrounds of the explanatory material or enclosed within speech balloons. Instead, the stripological convention they exploit is that usually reserved for the transcription of nonlinguistic sounds or noises, like the "boom" of an explosion.[28]

The first result of this procedure is to de-textualize the laughter. It becomes a nonlinguistic element in the strip which can then be represented paravisually (the linguistic element is not completely eliminated, however, since the signs in question need to pass through a linguistic decoding in order to yield their signification of laughter). As elements which operate within the visual parameters of the strip, they can change their size and placement to fit in with other visual elements, hence the larger characters surrounding Nasser's head, the medium-sized ones immediately below, and the smaller ones in the two mirror images on the bottom.

If the characters signifying laughter had been placed within speech balloons, they would have had to be attributed to individuals, or at the most to groups of individuals. Instead, by being assimilated to background noises, they become part of the total environment, in the air, surrounding and infusing the whole scene. This also contributes to their synchronicity with the other signs on the page. In a comic strip, one accepts the idea that the different modes of expression, visual or verbal-textual, constitute parallel narratives, in essence, that they are synchronous with one another. By adopting a third mode of expression (that normally associated with background noises) for the laughter, the authors of the Egyptian comic book make this element, too, synchronous with the others.

But the laughter is not only personally undefined; it also leaks out across the frames. Not only are the characters in question present in several frames, but many of them actually cross the barriers separating the frames. The laughter is the chief unifying element in the page ensemble. It is, as a result, the primary means of communication between Nasser and his audience. And it is perfectly mutual. It is clear visually that Nasser laughs (we see him laughing in the medallion), and it is equally clear that the audience (or we might better say, the audiences) is also laughing. Only the photographers maintain the seriousness of high politics; most of the other figures are either smiling strongly or laughing out loud.

The laughter brings all the Egyptians together with their leader. It creates a communion between the people and their president, for it is this couple which the Suez Canal page really celebrates. Here, then, is the explanation of the page's dual organization, which even bisects the central medallion. Its visual binarism reflects the essential duality of leader and people which dominates it.

The message is transmitted most forcefully in the medallion. This central circle is not devoted exclusively, as one might expect, to a cameo of Nasser. It is bisected, and the lower half contains four large figures representing three Egyptians of the popular classes and one middle- or upper-class individual. The medallion indicates what is most important on the page. This one states that the crucial reality is not Nasser giving a speech or Nasser nationalizing the Suez Canal, but the couple, Nasser and the Egyptian people.

That we are dealing here with a couple, that is to say, with two coequal actors, can also be seen in the fact that the people on this page face the reader. They are not turned into a passive audience. This phenomenon is, in fact, general in *Jamâl 'Abd al-Nâsir*. And if one of these two actors must turn his back to the reader, it is not the audience but the speaker, Nasser.

This relationship between Nasser and the people dominates *Jamâl 'Abd al-Nâsir*.[29] For example, in the page which chronicles the defeat of the Egyptian army in the Sinai (fig. 3.4), we saw that Nasser appeared as an actor on a level at least equal to that of the Egyptian soldiers. On the Jerusalem page (fig. 3.2), of course, Nasser was replaced in the central medallion by the holy city. The people shown on this page, however, are not the people of Egypt but those of Palestine. Hence Nasser cannot form a couple with them. One can argue by extension that Nasser is for his people what Jerusalem is to the people of Palestine: the crystallization of their identity.

The mode of communication between the Egyptian president and his compatriots is the emotion of laughter, just as Nasser's fundamental communication with the defeated Egyptian army is his emotional participation in the fact of their defeat. The same is true on the last comic page of the text, the one displaying Nasser's funeral procession (fig. 3.5). Here it is Nasser's flag-draped coffin which dominates the central medallion, though it is surrounded by soldiers and onlookers. What ties the groups of mourners, both individuals and crowds, together is the grief they express in their tears and their words.

Not only do Nasser and the people form a couple, but the essential mode of communication between them is nonrational. This notion of a lone leader enjoying a mystic communion with his people, free of any parliamentary or electoral formalities, is not a new one. It is one of the components of fascism—but of fascist theory more than of fascist practice. Nor is this meant to suggest that Nasserism is a form of fascism. The dissimilarities are considerable.[30] But this idea of the leader as direct representative of the people, so heavily exploited in Europe by the antidemocratic right, is clearly one of the major ideological messages transmitted by *Jamâl ʿAbd al-Nâsir.*

One difference is quite striking, however, between the presentation of the Egyptian leader in this biography and that associated with so many twentieth-century dictators, of both the Right and the Left. Many modern dictators cultivate the image of never being wrong, of only succeeding in their activities. This is far from the way Nasser is presented in this comic text. Nasser's communion with his people is so close that he shares their tragedies as well as their triumphs. He does not stand above them as all-knowing or all-wise. The Egyptian leader's closeness to the people is further reflected in the frequent use of his first name without other titles or appellatives, both by the narrator and by the people. This populist relationship between Nasser and his people is also fundamentally extraconstitutional. One may even see the continual emphasis in *Jamâl ʿAbd al-Nâsir* on this direct relationship as a form of compensation for other forms of legitimization.

Speech vs. Writing

The Suez Canal page highlights another important aspect of the comic-strip biography: its emphasis on the oral. On this page, as we saw, Nasser is linked with his Egyptian audience, fundamentally through laughter, the graphemes of which leak out across the frames. Since these laughter letters are not presented in the normal textual way, they are read more as sound than as purely written text and are distinguished from the other letters which form part of the text of the strip. Hence the laughter is an essentially oral phenomenon, and its central signifying role serves to valorize the oral. Of course, even without the laughter, the page celebrates Nasser's oral communication with his people.

The oral basis of Nasser's relationship with his people, what one could call the politics of orality, is reinforced throughout the comic strip, both positively and negatively. Positively, the politics of orality is manifested on other occasions when Nasser addresses his audiences. For example, the establishment of the United Arab Republic is celebrated with a half-page composition showing Nasser addressing two popular audiences at the same time, one in Cairo and one in Damascus. Images of Nasser addressing his people, speaking into a microphone (and with his words in a speech balloon), are legion.

But the biography of Nasser also stresses the oral by avoiding its opposite, the

3.6. *Historical synchrony: war is declared.*

3.7. *Pictographic balloons, the 1956 War.*

textual. At no time are newspapers, proclamations, or other texts used as both images of objects and textual messages, as they are used, for example, to announce the coming of the Second World War in the *Histoire de France en bandes dessinées* (fig 3.6).[31] There is nothing in the nature of Egyptian society that would make such an application inappropriate. *Al-Ahrâm*, with its easily recognized logo, makes an excellent newspaper of record, and we saw it used in this way in the Egyptian story of Ramsîs.[32]

This orality, of course, also has a populist content. In all civilizations, writing is first and foremost an appanage of the elite, whatever its penetration among the masses, while oral transmission retains a more popular character. It is not a coincidence that so many humble Egyptians are shown enthralled by Nasser's speeches.

But *Jamâl 'Abd al-Nâsir* goes even further than this ideological hegemony of the oral over the written. It actually seeks, where possible, to detextualize (in the sense of reducing the role of the written text) the comic strip itself. For example, on page 14 we find an interesting stripological innovation (fig. 3.7). In the treatment of the Israeli invasion of 1956, we see Nasser, characteristically, speaking into a microphone. But the ''speech'' balloon attached to the Egyptian president is not a *speech* balloon at all. Instead, it is completely filled with a picture of Moshe Dayan in front of a group of Israeli soldiers in combat gear. So completely does this picture fill the balloon that it looks more like a frame than a balloon. Only its tail linking it to the speaking Nasser establishes it as a signifier of speech.

Of course, a number of familiar themes are carried by this set of images. First, Nasser is speaking to the Egyptian people, shown below him to the left. In addition, the "image balloon" creates a synchronicity between historical events. The image of Dayan and his soldiers, because of its mimesis, signifies not only the content of Nasser's speech but also its referent, the historical reality of the Israeli military actions. And as usual, Nasser is the figure through which the external event is mediated.

But something else is going on here. The text of Nasser's speech has been replaced by a picture. Rather than presenting the speech of the Egyptian president through words (which in this case would have to be written words), it is communicated through pure imagery. The balloon is an icon for its message. The result is a radical detextualization of Nasser's speech. Though there are some similarities, this phenomenon is different from the use of pictures in the thought balloons of *Ramsîs*. In the story in *Mîkî* magazine, because of the doubling of pictographic and linguistic signs, images do not replace a text, they supplement it.

This replacement occurs again on the very same page. Just above the center of the page, we observe a frame which consists of Nasser's head and a thought balloon which is an image of advancing tanks (Israeli ones, it is clear in context). Again we have synchronicity mediated through the Egyptian leader and again the replacement of linguistic text with imagery, of graphemes with icons. Examples of this procedure (all involving Nasser) can be found on two other pages (9 and 11).

The general effect of this de-textualization is to pretend to subvert the gap between the symbol and its referent, between the historical-biographical text and the historical reality it claims to transmit.[33] The denial (or simply the occultation) of this essential mediation parallels the elimination of those which separate Nasser from the people. Related to this is the fact that so many events are evoked through Nasser that his intelligence appears as the central link, the principle of coherence in the historical narrative.

Life and Death

If textuality connotes the recorded and hence the historical and completed, orality signifies life. The last page of *Jamâl ʿAbd al-Nâsir* (fig. 3.5) represents the mortal remains of the Egyptian leader in a form of communion with his grieving people. That this is a communion with a still-living figure and not the expression of emotion in the presence of a corpse is represented through the cries of the mourners: "You will remain eternally in our hearts and minds, O Abû Khâlid." At the bottom, in the center, stands a picture of Nasser, acting as a pendant to the image of Sadat in the top center. The Sadat frame explains that Nasser has died, and Sadat himself quotes the Qur'ân (Sûrat al-Fajr, verses 27-30) on the repose of the soul with God.

The frame with Nasser, however, counters this. Below the hero's serenely smiling countenance stands this text: "It is said that ʿAbd al-Nâsir died. But ʿAbd al-Nâsir . . . is the revolution and the hope of his people. And the revolution stands; and hope does not die." Nasser is a living presence on the last page of the strip.

The reason he is alive is fundamentally political: the identification with Egypt expressed through the communion with its people. At the top of the page, we read that "the heart of Egypt stopped beating," a phrase that creates an identity between Nasser, who has just died of a heart attack, and his people, whose emotional reaction mirrors the cause of his death. The presentation of Nasser's death thus reflects, like the rest of his comic-strip biography, a set of stripological choices. And these choices are not innocent. They express a view of the man, of his relation to his people, and of history.

4

Machismo and Arabism:
Saddâm Husayn as Lone Hero

A life in strips can be history. It can also, more obviously, be adventure or myth. Each vision implies its own forms of political legitimization, just as these, in turn, rely on appropriate stripological techniques. The comic-strip biography of Nasser wraps its hero in all the richness of historical narrative.[1] That of his younger colleague and fellow pan-Arab, Saddâm Husayn, becomes an adventure, itself approaching the forms of myth. The adventure and its essentially solitary protagonist promote a distinct set of values: that of the Arab "hero" as he was conceived in the days before Islam and as he has remained in the consciousness of the Arabs.

Saddâm Husayn became the leader of Iraq and of its ruling Baath party in 1979. This political group, founded by the Syrian Michel ʿAflaq, has always defined itself in pan-Arab terms. For the Baathists, Iraq is a "region" in the Arab "nation."[2] The choice of originally pre-Islamic values ideally suits the combination of Iraqi national reality and pan-Arab vision.

Given the cult of personality surrounding the Iraqi leader (the government even distributes Saddâm Husayn watches), increasingly intensified after the beginning of the war with Iran, and the enormous resources devoted by the regime to mass education and propaganda,[3] it is not surprising that Saddâm Husayn should be the subject of a comic-strip album. It is equally a testimony to the productivity and the sophistication of Iraqi writers and illustrators that this portrait of Saddâm Husayn is apparently the only such comic-strip biography conceived and produced exclusively by Arabs in an Arab country.[4]

The Making of a Lone Hero

Our text, entitled *al-Ayyâm al-Tawîla* (The Long Days), is based on a work of the same name by ʿAbd al-Amîr Muʿalla. Labeled a "novel" (*riwâya*) on its cover, Muʿalla's book is a partly fictionalized account of a period in Saddâm Husayn's life before the second (and successful) Baath revolution of 1968 and his rise to power. Though the central character of this novel is called Muhammad Husayn al-Saqr and the leader of Iraq is known as Saddâm Husayn, it is clear to the Iraqi reader, both by the facts in the book and the context of its presentation, that its hero is the leader of the country. This semidisguise permits Muʿalla to take whatever liberties he wishes with the life of his protagonist, while permitting the identification with the historical personage essential to the latter's legitimization.[5]

The comic-strip album, drawn by Adîb Makkî, was adapted "freely," as the title page puts it, from Muʿalla's novel, but only from the first of the three volumes of that work. The album, however, is not presented as the first volume or part of a larger work but as an independent text.[6] From a literary point of view it possesses its own unity, with appropriate closure (as does the first volume of the novel).[7]

To this shorter narrative the anonymous adapter has added a number of other changes, some of which, such as the omission of many details and descriptive passages, are clearly associated with the adaptation to comic-strip form. Others, such as the transformation of incidents or even the omission of characters, shift the emphases in the text and help to shape the image of the Iraqi leader presented in the comic strip. One shift is both immediately generic and directly visible: the hero of the strip is even more readily identifiable than his novelistic alter ego. His face is clearly that of a younger Saddâm Husayn.

The story is relatively straightforward. Our young hero, we shall call him Husayn (the name element common to both identities), is ordered by the Baath party to participate in the plot to assassinate the Iraqi dictator ʿAbd al-Karîm Qâsim. Husayn and a small group of comrades riddle the tyrant's car with bullets. Miraculously, the dictator survives and Husayn and the other would-be assassins must flee Qâsim's police. After an initial period with his colleagues in a prearranged Baath party hideout, Husayn, wounded in the leg, decides to make his way to safety. He flees first to his family home in Samarra and then across the desert to Syria and safety. The story ends with his safe arrival in the Syrian border town, Abû Kamâl. As the sun rises, the hero declares: "It is a new day, after long days" (p. 67).

Historical contextualization is kept to a bare minimum. The reader is told that there was a popular revolution in 1958 but that its "fruits" were stolen by Qâsim. The tyrant and his henchmen set up a ruthless dictatorship; opponents were jailed, tortured, and killed. Against this regime, the Baath party plotted revolution (pp. 10–13). After this brief discussion, neither the historical nor the larger political contexts are ever evoked again, as the text concentrates exclusively on the adventures of its hero. More important perhaps than the brevity of this historical discussion, however, is its narrative ordering, which prevents it from acting either as parallel to or completion of the dominant narrative of the text, the adventures of Husayn.

One notices immediately, to borrow Gérard Genette's terminology, that the "story" (the sequence of events as they have taken place) is not identical to the "narrative" (the sequence of events as they are presented in the text). The opening pages of "The Long Days" provide us with examples of both prolepses (events presented or alluded to in the narrative before their occurrence in the story) and analepses (events presented or alluded to in the narrative after their occurrence in the story).[8] The historical discussion combines both prolepsis, analepsis, and synchrony.

The album properly speaking begins with a proleptic vision of our hero at what is, in effect, the last stage of his escape into Syria. First we see the soldiers who are searching and, on the following pages, Husayn and his companion as they reach the border town of Abû Kamâl. The first political allusion comments on the image of the policemen: "The time: 1959. Iraq is under the shadow of the rule of the dictator, ʿAbd al-Karîm Qâsim" (p. 7). This prologue completed, the text returns to the dominant narrative sequence and begins the story of the young Husayn, contacted by the Baath party. Almost immediately, however, the synchronic mode enters with the description of life under Qâsim's dictatorship. Its initial words echo those of the first political allusion: "The year: 1959. A dictator was ruling Baghdad . . . " (p. 10). But the two 1959s, though both invoke synchrony, are not the same. The first takes place at the end of the story, the second at its beginning. Their principal effect is to frame the diachrony of the adventure into a historical synchrony. Events move, but not history. The important changes are not in the life of the nation but in that of the hero. His story has been separated from that of history.[9]

Yet the linear nature of the historical process is evoked shortly afterward through an analepsis back to 1947 and the foundation of the Baath party. The next event pictured is the revolution of 1958. But the relationship between the struggle of the Baath and the overthrow of the monarchy is left carefully ambiguous (pp. 11–12).

Thus the small amount of historical linearity present is twice removed from the dominant narrative and subordinated to a synchronic evocation of the setting of the adventure. The contrast with Nasser's strip biography is striking. There the linear narrative, essentially free of analepses or prolepses, carried forward both the life of Nasser and the history of his country. The leader is fused with the history of his nation. Saddâm Husayn, by contrast, is removed from the history of his. (This evacuation of history spares "The Long Days" the stripological challenges involved in the representation of a full historical narrative and by the same token obviates the need for the kinds of solution adopted in *Jamâl ʿAbd al-Nâsir*.) Most of the historical material appears in the familiar mode of explanatory texts, accompanied by illustrations which are not strictly necessary for its comprehension. Only one page displays a Nasserian attempt at the visual representation of historical phenomena. The revolution of 1958 fills one of the few, and the only historical, full-page frames. The bottom half of the frame brings together a set of scenes of an essentially anonymous popular uprising. The top half of the frame is a deserted street, shortly after sunrise, as flocks of birds

3.2. *The loss of East Jerusalem.*

3.3. *The Suez Canal nationalization speech.*

3.4. *Defeat in the Sinai.*

3.5. *Nasser's funeral.*

4.2. *The hero at the end of the adventure.*

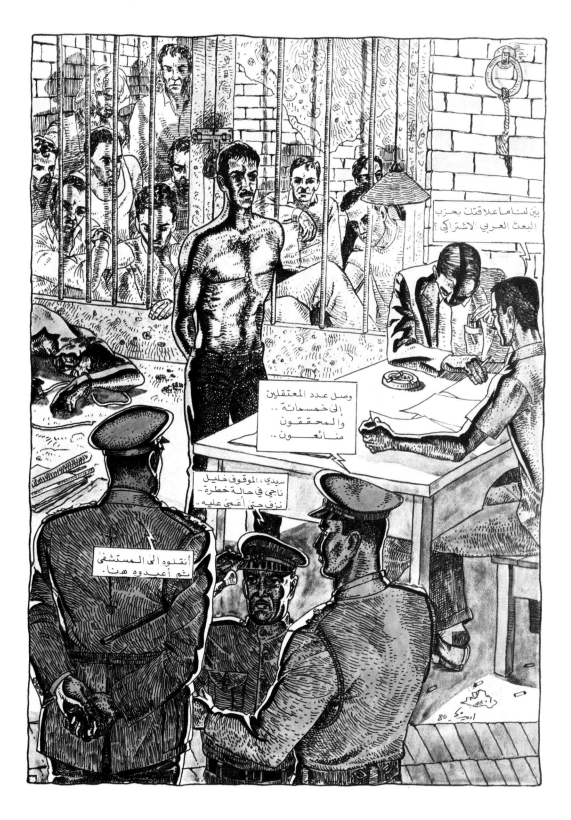

4.3. *Interrogation scene.*

4.5. *The hero dreaming and awake as his saga ends.*

9.1. *The Mâjid look: a cover by Hijâzî.*

take off from the rooftops (p. 12). The message is synchronic and iconographic: the revolution is the dawn of a new day.

But this full-page frame is an exception. Rather than the story of Iraq or even of the Iraqi Baath, "The Long Days" gives us the story of one man, and its presentation further accentuates the protagonist's separation from his fellows. Husayn is a lone hero. Concentrating on a brief episode in the Iraqi leader's life (he is never shown either older or younger) gives him some of that atemporality and agelessness often associated with traditional comic-strip heroes.[10]

The young man starts out as a dutiful and disciplined party member. He is but one of seven men chosen to fire on the oppressor of his country. Only as the plot takes shape are "the magnificent seven" gradually replaced by "the lone ranger." Husayn, while remaining respectful of his hierarchical superiors, begins to display leadership qualities. After the proposed attack has been outlined, he suggests that the gunmen first fire into the air to warn away onlookers and prevent innocent casualties. The suggestion is adopted (p. 17).

The failure of the assassination attempt propels the hero further into the limelight. Structuring the story around a failed action, one in whose planning the young hero played no role, can only discredit the older leadership of the party. And the direction of the hero from this point onward is away, both physically and symbolically, from this bloody failure.

More concretely, when the getaway car does not arrive as quickly as expected, Husayn runs to hail a taxi (p. 22). In the hideout, he directs the removal of the bullet from his own leg (pp. 25–26). Of greater significance, Husayn begins to disagree with his superiors. While they wish to remain where they are, he insists that their hideout is not safe and that it is only a matter of time before the police locate it. He leaves first, on his own; the rest of the group departs later. The correctness of Husayn's advice is borne out when Qâsim's police enter the hideout shortly after the last Baathists have departed, a point absent in the novel and added in the strip (pp. 27–29, 33).

From this point onward, Husayn goes his own way and makes his own decisions, effectively emancipated, not only from his immediate superiors but also from the Baath party apparatus as a whole. "Do I ponder until the leadership of the party takes some measure?" he asks himself while still in Baghdad (p. 31). The negative answer he provides through his own actions.

The essential solitude of Husayn's quest already present in Mu'alla's novel is even further strengthened in the comic-strip version. In the novel, Husayn makes the final journey across the desert to Syria in the company of a guide who does not know his identity and a friend, Tâlib, who does.[11] In the strip version, Tâlib is missing. Husayn, traveling incognito, is more truly alone.

All of this adds up to a considerable separation of the national hero, not only from his people but even from the Baath party, and suggests its own distinctive form of political legitimization. Nasser, as we saw, was defined through his membership in the couple, leader-people. The mode of legitimization was populist and plebiscitarian. The Husaynian text, by contrast, suggests the solitude of power; a leader alone, above

4.1. *Husayn is wounded.*

party and people. The specifics of the legitimization itself argue from the personal characteristics of the leader, not from his popular support.

How does this valorization of personal rule fit with the larger Baath ideology? One answer is provided in the iconography of the strip itself. As we saw, the revolution was metaphorically defined through the flight of birds at dawn. This distinctive image appears twice more.

As the group of gunmen run from the scene of their unsuccessful attack, Husayn is wounded in the leg by a bullet (see fig. 4.1). This event is crucial, since the wound will serve as the hero's telltale mark and point of weakness (his Achilles heel, if one wishes) throughout his flight. The wounding of the hero is represented by a dramatic closeup frame of the lower part of his leg being ripped apart by the bullet. The frame to the left (the next frame in Arabic sequence) shows Husayn stumbling, as a more badly wounded comrade falls. The relationship between the two frames is a clear narrative one. But just above the frame of Husayn's wounding is a small horizontal frame, very unusual in size and shape, showing a set of silhouetted rooftops from which a flock of birds is taking off, against a backdrop which could, in strictly visual terms, be either sunrise or sunset. The context tells us that it is dusk, not dawn (p. 21). This small frame has no real place in the narrative. It is not drawn from Muʿalla's novel. Its only function would seem to be as a visual metaphor attached to the wounding of the hero in a highly dramatic stripological juxtaposition.

The third appearance of this image is narratively the clearest. In the last frame of the text, occupying a full page, the young hero stands by an open window as dawn creeps over a sleeping Arab city and birds take flight in the distance. A Syrian flag is barely visible. As the hero says (p. 67), "It is a new day" (fig. 4.2). The new day marks the end of the hero's travail; he is free. When this final page is associated with the other two, another message emerges. Saddâm Husayn *is* the revolution, the new day we first saw in the visualization of the aborted revolution of 1958. The link is created when the hero receives his wound. If the first hope, the first flight of birds, was confiscated by Qâsim, the second hope, Saddâm Husayn, has escaped the dictator, carrying the future of the Iraqi revolution with him.

Shadows pervade "The Long Days." One of the most distinctive visual features of the comic strip is the way light and shadow are dynamically integrated into the color schemes of the frames. As in impressionist painting, shadows are never gray or merely a darkened version of the light. They take on other hues: purples, dark blues, sometimes even greens. Lit portions are often marked in yellow. In a few night scenes, the whole frame (or most of it) is in a virtual monochrome of colored shadow (e.g., pp. 33, 35).

More commonly, light and dark divide the frame, and monochrome shadow is often used to set off less important characters or background. The division of the frame by zones of light can even replace natural coloring with separate monochrome bands, as in a highly dramatic full-page (p. 32) interrogation scene (fig. 4.3). A group of prisoners in a cell in the background is largely gray. The front of a standing figure reflects the yellow of the policeman's lamp, but his back is shadowed in dark pink, as is a crumpled figure behind him. Three officers silhouetted in the foreground are largely blue. The coloration, like the scene itself, is sinister. This is a relatively unusual way of using color in comic strips, even more so in Arab comic strips. In the Nasser biography, for example, bright colors predominate and frames are usually evenly lit.

But if, as we saw, revolution in the Husayn strip was dawn, then it is not surprising that Iraq is bathed in shadow. After all, the text began: "The time: 1959. Iraq is under the shadow (*zill*) of the rule of the dictator, 'Abd al-Karîm Qâsim." And in the accompanying frame, a single soldier (who is participating in the hunt for Husayn) casts a large blue shadow behind him (p. 7). Particularly striking in this use of shadow is its reversal of a traditional Islamic position in which shadow was a positive signifier of sovereignty, suggesting protection. The context of the strip makes no such positive association possible.[12]

But the privileged reflector of light and shadow is Husayn himself. More than that of any other figure, his face is clearly divided into strong bands of light and dark. To him is reserved the clear division of the face into strong stripes of color, sometimes two, often three. The most striking example of this phenomenon is the last page (67), in which the rising sun divides the face of Husayn into yellow, red, and green, like the colored stripes of a flag. Above this, a second image of his face is divided into yellow and flesh tones (fig. 4.2). The contrast between the darkness of tyranny and the light of hope is reflected on and embodied in the face of our hero.

There is, however, one sense in which the future leader is dependent on others, and hence a corresponding intermediate group is implicitly associated with his rule. The strip devotes considerable attention to those, family and friends, who, at the risk of their lives, aided Husayn in his flight. The alert Iraqi reader (and the political culture of the Arab world promotes this kind of alertness even among general readers) would note that many of these figures or their close relatives occupy important posts in the Iraqi government. Their legitimization as such derives from their role in Husayn's saga.[13]

Machismo and Arabism

To say that Husayn is valorized as an individual is also to say that he is valorized for individual characteristics. What is perhaps most striking in the virtues attributed to our hero is their correspondence with a set of values of pre-Islamic origin, known in the Arab tradition as *muruwwa*. The Arab culture of the Jâhiliyya, the period before Islam, was a kind of Golden Age marking the origins of the Arabic language and poetic traditions, in effect, of the Arab identity. Despite the importance of the Prophetic mission and the rise of Islam, the Jâhiliyya has remained a central cultural focus and referent for Arab societies, down to the present day. Though dominantly tribal in organization, Jâhiliyya society held a certain kind of individualistic hero in high regard: the lone adventurer, who could even operate against the wishes or interests of the tribe. The poet Imru' al-Qays is the best-known example. Indeed, the general atemporality, the relative dearth of historical contextualization, in the Husayn strip facilitates an association with this pre-Islamic Golden Age. An association could also be made here between the "Long Days" (*al-Ayyâm al-Tawîla*) and the "Ayyâm al-ʿArab," the famous "Battle Days" of the pre-Islamic Arabs.[14]

Muruwwa, sometimes translated as "manliness," consists in a combination of virtues adapted to the life of the desert: courage, loyalty, and hospitality.[15] In effect, these virtues are either directly embodied in the hero or associated with the success of his quest. As a group, they are the values most consistently promoted by "The Long Days."

Husayn's courage, frequently combined with a manly savoir faire, is shown repeatedly. When the group of Baath gunmen reach the hideout, the wounded Husayn calmly informs his fellows that he knows the bullet is still in his leg because he had been taught in the village that only the presence of a bullet would make pain multiply in the body. He requests a razor and says that if a friend cannot remove the bullet, he will do so himself. After the removal of the bullet, his friend calls him a hero for having borne the pain (pp. 25–26). This is the first time that Husayn attains that verbal status, and it is in association with physical courage and machismo.

It is worthy of note that Husayn's response to the praise is itself personalized and directed to the idea of manhood. One might have expected him to respond with a typical patriotic piety, such as "I would bear more than this for our noble cause, for the freedom of our people." Nasser's response when shot, for example, was in this vein.[16] By contrast, Husayn answers: "Pain disappears with the passing of time. But

tyranny extinguishes the resolve of men" (p. 26). It is hardly surprising that the term
men (*rijâl*) refers to the masculine representatives of the species. In Freudian terms,
one would say that tyranny castrates.

Husayn's machismo is made even greater in the strip than it was in the novel. In
Muʿalla's version, when Husayn tells his uncle about his wound and its treatment,
tears of compassion form in the eyes of the older man. His nephew then asks for medicine to treat the inflammation. In the strip version, the uncle's tears and the nephew's
request for medicine have both been eliminated. Instead, the uncle simply inspects
the wound (p. 30).[17] Perhaps even clearer in this regard is the elimination in the comic
strip of an incident when Husayn, being pulled along by an unsuspecting friend, cries
out in pain.[18] The comic-strip hero is made of tougher stuff.

Husayn shows a bedouin sang-froid and resourcefulness on other occasions as
well. When he cannot ford a stream without being detected, he ties his belongings to
his head and swims it (pp. 49–50). Later, crossing the desert, he shows a better knowledge of animals than his bedouin guide. When wolves approach at night, the latter
can only think to light a fire to frighten them away, even though this will attract the
attention of the border guards. It is Husayn who has the solution: if the two remain
immobile in the dark, the wolves will leave them alone, since they only attack prey
that moves (pp. 63–64).

Husayn's manly courage is clear. But the other virtues associated with *muruwwa*,
loyalty and generosity, come out more clearly in his relationships with others. It is the
loyalty of friends, relatives, and colleagues which makes his escape possible. Allegiance to family and friends takes precedence over that to the state. When an uncle
accidentally sees from his window Husayn's participation in the assassination attempt, he is stunned and deeply concerned. But it never seems to have occurred to
him for a moment to turn in the would-be assassin (pp. 20ff).

Of all the pre-Islamic virtues, hospitality is probably the one on which the Arabs
pride themselves most and which they consider to be most distinctive to themselves.
This last trait demands acceptance of strangers as guests—their nourishment, shelter,
and, perhaps most important, protection. Fleeing across his country to Syria, Husayn
is forced to rely upon this virtue. But since he is an outlaw with a price on his head,
the virtue of hospitality is severely tested in a context of progressively increasing danger. The first time, Husayn has but to request his due. He is taken in, sleeps, and we
see that he is sent off cheerfully the next morning (pp. 43–44). The second time, he
arrives at a wedding and is, of course, invited in. But suspicions have begun to
mount. One of the men at the wedding party says to another that he is sure he has
seen their strange guest's face somewhere (pp. 45–46).

On the third occasion, our hero is found prostrate and exhausted on the river-
bank after having swum the river with his wounded leg. When he is asked who he is,
he answers: "A man with no power and no strength, who is asking refuge with the
Arabs." The term ʿ*Arab* is ambiguous, since it can signify both the Arabs and the bedouin. He is taken in, but his host submits him to an interrogation, suspecting
strongly that his guest has been involved in some crime. Husayn's answer invokes the
rights of the guest: "Let us say that you are right, and that I did kill a man and sought

refuge with you. Do you wish to turn me in while I am in your house?" With this, of course, the host allows the hero to go on his way (pp. 51–52). Hospitality has triumphed over danger.

A village *shaykh* is quizzed by a police officer who wants to know the identity of his three guests (one of whom was Husayn). When the *shaykh* declares that he does not know them, the policeman is disbelieving: "How marvelous. A host who does not know his guests!" The reply of the *shaykh* sets the matter straight: "If your Honor came to me, would I refuse you hospitality?" The *shaykh* then proceeds to invite the official to his home (p. 64).

These hospitality trials, however, are not evenly distributed through the text. They begin at a clearly marked point — after our hero has adopted Arab bedouin garb, with its distinctive headdress. In effect, the comic strip does more than promote pre-Islamic Arab values; its hero passes through what we can call a zone of Arabism and takes on an Arab identity, understanding this last as a reference to the bedouin Arabs. This is accomplished in the course of two journeys, the first from Baghdad to Samarra and the second from Samarra across the desert to Abû Kamâl in Syria. More is involved here than clothing. By leaving the city, the hero has left the zone of the modern bureaucratic state dominated by the tyrannical Qâsim and entered a more natural world of Arab life and Arab virtue, conceived as the opposite of bureaucracy. When asked for his identity card, the disguised Husayn responds: "We here do not carry an identity card. This is our land and we are the sons of its tribes" (p. 48). It is as if, in the course of his quest, he had to pass through a communion with his ancestors, rebathe himself in the essential qualities of his ethnic heritage.[19]

Even more, this journey becomes the climax, if not the essence, of his saga. Though the trips through the wilderness represent slightly less than half the text, they are clearly its most important part. We noted earlier the presence of a prolepsis in the beginning of the album. In effect, the narrative begins with the end of the story: Husayn's final flight through the desert to Syria, an introductory segment which ends with his safe arrival in Abû Kamâl. Placing this episode at the beginning of the text foregrounds and privileges it, especially since the prologue was not even present in the novel. All the more so, since the title page of the album figures a scene from this flight across the desert and the end papers show Husayn in bedouin garb mounted on his charger. Finally, this last phase of the story is the one in which Husayn, by both his garb and his setting, is at his most bedouin Arab.

The issues are drawn clearly in the first frame of the album. A bedouin, august as a Saudi prince, his head framed by a tent flap, stares down at a photograph in his hand, while a police officer opposite, in modern uniform, watches his eyes anxiously. Good faces evil; Arab tradition confronts the agent of the bureaucratic state. Between them is the picture of Husayn.

In "The Long Days" the modern bureaucratic state is completely identified with Qâsim's tyranny. In fact, as he escapes from the clutches of oppression, Husayn progresses away from the zone of danger and tyranny, the state. His first refuge is modern civil society, the network of his friends and relatives. Only then does he accede to the zone of pure Arabism. An interesting view of contemporary Arab society emerges. The state, on top, is alien and hostile. The true source of protection is the network of family and regional loyalties, ʿasabiyya. Beyond this, as a romantic ideal, lies the bedouin Arab tradition, a zone of ultimate dignity and freedom.

The criticism of the state becomes an opposition between nature and culture. The bedouin Arab is, of course, closer to nature. And light, an important recurring element, further reflects this. If the natural light of dawn dispels the darkness of dictatorship, artificial light represents the intrusive power of the state. Lamps tend to be of two kinds. The most common is an overhead lamp which casts a clearly marked pyramid of light and is almost exclusively associated with police investigation and interrogation. On the first page, the officer coordinating the search for Husayn is divided by such a light. The same overhead lamp is the unique source of light in the full-page torture and interrogation scene discussed above, just as it is in three other interrogation scenes later in the story (pp. 32, 53, 59). The same type of overhead lamp lights the interior of a prison and the hideout while it is being ransacked by the police (pp. 60, 33). The only exceptions to this direct association of overhead lamp and police investigation are two representations inside the hideout, one of which also signals the danger of police intervention (pp. 26, 29). Sinister as well are the headlights and the searchlights of the police in the desert (e.g., pp. 62, 63, 66). By and large, artificial light identifies culture with the oppressive state.

This negative view of the state is not unproblematic, considering that the hero is now himself the head of such a bureaucratic state, served by modern machines and uniformed policemen. It is logically possible for a reader to associate the bureaucratic state castigated in the album with that of Saddâm Husayn and the protection afforded the outlaw with that provided to more recent opponents of the regime (like the Kurdish rebels of the Barzani family). Of course, the official reply would be that Qâsim's regime is clearly represented in the strip as a brutal dictatorship, whereas Saddâm Husayn's would not be. But this last point remains only on the level of implication, since nothing in the strip, even on the level of promise or ideal, directly indicates it.

Nor is the visual representation of the relationship between Qâsim and his police apparatus without ambiguity. On the first page, for example, we see two police agents in their offices, and on the wall behind each officer a framed picture of the leader—except that in both cases it is impossible to see the leader's face and, hence, his true identity. The nature of his rule is iconographically indicated in one of these two frames by the visual balancing of the picture against a set of handcuffs (p. 7). These unrecognizable portraits grace other official offices (e.g., p. 64). The official picture of the dictator himself (smiling, interestingly enough) only appears once, on the wall on the edge of a large downtown Baghdad street scene. Here the official portrait, which looks like a photograph inserted into the drawn text, is clearly described by a highly unusual speech balloon stating: "The name of the dictator was ʿAbd al-Karîm Qâsim" (p. 10). This iconographic avoidance produces interesting results. Normally, the use of a photograph might signify authenticity. (We shall see that this is the case in other strips.)[20] But here as the only photographic representation in the album, its effect is to pull the official portrait of Qâsim away from the otherwise consistently represented, drawn universe of the strip. As such, it reinforces the iconographic absence in the portraits.

Why is Qâsim's official face so systematically occulted? Representing him frequently would have served to identify him more concretely with the repressive behavior of his police. The problem lies in the fact that in the contemporary Arab world (but, of course, not only there), the ubiquitous presence of the icon of the leader is both a major manifestation of rule and a creator of legitimacy. The visual representation of Qâsim's official portrait would have risked legitimizing his authority. But, by the same token, his nonrepresentation cuts the tie between bureaucratic state and dictator, giving the former a potential projectability into other regimes. The same tendency is increased by the fact that the real Qâsim speaks no words and takes no actions in the strip itself. He is not shown, for example, ordering the capture of the men who tried to assassinate him. The repression remains largely anonymous.

The valorization of the hero Husayn (and thus by implication the legitimization of the leader Saddâm Husayn) operates in opposition to the state, which in turn suggests two logical possibilities. The first would be that Saddâm Husayn's rule is not based on the bureaucratic state but on other forms of cohesion. The strip here would suggest more personal and clan loyalties. The second possible interpretation would be that it is the successful opposition to the state that later gives one the right to run it.

On a more obvious level, of course, the hero is validated through the positive evocation of bedouin Arabism and the legitimacy of Saddâm Husayn's later government is, therefore, attached to that notion. And this type of Arabism is ideally suited to the ideology and position of the Iraqi Baath regime. Any reference to the Jâhiliyya and the life of the Arab bedouin, a heritage shared by all the modern Arabs, is automatically pan-Arab, a tendency further stressed by the fact that the text is completely in *fushâ*, without Iraqi dialect.

Yet the distance from this Jâhiliyya heritage varies from one Arab state to another. Such a pan-Arab evocation, for example, would not concord well with the sense of Egyptian identity. The realities of life in the Nile Valley are too far from those of the desert, itself more often the source of the national enemy. Hence the pan-Arabism of *Jamâl ʿAbd al-Nâsir* is never associated with bedouin or Jâhiliyya life. Iraqi realities, by contrast, are closer to those of bedouin Arabism. True, Mesopotamia has always lived on its rivers. But Iraq borders Arabia, and its population includes the largest percentage of settlers from the original Arab conquests and migrations of the seventh century. Even before the Arab conquest, much of Iraq's territory was occupied by authentic Arab tribes, and it continues to be. Hence "The Long Days" can be both Iraqi and pan-Arab.

Indeed, this duality would have been eliminated by too close a relationship. In a production associated with one of the states of the Arabian peninsula, the valorization of bedouin life-style, especially in contrast with the modern state, would no longer signify pan-Arabism. There the romanticization of the bedouin would suggest a purely local, Arabian reference. As we shall see, this is what happens in the United Arab Emirates' children's magazine, *Mâjid*.[21]

Rite of Passage

It has become evident that more than politics is involved in the Husayn comic strip or that politics itself is resolved into a rite of manhood. We have already seen how the older generation's failure emancipates our hero. Even more, the entire process—participation in the assassination attempt, the wound, the flight to Syria— functions as a rite of passage. In the course of his quest, the hero leaves the city where he was born and even changes his identity. When he reaches the Syrian city, the process is complete. He recovers his old identity and sheds his Arab garb. What has changed? He has become a man.[22]

Visual juxtaposition tends to be thematic. Thus it is that the most unusual combination within a single frame both ties together the Baath and the Arab themes while redefining the sense of the hero's personal quest. While riding between Baghdad and Samarra, Husayn hears shots cutting through the night sky. It is a wedding, he concludes (p. 45). The next frame (p. 46) consists of two scenes joined in the center by the figure of the mounted hero (fig. 4.4). Husayn and his steed are facing directly toward the reader. Their movement from the back to the front of the frame is given greater depth by the protrusion of the muzzle of the horse forward from the frame to a position in front of it, where it blocks the frame below. Such movement from the back to the front of the frame, unmixed with left-right motion, is highly unusual in our strip. The only other example is the dramatic forward motion of Qâsim's car, as the assassination attempt begins (p. 18). As we shall see, this parallel is not fortuitous. To Husayn's left (our right) is a traditional Arab wedding feast, lit by candles. In the foreground of this scene is a traditionally dressed Arab, his rifle pointing upward. The balance of the frame, Husayn's right (our left), is a drawing of the Baath gunmen firing their automatic weapons.

The text explains the juxtaposition. Husayn muses: "The shots which I fired were also shots of a wedding (*farah*) but it was a wedding which was not completed." *Farah* also means "joy," but the visual context and specific reference make it impossible to eliminate the meaning of "wedding." The metaphorical association of traditional Arab wedding and assassination attempt links the two major political themes of the album: Arab tradition and the revolutionary action of the Baathists. Much in the album, however, suggests a deeper psychological, even unconscious, level of meaning. Despite its title (*Ayyâm* refers to the combined unit of night and day), "The Long Days" could be considered one long night. Night falls as the gunmen flee from their failed assassination attempt. Though there are many sunrises and sunsets in the story, the sun does not rise definitively (and on the level of the deep structure of the story) until the dawn of closure in the giant final frame. The hero's journey is one across a metaphorical night of danger to a new day.

More precisely, the entire story (almost the entire narrative) is framed in a dream, all the more significant in that this oneiric element was absent in the novel and added in the album. At the end of the initial prolepsis, after our hero arrives in Abû Kamâl, stands a large complex frame (p. 9) (fig. 4.5). Its top right corner shows the hero, his head on a pillow, eyes open, thinking: "Those days. The long days." Immediately below this, we see a second Husayn, head still on the pillow, his eyes shut, and the image of a peaceful village emerging from his head in a swirl of cloudlike shapes, indicative of the dream state. Husayn's "dream" includes, then, all the action of the story which follows, because the frame is not closed—he does not "wake up"—until the final image of the album (fig. 4.2). There, above the triumphant image of the standing Husayn watching the sunrise, floats a second, smaller picture, visually surrounded by the colors of the first, of the same recumbent Husayn, but now relaxed, awake, and smiling. Thus the visual imagery, like the written text, sends the reader back to the moment, at the end of the prolepsis, when the hero fell asleep. It is almost as if the entire experience had been a dream.[23] The predominance of shadow also does nothing to break this mood, and the dark pastels, the frequent use of gray and dark blue, help to create an atmosphere of mystery and unreality.[24]

A dream state, of course, suggests unconscious content. But this dream world is not one of absolute subjectivity. Framing the story within the dream—or, if one wishes, the memory of the hero—would normally reflect it through his consciousness and hence place it, at least partly, in the first person. Yet the entire narration remains third-person and the narrator, external to the story. There is created a zone between subjectivity and objectivity, a region of myth and liminality, like that between night and day, between dream and reality.

This zone is also one of multiple identity. We have already observed how Husayn took on another personality in his flight. More striking is the visual doubling embodied in the sequence enframing the story. Each tableau includes two pictures of our hero, a doubling which makes the paired heroes both different and the same. This doubling, which stands guard at the beginning and end of the story, is strangely reflective of the pact defining the historicity of the strip. Muhammad Husayn al-Saqr, who lives the adventure, and Saddâm Husayn, who leads Iraq, are a doubled personality, different but the same. Considered internally, the creation of an alter ego strengthens the sense of liminality associated with a rite of passage, just as it reinforces the psychological, mythic dimensions of the adventure.

Text and image work together to define the assassination attempt as a wedding, or rather as an attempted wedding, an unconsummated marriage. The visual and textual locus of this bisociation, Husayn, was also the person (another change from novel to strip) who suggested that the action begin with shots in the air, in effect, as in a wedding feast. The parallel is an interesting one, with its suggestion of violent penetration, but is nevertheless imperfect, since the blood of defloration signals the consummated marriage, while the assassination attempt was incomplete despite its bloodiness.

The phallic role of the gun in this rite of manhood is indeed marked throughout the album. Not only are the blazing guns dramatically foregrounded, as one might expect, in the images of the attack itself, but two previous frames show the Baathists posing with their guns, in virtual revolutionary portraits (pp. 18, 19). More telling perhaps is the image accompanying the historical statement that the Baath party was preparing a revolution against Qâsim's system (p. 11). Rather than party militants preparing or distributing clandestine literature, the frame presents a group of men sitting around a table covered with a variety of weapons: rifle, submachine gun, pistol, grenade. It is clear what is meant by revolution. Later evocations of the assassination attempt are likewise symbolized by the visual image of the gun, sometimes without even an indication of who is holding it (pp. 35, 45).

The marriage parallel suggests other meanings. If the assassination attempt is a failed marriage, then the promised bride would have to be Iraq, now in the arms of the dictator. Killing the dictator father in order to marry the mother would give the entire ritual an Oedipal flavor, though Oedipal here would have to be understood in the sense of the Freudian complex, not the original Greek myth, since there are crucial elements in the latter, like the problem of fate, which have no place at all in our album. Of course, there are other mythic parallels, especially in the Islamic tradition.[25] Our hero's flight recalls that of the Prophet Muhammad, who fled across the desert from Mecca, locus of pagan tyranny, to the freedom and security of Medina, also with would-be assassins on his tail. The hero of *The Long Days*, of course, bears the first name Muhammad. But this sacred parallel is left curiously undeveloped in the album. The author could have noted, for example, that his hero (since this was actually the case for Saddâm Husayn) like the Prophet was orphaned and raised by his uncle.[26] Yet this curious parallel is never mentioned, keeping the Husaynian myth of legitimization on a purely secular level, concordant with the valorization of the Jâhiliyya. Nor is it coincidental that Islamic references and symbols are completely absent from the strip. The closest one comes is the occasional outline of a mosque, never playing a prominent role, in the background of a cityscape (pp. 23, 46, 67).[27]

Paradoxically, Husayn's rite of passage begins with a failed rite of passage, which, of course, makes his own personal adventure possible. The reason the first failed was because it was still within the house of the father (the Baath party) and thus did not really test the manhood of the hero. Hence our hero, like the hero of many a tale, begins with a lack, produced by the initial failed passage.[28] This lack puts him in danger of Qâsim's police. Its physical manifestation on the body of the hero himself, the telltale leg wound, is, of course, also the result of the failed attack. But the problem is not eliminated by the help of a mediator, as is so commonly the case. Playing that role is the entirety of traditional Arab society. To cure his lack, Husayn must risk his identity as a modern urban Arab Baathist by plunging himself into the metaphorical past of bedouin Arab existence. It is only after having done so that he can be reborn as a new, unified individual who has bypassed the division between old and new Iraqi society. It is this that fits him for the leadership of his country, just as it makes him a man.

5

Radicalism in Strips:
Ahmad Hijâzî

History is not the only vehicle nor the celebration of national heroes the only occasion for political comic strips. Nor are the political positions of Arabic strips limited to the promotion of ruling groups and dominant values. Highly critical political material has successfully crept into Arabic comic-strip production.

Between Strips and Editorial Cartoons: *Sî Juhâ*

The closest relative of the overtly political strip is the editorial cartoon (sometimes referred to as the political cartoon). Like a strip, an editorial cartoon is an image, usually combined with words, often in balloons. Indeed, with both cartoon and strip, it could be argued that the greater the virtuosity of the visual language, the less need there is for verbal language.

But the editorial cartoon is distinguished from the strip by a number of features, some strictly formal, others less so. The strip, as its name indicates, consists of a sequence of frames which must be read together and in order, whereas an editorial cartoon is normally a single, self-contained frame. While the content of a strip is not normally limited, the sequencing of frames steers toward narrative (it is sometimes even necessary to add a narrative dimension to material which might otherwise not possess it).[1] The editorial cartoon is generally a direct commentary on current events and any "story" which its images might tell becomes subordinate to such commentary. But as is so commonly the case, reality does not divide itself up as neatly as theory, and there are a variety of intermediate forms, creating an effect of continuity between cartoon and strip.

What happens, for example, when editorial cartoons combine four, five, or six frames, or when strips turn into commentaries on current events? Typical of such intermediate forms is the series *Sî Juhâ* (Mister Juhâ), which appears in the Tunisian bilingual weekly, *Le Maghreb/al-Maghrib al-ʿArabî*, with scenario and drawings by Faysal al-ʿIshsh.[2] Usually with six but occasionally with nine frames, *Sî Juhâ* follows the dialogue of two, rarely three or four, characters rendered in balloons in Tunisian dialect. Juhâ himself, based on a well-known Arabo-Muslim traditional comic figure (a point to which we will return later[3]), represents half, and usually the more intelligent half, of this dialogue. The brief strips, however, are essentially nonnarrative, generally consisting of commentaries on current problems (from international politics to purely Tunisian developments). Further, and this is linked to their largely nonnarrative nature, they are not really visual. If the drawings were eliminated and the dialogue left with the name of each speaker, the argument would be just as easy to follow and the political commentary just as evident.

Perhaps most striking in the entire project is the political role assigned to Juhâ. He is generally the most sensible speaker and the one whose political interpretations remain as the most founded—in marked contrast with his traditional and still-living image (as one can find it today in postcards sold on the streets of Tunis). Juhâ is most commonly a fool, and in certain situations, at most a wise fool.[4] Either a certain cynicism or even an unconscious ambivalence about the essentially conformist political line results from this confrontation of roles.

Ahmad Hijâzî

One figure has effectively assumed the range of production from editorial cartoon to strip, the Egyptian Ahmad Hijâzî. Moreover, Hijâzî has combined this relatively modest achievement with a far more important one. More than any other figure, he has succeeded in producing and circulating to wide audiences comic strips with political and social criticism, ranging from the basically acceptable (and hence conformist) to the subversive.[5]

It is relatively normal in the Arab world, at least in countries such as Egypt which tolerate an opposition press, for editorial cartoons to take antigovernment positions, except as regards the person of the head of state. In the world of children's magazines and comic strips, subject as they are to far greater pressures for conformity, genuinely radical politics are virtually unheard of.[6] Hijâzî has delivered his political messages through children's stories published initially in *Samîr*, the widely read Egyptian children's magazine produced by the government-owned publishing house of Dâr al-Hilâl. In more recent years, Hijâzî's politics have become more evident (or editors have finally begun to figure out what his stories are really about). The recent series executed for the *Majallat al-Shabâb* (Youth Magazine) was refused by that magazine and published in the newspaper of the Egyptian Left opposition, *al-Ahâlî*.[7]

A child of the Egyptian Delta, without higher education or any formal art training, Ahmad Hijâzî went to Cairo at the age of eighteen in 1954, to begin his career as illustrator and cartoonist. One of the best-known editorial cartoonists of the Arab world,[8] Hijâzî has drawn for mainstream Egyptian magazines such as *Sabâh al-Khayr* and, in recent years, on a regular basis for *al-Ahâlî*, in which he attacks the *infitâh*, or economic open-door policy, the United States, and Israel.[9]

Hijâzî's intense involvement with children's literature began in 1965 with his association with the leading Egyptian children's magazine of the time, *Samîr*.[10] For this magazine, Hijâzî authored, as both scenarist and illustrator, a number of long series, "Tanâbilat al-Sibyân" (The Lazy Boys), to which we will return. In 1979 he participated in the founding of *Mâjid*, now the most important children's magazine in the Arab world. He has remained the leading illustrator and the closest thing to a number-two man for that weekly. For *Mâjid*, however, Hijâzî serves mostly as illustrator of stories written by others.[11] Hijâzî's independent creations, those in which he is both scenarist and artist, have been largely published under other auspices. It is these exclusively Hijâzîan creations which most clearly reflect his politics and which will form the subject of this chapter.

Ahmad Hijâzî shares many of the basic positions of the Egyptian Left: hostility to imperialism, suspicion of international business. But he extends his analysis to less widely accepted positions: a critique of nationalism and even patriotism, hostility to militarism, the state, and all modern forms of authority and hierarchy. His concern for children and his thoroughgoing anarchism show in the remark he once made to us that the principle of authority should be banished, even in relations between parents and children. The cult of personality and the worship of the state, even in the guise of the nation, are the antithesis of his most deeply held convictions. For Hijâzî, however, political matters are always associated with personal ones. Justice is as much a question of personal maturity as it is of politics in the larger sense.[12]

It goes without saying that such radical positions are not easily inserted in material destined for children. Instead, elements of this ideological mix have permeated different strips to greater and lesser degrees.

The Comic Strip as Editorial Cartoon: Hijâzî

Given Hijâzî's double life as political cartoonist and producer of comic strips, it is not surprising that he has created political cartoons in comic-strip form. Most are similar to the Tunisian *Sî Juhâ*, in that a modest number of frames (four or six) are used to transmit a dialogue between two individuals without visual motion or development through the frames.[13]

Occasionally Hijâzî creates a true strip. Mocking the government's referendum propaganda, Hijâzî produced for *al-Ahâlî* a fifteen-frame ministrip which presents in germ many of the themes developed in his full-length visual narratives (see fig. 5.1).[14] On the television, a young woman, the teacher Nazîha, gives a short course for housewives on how to get fresh use out of old or discarded items—except that in this case, the object is the word *no* (*lâ*), represented by a large cardboard cutout of the two linked letters. Step by step, Nazîha shows how to cut off pieces of the letters and re-arrange them into a new pattern, "and in this way, you will have made from the old *no* (*lâ*) a new *yes* (*na'am*), which looks really beautiful, and which you will find useful the day of the referendum."

On the most obvious political level, the name Nazîha mocks the government's claim that it will watch over the rectitude (*nazâha*) of the referendum procedure, a very vulner-able point, given the previous history of elections in Egypt. (An earlier cartoon had pic-tured a woman, "Nazîha, the person responsible for the uprightness (*nazâha*) of the elec-tions.")[15] The piece functions as a true comic strip, since the visual language, skillfully exploiting the graphic economy of the Arabic script, is as important as the verbal. In fact, a masterful comic bisociation is created between the balloons, which remain on the purely practical instrumental level ("trim a piece of this, add a piece of that"), and the image which, by the eleventh frame, we perceive clearly is being changed from a *no* to a *yes*, giving the political dimension to the strip. The two do not come together until the very last frame, when the balloon speaks of the referendum.

More than just the referendum is being pilloried. The television image becomes total reality. In the first frame we see the woman within the television set, though her balloon reaches outside it. In the second and all successive frames, the mediating tele-vision has disappeared, as its images completely fill the visual space. As important as it is comic is the satire on the allegedly public service, practical self-help television program. The patronizing sweetness of the beautiful announcer is the newest form of political propaganda. The interested nature of mass media and their use to infantilize and control the Egyptian population are recurring themes in Hijâzî's strips.

The Tanâbila Come to Egypt

Hijâzî's longest strips are those devoted to the Tanâbila. Here political content must be carefully woven into a story that functions perfectly on the narrative level and will delight children of all ages, as the expression goes, while providing the more se-rious minded with ideological food for thought.

Perhaps as a result of these constraints, the ideological message inherent in the Tanâbila series emerged only progressively and in layers. In the earliest series, enti-tled *Tanâbilat al-Sibyân* (The Lazy Boys), the radical view of Egyptian society is almost smothered by a moralizing and essentially conformist plot line. The second, *Tanâbilat al-Sibyân wa-Tanâbilat al-Khirfân* (The Lazy Boys and the Lazy Lambs), by contrast, de-velops a masterful satire of Egyptian society, and especially business circles. Its con-clusions are anything but optimistic. Hijâzî's third foray into the world of the Tanâbila

5.1. *Ridiculing the referendum: turning no into yes.*

is an expansion of a fragment of a tale enframed within the first series. Published as *Tambûl al-Awwal* (Tambûl the First), it is a thoroughgoing and radical (in the etymological sense) attack on the political and social order.[16]

Tanâbilat al-Sibyân reads like a struggle against a censor, internal or external. Or is it just the hesitation of a new writer finding his voice? Whatever the reason, the narrative is loosely constructed and episodic. An enframed movie plot is deliberately left uncompleted. Perhaps more important, the ideological tone is not consistent: two visions of Egyptian society struggle against one another.

The Tanâbila series begins, curiously enough, with two elements. The first is a fairy-tale setting, "once upon a time" (*kân yâ mâ kân*), and the statement that the events take place "in the land of the Sultan" (*Samîr*, 1977, no. 1095). This is another place with another system of government (there are scarcely any sultans left in the region, and it does not appear that Hijâzî is making reference to the Sultanate of Oman), whose political realities might not relate to those of modern Egypt. This political distancing drops off quickly to reappear only for small parts of the text, creating a general hesitation between fairy tale and realist conventions. The second element is more consistent, transcending all the adventures of the Tanâbila: a popular demonstration against the lazy trio (1977, no. 1095).

In effect, pushed by an angry populace and seconded by the ruler, the Tanâbila, three fat children, are being thrown out of an imaginary yet clearly traditional Middle Eastern land. The complaint: they always eat and sleep but never work. A clear moral position is posited, and developed across the series: everyone should work and only those who work should eat. The principle sounds socialist but is susceptible to either socialist or capitalist applications. In the course of the story, Samîr, namesake and positive hero of the journal, seeks to inculcate an essentially socialist view of work while the Tanâbila eventually adopt a capitalist one. Much of the ideological tension present in *Tanâbilat al-Sibyân* derives from the confrontation of these two applications.

Ejected from the land of the Sultan, the sleeping Tanâbila are put out to sea in a boat, where a first lesson in work awaits them. To eat they must catch a fish, clean it, and cook it, using the tools and supplies conveniently present in their craft. The fortune of the waves takes them to Alexandria in the summer (and hence into the fiction of realism), where they find the beaches filled with crowds of vacationing sunbathers. There they also meet Samîr, who corrects their initial impression that they have landed in a country of lazy people (*tanâbila*) like themselves, explaining that the vacationers are hard-working employees taking a break so that they can joyfully return to work. There follows a series of attempts on the part of Samîr to change the Tanâbila into hard-working individuals. Evading Samîr's efforts leads the tubby trio into a series of adventures in Egypt. There they stand out both because of their round forms and their double-pointed hats, the clothing of "the land of the Sultan" from which they came. These distinctive visual features indeed mark them through all the Tanâbila adventures (fig. 5.2).

In Alexandria, the thing the Tanâbila want to do is eat. They abandon Samîr and indulge themselves at a fancy Alexandrian restaurant. When they cannot pay the bill, they are beaten and thrown into the kitchen to work off the price of the meal at ten piasters a day per person. Finding this too much work for too little money, they run

5.2. *The Tanâbila.*

away, only to be picked up by an agricultural labor contractor. They are hired (now at only seven piasters a day) to fight a boll weevil infestation in the cotton crop. Since they do their work so badly, they are beaten instead of being paid. The lesson continues: a peasant family takes them in but the father explains that, like his own children, they will have to work if they expect to be fed.

In the cotton fields, the Tanâbila are reunited with Samîr, who has volunteered to fight the boll weevil as a national duty. As he explains it, the cotton crop must be saved so that the government can sell it for the hard currency which the country badly needs. This, of course, is a socialist justification of work, labor in the service of the collectivity. The Tanâbila, by now, have also learned the necessity of work. As they explain it, to eat one needs money and apparently one cannot get money without working, the capitalist system.

The Tanâbila, who are beginning to learn their way around Egypt, are offered work as television actors. They draw large salaries and drive big cars. Accordingly, they respond disdainfully to Samîr's argument that it is better to work in the cotton fields in the national interest. "You are wasting your time fighting the worm . . . Are you the one who is going to save the crop? There are many others fighting the worm" (1977, no. 1105).

As millions of Egyptians fall in love with the Tanâbila television series (an apparently inane set of songs and dances), the three become stars. They decide to go back to the Alexandria restaurant where they had been beaten and forced to work in the kitchen. Upon arrival, their changed status is obvious: the waiter who beat them has been fired and the restaurant has been renamed in their honor—the staff wear Tanâbila uniforms. The owner fawns over them like royalty and is happy to rehire the original waiter on their request. The Tanâbila are also involved in an automobile accident. The collision destroys a truck and they are badly injured. Their hospitalization forms the occasion for further popular lionizing.

Samîr, returned from his volunteer work in the cotton field, sets off to find the driver of the destroyed truck. At the same time, the Tanâbila begin work on a movie project, and after a brief indication of cameras rolling, the strip shifts to the plot of the movie itself, which becomes a story enframed within the larger *Tanâbilat al-Sibyân* series.

In the film, the Tanâbila, in a sense, play themselves. They have the same names and the same basic behavior pattern. But the setting has become fictional: a kingdom of which Tambûl is the sultan. Thus it doubly echoes the series' prologue in "the land of the Sultan." A hopelessly selfish and lazy monarch, Tambûl does nothing but eat and sleep while his two fellow Tanâbila are locked away in prison and his people are in tatters, starving. The locale is nowhere, but there are references which make one think of Egypt. When one of the poor speaks of revolution, he is answered: "But our people does not know how to make a revolution, because they are a nice people" (1977, no. 1113). The social satire is severe, the class system pronounced, virtually feudal. Tambûl stuffs himself with fancy dishes, and we see that the office of supply for the citizenry is distributing *fûl* beans, a staple of the Egyptian lower classes.

The system shown is perfectly despotic, but its political referent is blurred by its placement within a film which is itself a fiction in relation to the dominant, realist fiction of the Tanâbila in contemporary Egypt. The political implications become stronger and clearer in the comic-strip expansion of this story, to be discussed later.

In the film, the two imprisoned Tanâbila escape and the populace has begun to revolt when the story is interrupted because the director is waiting for the writer to finish the story. But the film is never completed. The producer has lost all his money gambling and the project is brought to a halt. By this time, Samîr has located the truck driver, expecting the Tanâbila to replace his truck for him. When Tambûl refuses, the other two Tanâbila claim that the role he has recently played has gone to his head. As the story ends, the Tanâbila decide to go back to the land of the Sultan and to give away all their property: one car to the truck driver, one to Samîr, and one to the movie director, their villa and its garden to their domestic staff.

The ending is morally satisfying in that good triumphs. But it is ideologically and psychologically problematic. It does not really fit the earlier behavior of the Tanâbila. Indeed, there are two levels of morality in the story. Samîr represents the pure justification of work. As a chorus of peasant children in the cotton field puts it: "Is there anyone in the world who does not want to work?" (1977, no. 1101). The emphasis on work and its implicit connection with the right to eat fits typical pedagogical moralizing as well as the Nasserite socialism dominant at the time. And on one level at least the Tanâbila seem to have been won over. When the film project is abandoned, they reply: "We have become accustomed to work . . . How can we sit idle for two or three months?" (1977, no. 1116).

But, as the series shows us over and over, their work is not like that of the rest of the Egyptians. Idealism aside, they receive far better rewards for their television work than either Samîr or any of the other agricultural workers. The comparison implies a class system and even suggests (as do the Tanâbila themselves) that those on the bottom of the pyramid are dupes, victims of bad luck or naiveté. If the Tanâbila have learned a lesson, it is the capitalist one of the need for money. It is abundantly clear that one is not going to get this in Egyptian society through physical labor. They live as members of the Egyptian elite, with arrogance and conspicuous consumption. Their example effectively subverts Samîr's doctrine of work for the collectivity. And there are numerous swipes at Egyptian class relations. The sycophancy of the restaurant owner is but one example. It is also clear that the peasants who work in the fields do not even get to consume the Tanâbila's television productions. When the latter arrive in the village looking for Samîr, the locals (unlike the Cairene population) do not recognize them, mistaking them instead for agricultural ministry officials—in effect, mistaking one branch of the elite for another.

The source of this injustice is also clearly shown. It is television, the media, the star system. In *Tanâbilat al-Sibyân*, finally, this critique (like the savage political satire sketched in the enframed movie) stands uneasily next to a conformist moralizing. This is not at all the case in later adventures. There, not only is the social critique more consistent but the attack on the media is deepened into an analysis of its connections to big business and its exploitative role in the consumer society.

Big Business and the Media:
The Tanâbila as Robber Barons

Does being a television personality count as real work? The reader of the first *Tanâbila* is left to wonder. A remark at the very beginning of the second sets the tone for that whole series. When the Tanâbila suggest opening a factory, Samîr's sister, Samîra, counters: "True work is that you be a worker not the master over work" (p. 3).

Tanâbilat al-Sibyân wa-Tanâbilat al-Khirfân (The Lazy Boys and the Lazy Lambs) is the longest of the Tanâbila series, running ninety-eight pages.[17] But it is also probably the richest. In a superbly drawn, tightly constructed, and richly comic narrative, Hijâzî weaves a broad and savage satire on Egyptian urban society. The specific target of his pen is the collusion of business, fraud, and the media. This focus gives the story, published under Nasser, a prophetic quality, since it targets developments that would become more important under Sadat and Mubarak.

The *Tanâbilat al-Khirfân* also deepens the personalization of the Tanâbila themselves. They are each given names: Tambûl, which means lazy; Shamlûl, which means lively and nimble; and Bahlûl, which means a clown or buffoon.[18] Under the variant vocalization Buhlûl, the latter is also the name of the typical representative of a classical Arabic character type, the wise fool or clever madman.[19] With names comes personal differentiation. Tambûl is the leader of the pack, the most inventive but also the most cynical. It is the other two (especially Shamlûl) who occasionally object to the fraud or victimization of innocent individuals, though the rationalizations of their comrades (usually Tambûl) always overcome their scruples.

This particular adventure of the Tanâbila revolves around the creation of a company to produce canned meat (*bluebeef* in Cairo dialect), or "luncheon," as it is often called in the Arab world.[20] As clever businessmen, the Tanâbila do not begin by building the factory or even collecting capital to build one. They begin at the true beginning in a consumer society. One of the Tanâbila asks Tambûl which comes first, the project or the publicity. The latter's answer: the publicity, of course (p. 4). The Tanâbila start with a free front-page story, obligingly provided by the newspaper's editor-in-chief. Soon they add paid advertisements to their continuing free media coverage. Jingles fill the airwaves, singing the praises of their product. The Lazy Boys' luncheon is made from fat, lazy lambs, a mark of its quality.[21] Soon all Cairo is dying to taste this delicious new product.

Meanwhile, the Tanâbila proceed to hire a staff, an activity also heavily covered in the media. The personal interviews used to select among the thousands of applicants are a rich satire of corporate manners. The honest worker who explains that he needs the job to feed his family but has never eaten *bluebeef* in his life is passed over. An attractive young woman has hit the right tone: "All day and night I think about *bluebeef*, while eating *fûl* I think of *bluebeef*, while eating fish I think of *bluebeef*, while eating meat I think of *bluebeef*, and when I meet my fiancé I think of *bluebeef*" (p. 6).[22] The Tanâbila also make one other, and rather different, hiring. They take on the most dangerous and skillful pickpocket of all Egypt, 'Alî 'Alîwa. When 'Alî's presence raises eyebrows, Tambûl explains that the former thief is going straight and they are giving him the opportunity to earn an honest living by making him head of accounting. This excess of generosity impresses everyone and adds to the Tanâbila's good name.

By now, with publicity covering Egypt, an enormous demand has been created and merchants have placed, and paid for, advance orders of Tanâbila luncheon. But of course, since there has been no real production, there is still no product. Accordingly, two merchants arrive at the Tanâbila offices to request the return of their advances. The Tanâbila apologize for the delay and cheerfully offer to refund the money. The merchants are sent to 'Alî 'Alîwa, who, as head of accounting, pays them out immediately in cash. In each case, 'Alî then follows the merchant, steals the money, and puts it back in the company's safe—a marvelous transformation of the idea of circulating capital.

A similar technique is used, under the close direction of the Tanâbila, with the employees' salaries. They are paid very handsomely but, as a company rule, must ride mass transit to and from work, apparently, as one employee opines, to teach them humility (p. 18). Once they are paid, however, 'Alî's gang of three pickpockets ride the buses and trolleys and rob all of them. Distraught, the employees, who have lost their month's income, beseech the Tanâbila for an advance on the following month. Graciously, Tambûl grants them half a month's salary. When this too is stolen, he grants a second advance, but by now the employees have decided that it is much safer to take taxis and they return unrobbed. The whole scheme functions like a parodic concretization of the Marxist notion of the exploitation of salaried labor. The bosses really are picking the pockets of their workers.

Meanwhile, the police are helpless. When the first merchant reports his very substantial theft (5,000 Egyptian pounds), the police round up all the pickpockets of Cairo and try to browbeat them into confessing. All, that is, except 'Alî 'Alîwa and his gang, for, as everyone knows, 'Alî has gone straight and his gang cannot do anything without him. They merely sit around and play cards all day in a coffee shop.

The Tanâbila's success brings with it its own problems. Everyone wants Tanâbi-

5.3. *Relabeling the canned meat.*

lat al-Khirfân Bluebeef, but there is none. "How could something like this go by us!" exclaims Tambûl.[23] "Impossible. How did we do all this publicity for *bluebeef* and forget to build a factory that will make the *bluebeef*?" (pp. 25–26). Our ever-resourceful Tambûl quickly finds the solution. They will purchase the regular, imported canned meat, remove the label with the brand name, and glue on one of their own. He does this immediately with one can; it is proudly presented to the media, which elaborately reports this first production from the Tanâbila factory (fig. 5.3).

Tambûl also makes a virtue of necessity. If people have found no Tanâbila luncheon in the market, they will suppose that all the production has been sold out, "and that is the best publicity" (p. 30). He places an ad in the paper assuring consumers that more cans will shortly be delivered to grocers and state shops (*jam'iyyât*). The Tanâbila then systematically organize the purchase, remarking, and resale of the imported meat as Tanâbila Bluebeef Luncheon. A number of problems arise, however. First, the Egyptian minister of supply is so impressed with the Tanâbilat al-Khirfân—he finds its quality every bit as good as the imported bluebeef—that he decides to protect this budding national industry by prohibiting imports. Fortunately, the Tanâbila are able to convince him to rescind this order, explaining that they like competition. The second problem is more fundamental. How can they continue to pay their employees when these employees have decided to only take taxis? Thus they decide to fire and replace all their employees, except, of course, 'Alî 'Alîwa. Even 'Alî's special treatment does not awaken suspicions. Instead, people interpret it as a mark of the quality of his service and a further sign of his wonderful rehabilitation.

The arrangement with ʿAlî is too good to last. One day ʿAlî's men are overheard in the café explaining how they systematically stole the workers' salaries. The streets fill with angry crowds, shouting: "Down with the Tanâbilat al-Sibyân," "Down with the Bluebeef of the Tanâbila," "No Tanâbila after today" (p. 48). The scene reads like a repetition of their ejection from the land of the Sultan in *Tanâbilat al-Sibyân*. But by now the tubby trio have become much more clever. In a series of frames we see the same two men in different public places, loudly repeating the same argument: that the Tanâbila are above suspicion, that everything is the fault of ʿAlî and his gang. We soon discover that with his usual sense of the power of publicity, Tambûl has paid the rumormongers. And the technique works; this version of events spreads and ʿAlî and his three followers end up in jail, while the Tanâbila are freed and back in business.

Without ʿAlî, our three heroes need a new source of funds to meet their payroll, and, of course, satisfy their gluttony. The solution this time is high finance. They decide to sell Tanâbila Bluebeef Company Investment Certificates. Their purchase yields a regular return, plus the chance to win prizes in a monthly lottery. Of course, the ever gullible public snaps them up. In the process, the comic strip has moved from a denunciation of business fraud to an attack on finance and the stock market.

The infuriated ʿAlî escapes from prison along with his gang, swearing vengeance on the Tanâbila. Since the Ministry of Interior has put a fat price on ʿAlî's head, the Tanâbila decide to make some more money and help catch ʿAlî at the same time. They print up and sell for one piaster each photos of ʿAlî ʿAlîwa, which are bought by the millions by Egyptians hoping to capture him and earn the reward. With this, the economic critique of *Tanâbilat al-Khirfân* has reached full breadth. No longer clear fraud or even deceptive securities practices, the last activity is actually perfectly legal free enterprise. In context, however, selling the photo also becomes morally reprehensible, and the amalgam brings all three activities into the negative category of fundamentally exploitative business activities.

But the Tanâbila take other precautions as well. They find three tattered urchins living on the sidewalk and take them in, wash them, feed them to their hearts' delight, and, once they have become sufficiently plump, disguise them as Tanâbila. They then send them to work in their place, fully confusing ʿAlî ʿAlîwa and his men. Eventually, ʿAlî's gang disintegrates as he and his men are killed or captured.

The Tanâbila's racket only comes to an end when the workers whose job it was to replace the labels on the cans of meat repent their misdeeds and confess the system to the police. Of course, for some time now, both Samîr, who caught on to the Tanâbila's schemes relatively early, and his sister Samîra have been trying to alert the Egyptian population and authorities. No one takes them seriously, however, and the only result of their activities is to land them both in jail. They have no real effect on the Tanâbila, nor do they meaningfully contribute to their downfall. As the sole representatives of lucidity and probity in the strip, they are singularly powerless.

The ending of the strip is in its own way equally bleak. As the Tanâbila are about to be captured, they remove their characteristic dark glasses and leave the three disguised street children, now physically indistinguishable from them, in their house while they go, as they put it, "on a small errand" (p. 98). The last two frames are crucial. The penultimate one shows three apparent Tanâbila with dark glasses in a jail cell. "Believe us, Officer," one insists, "we are not the Tanâbila, they went on a small errand," while a second bemoans their fate, wishing they had stayed on the sidewalk. It would seem that these are the urchins. The last frame shows three more apparent Tanâbila in a boat, now without glasses. One suggests that they remove the clothes which had almost gotten them into trouble, while another exclaims: "Thank God the officer knew the truth and arrested the real Tanâbila. And we came out from this and emerged innocent" (p. 98). Then are the three in the boat the urchins and the three in prison the Tanâbila? We are left with a paradox. Each group suggests that the other is lying and both cannot be sincere. Has justice been done? Though the reader is left with the nagging suspicion that the Tanâbila have, in fact, gotten away, one cannot know for sure.

Nothing could be further from the traditional ending of a children's story or comic strip, where the plot is tied up neatly and good clearly triumphs over evil. The saccharine conclusion to the first Tanâbila series is a good example. Hijâzî's deliberate ambiguity in *Tanâbilat al-Khirfân* associates him (at least, as far as his ending is concerned) with contemporary narrative sensibilities. The Arabic literary tradition knows of tricksters, charlatans, and disguises of identity. The ambiguity in these texts, however, is never left with the reader. The famous *maqâmât* are the clearest example. Typically, in the last scene, the trickster is discovered or himself unveils his true identity. Hijâzî's equivocal ending is closer to those of the contemporary Egyptian leftist novelist Yûsuf al-Qaʿîd. In so many of al-Qaʿîd's novels, as in Hijâzî's strip, one is left with a nagging sense of injustice, fed by an uncertainty over the denouement. Need we add that for children's literature such a procedure is politically and aesthetically radical?[24]

Tanâbilat al-Khirfân and Egyptian Society

One of the most striking features of *Tanâbilat al-Khirfân* is the constant play of reality and illusion. Things are seldom what they seem. The first illusion is the basic one: the Tanâbila Bluebeef is not the Tanâbila Bluebeef. Its initial absence from the market is taken to mean that it has sold out, when in truth it has never appeared. All along, of course, the media support this climate of falsehood. ʿAlî ʿAlîwa is considered a repentant thief when he is purely and simply a thief. The salaries of the employees are illusory, since they return to the company's coffers. When the populace first rises against the Tanâbila and angry crowds surround their offices, the trio realizes that the only way for them to get out unscathed is to appear to be arrested. Accordingly they are led out by the police, and the populace, believing they have been arrested, disperses satisfied. In effect, the people are constantly duped. Grooming and masquerading the three urchins as Tanâbila creates the ultimate illusion and permits the ambiguous ending in which reality and illusion, truth and falsehood, have become hopelessly intertwined.

Fraud, misrepresentation, the juggling with reality, one would conclude from

Hijâzî's narrative, are closely woven into the texture of Egyptian society. Again, this brings his position close to that of the leftist al-Qaʿîd. In *War in the Land of Egypt*, the son of a village watchman trades identity with that of the son of the village ʿumda, or headman, in a corrupt scheme that has everyone misrepresenting the true reality. And the whole matter is never properly disentangled. A similar question of bureaucracy and faked identity appears in *It Happens in Egypt Today*.[25]

Attempting to evaluate the importance of this phenomenon inevitably risks unfairness (especially since fraud is in no sense uniquely Egyptian). In private conversations, however, numerous Egyptians of different political persuasions have repeatedly insisted to us that the visits of dignitaries to factories and other projects are commonly the occasion for widespread misrepresentation of the origin of products, the true progress of projects, etc. It may well be that Hijâzî has called attention to a particularly Egyptian way of doing things.

He has certainly hit close to home. Bertrand Millet has shown clearly that many of the comic-strip series published in *Samîr* as the original creations of Egyptian scenarists and artists are indeed either translations or readaptations of European strips.[26] This, of course, is the magazine for which Hijâzî worked and in which *Tanâbila* was published. How ironic then becomes a passage of dialogue among the Tanâbila. Shamlûl protests tearfully: "I am crying because we are liars. We wrote our name on imported *bluebeef*, that is, we stole the effort of others." But Bahlûl replies: "Shame on you for thinking this way, O Shamlûl. You have to understand that commerce is cleverness. And note that we also have tired ourselves out. We made advertisements, we printed paper with the brand name of the Tanâbila on it, and we bought glue" (p. 31). Indeed, this passage functions better as an attack on plagiarism, because while the Tanâbila have stolen from many, they have not really, in strictly economic terms, stolen the effort of the foreign manufacturers, since these manufacturers received the market price for their *bluebeef* when the Tanâbila bought it. But Hijâzî thinks in moral, not economic, categories.

Of course, the notion of fraud and illusion in *Tanâbilat al-Khirfân* is closely tied in with the role of the media. In effect, Hijâzî's text reflects a strikingly modern and sophisticated critique of the workings of advanced capitalist society. The notion of consumer sovereignty that is so dear to neoliberals, says this point of view, is a pure illusion, since the consumers are manipulated, their desires created, by the all-powerful media. Even the notions of democracy and liberty then become meaningless. The media, with a blend of advertisement and news, control the population far better than any police.

The strip shows the manipulation of the average Egyptian household (in this context, effectively urban). As the placidly happy family unit drinks in the Tanâbila jingles, it is the children who react first. They want to taste the *bluebeef* of the Tanâbila (e.g., p. 18). In effect, the population likes the product before they have tried it and it becomes immensely popular, despite its striking similarity to the previously available imported luncheon. Competing vendors, from butchers to *fûl* sellers, complain that no one is buying their products (p. 34).

This mild collective hysteria even extends outside the borders of the country. An

5.4. *The Tanâbila protected by the police.*

Egyptian student in East Germany greets his family through a radio program. He is studying hard and the only thing he lacks is the Tanâbila canned meat. A foreigner wants to come to Egypt to see the Pyramids, the Sphinx, and the antiquities, but also to eat Tanâbila *bluebeef* (p. 36). The campaign for the Tanâbila Company Investment Certificates has similar results. Family members virtuously decide to give up cigarettes and candy and to devote household economies to the purchase of Tanâbila securities (p. 61). Television is particularly targeted for its encouragement of passivity. To turn the urchins into fat lazy children like themselves, the Tanâbila can do no better than to plant them in front of a television set (p. 78).

Of course, the media are not innocent in this system. Hijâzî effectively shows their collusion with business groups and service to the powerful. Curiously, the *Tanâbilat al-Khirfân* functions as a denunciation of the consumer society associated with the Egyptian *infitâh*, begun under Sadat and continued under Mubarak. But the *Tanâbilat al-Khirfân* was written under Nasser's policy of relative autarchy and state socialism. The strip's precocious targeting of nascent developments makes it even more devastating today than when first written. The eagerness of the population to buy Tanâbila Investment Certificates can even be connected, if one wishes, with the response to the Islamic Investment Companies.

The third member of the triad, of which the first two are business and the media, would logically be the government. The latter is barely present in Hijâzî's text, except through the minister who rushes to aid the apparently successful industrialists. The state is essentially represented in *Tanâbilat al-Khirfân* through the maintenance of order and the institutions of the police and the courts. The only role played by the judiciary is to convict Samîr and Samîra for their attacks on the Tanâbila. The courts in no way help to establish justice.

Nor do the police. The helplessness of the forces of order goes further than the usual Keystone Cops comic ineptitude. In a naïve and unreflective way, they only serve the rich and powerful. It never occurs to them to suspect the Tanâbila, even when ʿAlî's pickpocket scheme is exposed and angry crowds are denouncing the corpulent capitalists. But when the Tanâbila need protection, the police bend over backward. We see (p. 64) each of our tubby heroes marching with an officer in front and a soldier behind (fig. 5.4). When it is a matter of dispersing the anti-Tanâbila demonstration, the police only reject the idea of arresting all the demonstrators because there are too many of them, not because it might be unjust (pp. 49–51). The behavior of the police makes a mockery of the official slogan, printed and repeated frequently throughout the strip: "The Police are in the Service of the People" (e.g., pp. 9, 33, 52). As Tambûl puts it, "It is the duty of the police . . . to protect the lives of the citizens, especially if they are famous industrialists like us" (p. 63). Nor, finally, are the police completely virtuous. When one of ʿAlî's gang drops a bag of food, the police who apprehend him eat it. When the criminal, in his deathbed confession, comes to the contents of the sack, the policeman adds that the chicken needed a little salt (pp. 70–71).

In effect, however (and it is perhaps this which makes Hijâzî's critique most devastating), the system extends to the Egyptian people themselves who become participants in it. Over and over again we see them motivated by greed. The Tanâbila employees are delighted with their jobs because of their high salaries. One important employee receives a bump on the head from a rock thrown during the anti-Tanâbila demonstrations. Every time Tambûl sees him, he gives him an indemnity of five pounds for the injury (a far larger sum then than today). Delighted, the worker arranges to be seen by his boss as often as possible. One day, in front of the mirror, he notes to his wife that the bump is almost gone. She solves the problem by hitting him over the head with a rolling pin so that the payments can continue (pp. 56–67). This is also how the Tanâbila understand motivation. They conclude that their main mistake, the one which caused their downfall, was their failure to pay sufficient bonuses to their most important workers, those who changed the labels on the cans of *bluebeef* (p. 97).

Whether it is the lottery or the reward on ʿAlî's head, the members of the public are led by their appetites, often imagining in advance how they will spend the money (p. 63). A group of children intend to go into business—the spirit of capitalism spreads (p. 64).

In effect, in Hijâzî's system of psychological motivations, greed and gluttony go hand in hand, the greed of the Egyptians reflecting the gluttony of the Tanâbila. But this parallel points to further relationships. Greed is associated with the world of money and of adults. Gluttony, or to speak in psychological terms, orality, is linked to that of children. A developmental view would see them as successive expressions of the same basic appetite. And in *Tanâbilat al-Khirfân* a subtle set of parallels and connections is established between the world of adults and that of children. The Tanâbila are, after all, children, with essentially childish appetites, successfully playing adult roles. This is shown by the fact that it is another group of children, the street urchins, who become their doubles. Even the names of the Tanâbila have a childish ring about them. The link between the two worlds, appropriately enough, is food made into an industrial, hence marketable, product—the concrete connection between the physical act of eating and the making of money.

But a far more general point is also being developed. The worlds of adults and children can be telescoped one into another because they have become more and more alike. The good people of Egypt, responding uncritically to their media and manipulated by the insipid jingles for Tanâbila luncheon, have become effectively infantilized. In this way, though they are participants in the process, members of a system, they are still its victims.

The glimmer of hope lies with a certain basic morality still inherent in the Egyptian population. In *Tanâbilat al-Khirfân*, this shows itself most clearly in the propensity to confess. The members of ʿAlî ʿAlîwa's gang confess once in a group and one confesses a second time because he believes that he is about to die. Of course, it is the confession of a group of workers which finally destroys the Tanâbila's empire. It is certainly not the state nor even the isolated crusading of Samîr and Samîra which produces justice but a basic, essentially religious morality remaining in the character of the Egyptian people—that is, unless one accepts the Tanâbila's argument that the fault was not bribing their workers well enough. Might this suggest that the continuance of a fundamentally corrupt system risks tainting what is left of traditional morality among the common people of Egypt?

The Tanâbila in Politics

Tanâbilat al-Khirfân is undoubtedly the most novelistic of Hijâzî's strips. *Tambûl I* (*Tambûl al-Awwal*) is a far more schematic text.[27] A reworking of the movie from *Tanâbilat al-Sibyân*, *Tambûl I* replaces the rich realism of the *bluebeef* story with an almost abstract story line that invites allegorical interpretation.

Even the material conditions of production have led to a foregrounding and refinement of certain Hijâzian techniques, giving them political implications not always present in earlier works. The earlier Tanâbila were all written for *Samîr* magazine and printed in that journal's customary alternation between color and monochrome pages. *Tambûl I*, partly rewritten and completely redrawn for the leftist publisher Dâr al-Fatâ al-ʿArabî, was printed in monochrome, that is to say, white, black, and a faded pink. White has been reserved exclusively for the speech balloons (some of which also have an imaginative use of black), leaving the illustrations themselves in only pink and black. To create the necessary differences in background and visual variety from frame to frame, Hijâzî has resorted to a series of abstract visual patterns, occasionally producing effects reminiscent of traditional Islamic art (fig. 5.5). The net effect is to link the lineally drawn figures with their background and bathe the whole in a feeling of abstraction.

The text begins with a bit of visual political science. Labeled "The Personalities of the Story," it is actually a description of society and the state. A series of picture groups, each group containing smaller and more numerous figures than the one before, sketches a kind of social pyramid (though the shape is more that of three hierarchically arranged horizontal strata) (fig. 5.6). With the exception of the three Tanâbila (as usual, visually almost identical), the groups also become less and less individualized. After the three Tanâbila, described as kings, come the eight ministers, who are differentiated by face and type of facial grooming. All have mustaches, all but one have beards as well, though in a variety of styles. None is clean-shaven, and all are highly individualized. The twenty-six soldiers who make up the middle register are moderately individualized, though all wear the same mustache. The bottom rectangle is a single frame containing a large indistinguishable clean-shaven mass. These are the people.

This visual representation of the class system (one might almost speak of three or-

5.5. *Monochrome design.*

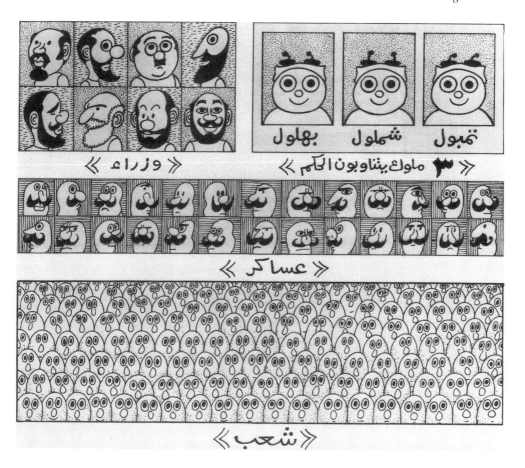

5.6. *The social hierarchy.*

ders in the traditional European sense) is both absolute and universal. The replacement of the sultan from the movie version (and, of course, the prologue to *Tanâbilat al-Sibyân* as well) with three "kings" further lifts the analysis from a purely Islamic context.

As the story opens, Tambûl is sending his two colleagues, Shamlûl and Bahlûl, to prison. He justifies his action in traditional political terms: the rule of one is better than that of three (p.1). Invoking the argument in this dubious context, however, effectively subverts it, turning it from a defense to an attack on all forms of monocratic rule, hereditary or otherwise.

Tambûl's behavior is not unique. We swiftly discover that when Shamlûl was king, he too had imprisoned his two fellow Tanâbila (p. 3). This point, one of many omitted from the earlier movie version, broadens the political satire. The common citizens themselves recognize that it makes no difference which combination of Tanâbila rule. Thus it is not the personal characteristics of an individual tyrant that count.

Tambûl I also constructs a wonderful satire on the actions of government ministers. The minister of transport carries Tambûl to the dinner table and from one dish to another. The minister of supply brings the food and the minister of agriculture tells the minister of health to wash the fruit correctly. The minister of culture tells jokes to the king to make him forget the problems of the country. Only the minister of interior (and apparently also the minister of finance) functions as he would in a real government. He is in charge of order, that is, repression. It is clear which ministries truly constitute the state (pp. 2–3, 13).

As in the movie version, Bahlûl and Shamlûl escape and are recaptured. Also as in the earlier version, their escape forms the occasion for the ceremonial derogation of the negligent jailer. In a scene reminiscent of the public degradation of Dreyfus, the faulty jailer is seated on a barber chair, in the center of a courtyard surrounded by soldiers at attention, while his mustache is shaved off (pp. 10–12). No longer a member of a privileged group, he has become an ordinary citizen. So much for military honor.

It is at this point that *Tambûl I* departs sharply from its predecessor. The later text features true revolutionaries and a true revolution. The revolutionaries have a secret hideout where they grow mustaches, in contravention of the public order limiting this privilege to the military. The revolution, however, is started not by the "party" but by a group of housewives angry over rising prices. As crowds surround the royal palace, Tambûl orders the army to fire on them. At first this disperses the population, but then the mustachioed revolutionaries emerge en masse from their hideout. These last, as the revolt began, finding that it was taking too long for their new members to grow mustaches, distributed ready-made ones which their comrades could paste on their faces. When the soldiers see the hairy-lipped revolutionaries, they take them for soldiers from another country. Brave against their own unarmed citizenry, Tambûl's soldiers turn tail at the thought of facing a foreign army. The revolution is successful; the people sit on the throne.

Meanwhile Tambûl goes to the prison, frees Bahlûl and Shamlûl, and the three flee. The revolutionaries search for them everywhere but cannot find them. Finally the leader of the revolution has an idea. This technique, present in germ in the prologue of *Tanâbilat al-Sibyân*, is much more fully elaborated in *Tambûl I*. First, the revo-

lutionary leader orders the head chef to prepare all the favorite foods of the Tanâbila. In a parody of a general organizing military operations, the leader commands the platters of different foods to be paraded through different parts of the city. As the instructions are being read out, we see the huge trays heaped with succulent tasties being carried by the tattered, famished citizens (fig. 5.7).

> The group of platters of potatoes with lean meat, squash with béchamel, and *mu-lûkhiyya*[28] with rabbits walk through the downtown streets. . . .
> The group of roast turkeys, stuffed ducks, and *fînû*[29] bread walk through the back streets.
> The group of fried fish, grilled shrimp, and boiled crabs walk in the main squares.
> The group of *ba'lâwa* with nuts, *basbûsa* with cream, gateau with chocolate, *sha'riyya* with milk, and *kunâfa*[30] with hazelnuts walk through all the streets. (Pp. 22–25).

Overcome by the smell of food and their own gluttony, the three kings emerge from their hiding place inside the throne, in effect concealed within the symbol of sovereignty. After stuffing themselves into unconsciousness, the Tanâbila are sent off in a boat. As they depart, the people declare that they will be governed by one of their own and "without jail or jailers" (p. 26).

There are elements in *Tambûl I* that could be assimilated with specific Egyptian realities. The revolt provoked by rising prices could be compared to the price riots of January 1977, just as the corpulence and gluttony of the Tanâbila remind one of King Fârûq (who was also exiled on a boat). But some of these points, like price-provoked disturbances, are historically very common. More important, Hijâzî's referents are far broader than Egypt or even the Arab world. The revolution he describes (carried out without firearms) is also against the army, which it eliminates as a privileged caste. As such, it resembles none of the "revolutions" of Egypt or any other Arab state.

Read on a surface level, *Tambûl I* hesitates between anarchist and what could be called Leninist or Blanquist formulations. On one hand, the attack on the state is thorough and the new society will be without means of repression. On the other, though the revolution is started by the populace, it is saved by the timely intervention of an organized revolutionary party. And the statement that the people will be governed by one of themselves reestablishes political authority.

But *Tambûl I* is not a realist narrative. The whole episode with mustaches as the center of political activity is comically ridiculous and begs a more symbolic interpretation. A mustache first of all is a sign of virility. But the sexist implications of the symbol are somewhat reduced by the leading role taken by the women in the revolution.

In *Tambûl I*, however, the mustache is also a sign of adulthood. The three Tanâbila are clearly infants. Their round, sexually undifferentiated forms (only their names suggest the male gender) and their oral fixation reinforce this. What they share in the opening tableau of our fictional kingdom with the common people is the absence of facial hair (fig. 5.6). They rule through hirsute adults who keep the people down by keeping them clean-shaven. That is why the act of growing a mustache for a common citizen is more than defiance; it is the overthrow of despotism. The state, run by children, keeps the population in a form of childhood which is subjugation. The revolution cannot be accomplished, then, without the coming of adulthood, of full political maturity (that is, educational and social development) of the common people themselves. Seen this way, the conclusions of *Tambûl I* concord with the analyses of *Tanâbilat al-Khirfân*.

Distinguishing the two texts is the role played in each by food. Already important in the earlier *Tanâbila*, food becomes fully dominant in *Tambûl I*. Food is, of course, the downfall of the Tanâbila, but of others as well. Bahlûl and Shamlûl escape when their jailer brings them their food. The other guards do not follow because they are eating. Food also separates the privileged from the underclass. When the negligent jailer loses his mustache, he loses with it his access to "vegetables, meat, fruit, soap, and chocolate" (p. 12). Finally, it is the high food prices that provoke the rebellion. Food has replaced money as the unique measure of exploitation, just as the game of reality and illusion gives way to unconcealed exploitation. Hence it is not the consumer society which is pilloried but the social order itself, with its basic exploitative character.

This emphasis on food has echoes on the Egyptian Left, and again, al-Qaʿîd is perhaps the best example. In al-Qaʿîd's *al-Harb*, a poor man invited to the ʿumda's house is struck by the abundance of food. The ʿumda's fleshy hand is also associated with meat, like the virtual consubstantiality between the tubby Tanâbila and their mountains of victuals.[31] For Hijâzî, however, food is less specific, since it associates the world of children with that of adults. For him, the politics of one are fundamentally the politics of the other.

The *Infitâh* in Strips

Tambûl I is at once both the most general and the most political of Hijâzî's strips. The sixty-six-frame narrative Hijâzî published in *al-Ahâlî* is both the most specific and the one which best ties together the politics of *Tambûl I* with the economic and social critique of *Tanâbilat al-Khirfân*. *Stimulating the Brain* (*Tahrîk al-ʿAql*) is a savage satire on

5.8. *Government officials as big children.*

contemporary Egyptian economic policy and effectively on the entire *infitâh*.[32] It could bear the subtitle "The Tanâbilization of Egypt."

The Tanâbila themselves are not present. They have been replaced by another series of comical childish figures whose spherical heads are capped by conical hats. While members of the official class are not as ridiculously corpulent as Tambûl, Bahlûl, or Shamlûl, they are quite stout and short-legged (fig. 5.8). Other characters, though slightly thinner, wear conical hats whose designs distinguish their professions. This is still, in a way, a world of children.

The story centers on a dialogue between the minister of economy and the administrative secretary of the Egyptian government. The minister, just arrived at the airport, explains that he really lives abroad, spending all his time going from one foreign nation to another in quest of loans. It is true, he admits, that much of the money thus collected goes into his own and other ministers' extensive travel expenses. But some is left over for the Egyptian people, and he has come to see whether this money is being well spent. He and the secretary visit government offices, factories, and the agricultural sector. The civil servants he finds contentedly asleep at their desks. This is a familiar topos in Egypt. The image is notorious of members of government bureaucracies wiling away the hours playing cards, doing crossword puzzles, or, less commonly, sleeping. It is well known that one of the main causes of this situation is the deliberate overstaffing of bureaucracies and the attempt to give employment to as many graduates as possible.

Hijâzî goes further, however, since the factory workers are also asleep and the peasants are happily frittering away their time in the coffeehouses. To the surprised minister, the secretary explains that the people are very happy: "This is happiness, that you sleep whenever you like" (frame 12).[33] The people of Egypt have suffered in the past the hardships of war and poverty, and "it is now their right to enjoy peace[34] and imported goods" (f. 10). As the secretary explains further, the people "used to produce food, garments, domestic goods, building materials, and arms to defend the country" (f. 16). But those days are gone. "We have abolished work," he proudly proclaims (f. 19). Everything is imported and paid for with loans. It is the farmers of Europe who till the soil and the Egyptians who gather in their products.

The minister sees a cloud on the horizon. The lender nations are insisting on repayment. The Egyptians will have to learn to work again so they can repay their debts. Songwriters will be hired to make a musical campaign to stimulate the masses and get them back to work. These media professionals are skeptical, however: "the people pass their time enjoying television programs and videocassettes" (f. 40). But the minister himself perceives a more serious problem. Stirring the people into activity is a dangerous proposition. Nations that are productive are more self-confident; they want a say in how they are governed and make life difficult for their rulers: "God protect me from the vileness of productive peoples" (f. 51).

Not to fear; the musical campaign is a failure. The lazy Egyptians just turn off their radios or their television sets. When the minister hears this, he declares that the problem was that the songs were domestically produced. In their place, the government will import foreign songs. While he is explaining this on the telephone to the secretary, we see the minister in his foreign hotel room, his arm around a floozy. His degree of concern is easy to guess.

This explanation of Egyptian economic policy is neat, even cute. But it departs from the usual leftist attacks on the *infitâh* in a number of ways. The most common charge against the economic open-door policy is that it permits the exploitation of Egyptian national resources by foreigners, who also get rich on the goods they sell to the Egyptian people.[35] The governing elites, according to this view, are simply paid off or controlled by foreign governments or bankers when the two are not the same.

Hijâzî's formulation, while it does not negate these factors, stresses other points. Indeed, his vision of a native population sleeping on the job while eating from foreign loans reads almost like anti–Third World propaganda or an argument against foreign aid. The crux of Hijâzî's system is the idea that a lazy, in effect demoralized and infantilized, Tanâbilized population is easier to govern. The contrast is striking with the Egyptian agricultural workers in *Tanâbilat al-Sibyân* who declared: "Is there anyone in the world who does not want to work?" All the themes of the Tanâbila series are drawn together in a nightmare vision of dependence and powerlessness.

6

Sacred Images:
Islamic Comic Strips

Islamic comic strips: the mere phrase seems a contradiction—or a provocation—in a religious tradition known for its hostility to the image, and with a history of avoiding iconographic propaganda. Can this form associated with Western secular mass culture be turned to Islamic purposes? Can Islamic themes be put in visual terms? Islamic sacred texts? Some marriages between the Muslim religion and the comic-strip form have earned the ire of the orthodox, but most have not. Islamic comic strips are not as anomalous as the name suggests; they are far more common than Christian comic strips in the United States, though perhaps not in Europe. The Islamic revival has meant that the availability of Islamic comic strips, both governmental and oppositional, has been steadily increasing.

There is a variety of ways in which Arab strips can be considered Islamic. Virtually all Arab strips and the children's magazines that carry them are Islamic in at least a passive sense, participating in a culture in which Islam is the hegemonic religion, if not always the dominant ideology. Even the secularizing, Westernizing *Mîkî* with its pervasive Pharaonism pays frequent lip service to Islam as a key element in the texture of Egyptian life.[1] Many other, otherwise secular magazines, like the pan-Arab *Mâjid*, include regular religion sections.[2]

Comic-strip materials are often Islamic in two other ways: first, when moral guidance is presented in Islamic terms or with Islamic legitimization, and second, when specifically Islamic topics are treated, whether religious discussions, historical evocations, or even the presentation of material from the sacred texts themselves, from the *hadîth* (traditions of the Prophet which report his words or actions) to the Qur'ân. Perhaps most clearly Islamic, at least in declared intention, are those strips which form part, often the largest part, of children's magazines which are Islamic in their titles, their self-proclaimed mission to spread Islamic faith and values, and their intended audience. It is no surprise that materials which are Islamic in the above two senses are most highly concentrated in these Islamic children's magazines.

The Islamic magazines featuring comic-strip literature for the longest number of years are the official ones, government sponsored and government supported. Since 1970, *Minbar al-Islâm* has been publishing a children's supplement, *al-Firdaws* (Paradise), which almost always includes comic strips. The monthly *Minbar* and its supplement are publications of al-Majlis al-Aʿlâ lil-Shu'ûn al-Islâmiyya (the High Council for Islamic Affairs), a department of the Ministry of Pious Foundations (Wizârat al-Awqâf) in Cairo. *Al-Firdaws*, which is aimed at children aged six to twelve, has a circulation of approximately thirty-five thousand.[3] Equally representative of "official" Islam is the slightly younger *Barâʿim al-Imân* (Blossoms of Faith), a supplement to *al-Waʿy al-Islâmî* of the Ministry of Pious Foundations and Islamic Affairs (Wizârat al-Awqâf wal-Shu'ûn al-Islâmiyya) in Kuwait.

The last decade and especially the last few years have seen an expansion of Islamic children's periodicals published by independent, nongovernmental Islamic associations. *Al-Muslim al-Saghîr* (The Little Muslim) has been, since 1984, the monthly publication of Jamʿiyyat al-Usra al-Muslima (Muslim Family Association), a privately supported Egyptian organization. The group's leader and the magazine's editor-in-chief is Marzûq Hilâl (his associates call him al-Hâjj, the honorific for those who have performed the pilgrimage to Mecca). The Hâjj's weekly children's television program, Nâdî al-Muslim al-Saghîr (The Little Muslim's Club), testifies to his integration into the Egyptian cultural establishment. *Al-Muslim al-Saghîr* aims a seasonally varied print run of ten to thirty thousand at children aged eight to fourteen.[4] Indicative of the Hâjj's resolute modernism is what happened one evening as we were sitting in his office. Everyone had a good laugh when he gently mocked a more conservative female guest, whose gloves were designed to prevent her physical contact with men, by ostentatiously enveloping his hand in a flap of his sport coat before shaking hers.

The clearest political coloration, however, attaches to the Egyptian children's monthly, *Zam Zam*, also created in 1988 and named for the holy well near Mecca where Hagar drew water for Ismâʿîl. The well is known as Zamzam (one word), but the magazine cover and logo are written as two words, though the magazine uses the logo Zam Zam and the word Zamzam interchangeably when referring to itself within its pages. Thus its title is both a specific referent and a reference to the holy place.[5] *Zam Zam* is a supplement to *Majallat al-Mukhtâr al-Islâmî*, an Islamist journal, whose connections reach to oppositional, though legal, Islamic circles. Its publishing house, Maktabat al-Mukhtâr al-Islâmî, handles figures such as the leading antiestablishment Islamist, Shaykh Kishk. And it is not surprising that al-Zuhayrî, who does so many of the Shaykh's book covers, draws *Zam Zam*'s best comic strips. Of course, al-Mukhtâr al-Islâmî also publishes independent but establishment personalities, such as Shaykh

Muhammad Mutawallî al-Sha'râwî. *Zam Zam* approvingly quoted a newspaper review calling it "the first independent Muslim magazine which treats the problems of the Muslim child in Egypt."[6] If this appreciation seems unfair given the far greater age of *al-Muslim al-Saghîr*, it gains in accuracy if we see independence as a euphemism for opposition to the political and religious establishment in Egypt.[7] Also created in 1988 is the independent Lebanese children's magazine, *Ahmad*, also called *al-Malâk Ahmad* (The Angel Ahmad).

Despite political and geographic variety, there is considerable similarity in the materials these Islamic children's magazines cast into comic-strip form. This convergence is due partly to the conformism so often dominant in Arab children's literature, partly to the choices and limitations that overtly Muslim publications put on themselves.

Basic similarity does not eliminate differences in tendency. The raison d'être of Muslim children's magazines is to replace the competing popular secular children's publications, be they native or imported-translated. In the new cultural discourses created by this children's literature, different magazines adopt more or less from their secular rivals and stick more or less closely to traditional Islamic messages and materials. *Zam Zam*, for example, presents a number of animal fables with a cynical but rather traditional political morality, in the absence of any Islamic referent or moral inspiration (1988, no. 2).[8] In another strip, turtles are involved in an adventure with no apparent religious or moral content (1988, no. 4). In a well written story splendidly illustrated by al-Zuhayrî (1988, no. 3), an Islamic referent is echoed by the kerchieflike veil worn by the mother bird (see fig. 6.1). Islamicization is a little more obvious in some other *Zam Zam* adventure strips, in which characters go to the mosque or cite sacred texts (e.g., 1988, nos. 1 and 2). But this most independent of Islamic children's magazines has gone farthest in the inclusion of essentially entertaining stories, which are in their basic nature neither religious nor moral.

Other magazines, and even *Zam Zam* for much of its comic-strip material, exploit a number of subject areas: contemporary political, educational (secular and religious), moral (modern and traditional), and religio-historical.

The purest political strips appear in Marzûq Hilâl's monthly, where the Hâjj writes all the scenarios.[9] The *intifâda* is an ideal topic: it is safely patriotic (support for the Palestinians is a consensus value in Arab society), it shows the Arabs in triumph, and it turns children (the audience of the strips) into heroes. Thus, also, has it been exploited by secular magazines.[10] The twelve frames in the February 1988 *al-Muslim al-Saghîr*, illustrated in color by Qadriyya Abû Shûsha, are not strictly speaking a comic strip, because they lack balloons. Instead, a third-person narrative occupies registers below each frame, coordinated with its subject. The narrator is identified as "an American commentator," and we see him in the last frame looking like a typical Western TV newsman, with his blond good looks, repeating his opening message: "The Palestinian *intifâda* is a time bomb, twenty years old, exploding now in the face of Israel." This personified narrator not only suggests factual veracity but accurately highlights the role of Western media coverage in the *intifâda*'s political successes.

6.1. *Mother bird with Islamic kerchief.*

Frames show children as well as men and women facing Israeli soldiers. One pictures a trio of uniformed school children with two soldiers behind them, while the text explains that the occupation soldiers follow the children in fear (fig. 6.2).

Stripological gaucheness echoes political embarrassment in a version of the *Achille Lauro* incident illustrated by Khâlid al-Safatî (November–December 1985). Not surprisingly, the story's title focuses on the U.S. interception of an Egyptian civilian aircraft, but more striking is the complete occultation of the Klinghoffer murder, which so incensed Western public opinion. The strip shows Egyptian officials negotiating with the Palestinian hijackers (called *mujâhidûn*, a more religious appellation than the more common *fidâ'iyyûn*). A frame without text shows Palestinians and Egyptians together on an Egyptian boat and the two following frames (both with balloons) show the interception of the Egyptian aircraft and the seizure of the Palestinians on the ground of a Sicilian airbase. Were negotiations with the Palestinians successful? Was the Egyptian government going to free them? Punish them? None of these questions is addressed in the narrative. The last frame of the story is at once the most ambiguous and the most telling. Coming after the image at the airbase, it shows only an Egyptian flag held aloft by an arm, emerging from the frame's border: a protest affirmation of Egyptian nationalism to balance the humiliation associated with the content of the previous two frames. The contrast with the triumphalism of the *intifâda* strip is marked.

Such purely political strips are rare in Muslim children's magazines. The October 1973 War sparked a rash of patriotic strips in the usually less political *al-Firdaws*. But

6.2. *The* intifâda: *Israeli soldiers and Arab schoolchildren.*

even in this time of war fever, the Egyptian periodical mixed the patriotic with other, more common Muslim comic-strip genres. Even before the Egyptian surprise crossing of the Suez Canal, a change appeared in the *al-Firdaws* strips, foreshadowing the war to come. A September 1973 story, written by ʿAliyya Tawfîq Mahmûd and drawn by Nabîl al-Ramlî, seems on the surface a typical moral tale, in which a girl is rewarded for returning a box she has found. The end of the story introduces the new element when we learn that the box contained letters from a son at the front to his mother, adding a patriotic element to an otherwise structurally typical tale of moral exchange.[11] The two November issues of 1973 each produced war stories.[12] In the first, a group of boys collecting dynamite to use against Israeli soldiers are saved when the enemy soldiers accidentally blow themselves up in a cave. Qurʾânic quotes in the middle (Sûrat al-Hajj, verse 38) and end (Sûrat al-Baqara, verse 190) of the story indicate that God protects believers and not unbelievers. Divine providence, not bravery or patriotic valor, saves our young heroes. In the second story, a child's paralysis is miraculously healed so that he can help a victim from the rubble caused by an Israeli raid. Again, patriotic fare is bent to religious purposes.

These magazines take their educational functions seriously, and the provision of general knowledge, especially scientific, is a frequent feature. In a regular series in *Ahmad*, a knowledgeable young man, ʿArif (a name meaning "one who knows") explains to a group of adolescents topics from moles to firefighting. This technique, conventional in Arab strips, is enlivened by the inclusion of photographs inserted into the strips themselves (e.g., 1988, nos. 14 and 21). Third World political economy is broached when ʿArif argues that his compatriots should eat their own fresh food rather than exporting it to be canned and repurchasing it at a higher cost, and that they should buy local products in order not to be dependent on others (1988, nos. 15 and 17).

Zam Zam, by contrast, usually inserts or attaches its general knowledge in narratives (e.g., 1988, no. 3). The greatest emphasis on education in all its forms characterizes *al-Muslim al-Saghîr*, the overwhelming majority of whose strips are devoted to such material. A number of strips feature father figures teaching younger individuals (e.g., 1985, nos. 28, 29, and 30). The most important teaching strip, and one of the most important series in *al-Muslim al-Saghîr*, is entitled "al-Faylasûf al-Zâ'ir wal-Shâtir ʿAtir" (The Visiting Philosopher and the Clever ʿAtir). The philosopher, with flowing white beard and traditional robes, explains a variety of subjects to his pupil: religious knowledge, historical data, the natural sciences (e.g., October 1985, February 1986, May 1986). The result of this pedagogical mixture is to define all these subjects into a larger category: that of general knowledge. Further, the choice of a philosopher (instead of a *shaykh*, for example) fuses the philosophical and Islamic traditions, while placing the entire curriculum under the sign of rational knowledge.

But a more subtle dialectic of tradition is being played out. Transmission of knowledge is patriarchal (from father figure to eternal son) but equivocal. The philosopher is not of our time; rather, he is outside time, hence his knowledge of all periods: he is a visitor, his clothes are timeless, he, apparently ageless. He functions, in fact, like the Islamic figure of al-Khidr.[13] But our philosopher, though clothed in the attributes of a venerable religious figure, belongs, through his title if nothing else, to a more secular tradition. Thus does the assimilation of religious to profane knowledge risk the replacement of the religious tradition with the scientific one.

Moral Tales

Our Muslim magazines give little space to unadorned practical religious instruction and prefer, when they do, to deliver these messages in narrative form. This does not mean that the daily practices of a Muslim do not find their way into frames and balloons. Nothing perhaps testifies better to the ubiquity of the comic-strip medium as a Muslim educational tool than the posters available in bookstores around the region explaining proper religious conduct. Among the best is a polychrome production by Ahmad ʿAbd al-ʿAzîz printed in Cairo. Sixteen of these twenty-one frames also appeared in a publication series by the Children's Culture Branch of the Safîr Company. This booklet version has reduced the frames to virtual illustrations placed within prose fields. The poster traces "A Day in the Life of the Muslim Child."[14] But our black-haired lad becomes more than a Muslim everyman. Iconographically, he is a comic-strip hero: his head in an Islamicized medallion in the form of an eight-pointed star, accompanying the title (fig. 6.3). The frames themselves take us through the boy's day from awakening and greetings to his parents through prayers, meals, school work, "sports," visiting the sick, etc. Only the boy speaks. Narrativizing text is reserved for words at the bottoms of the frames, which, when combined with the pictures, identify the daily-life scenes. These present-tense comments blend prescription with narrative: "He gets up to perform the dawn prayer," "he goes to the mosque," "he helps his mother at home," etc. From the mouth of the boy come only pious for-

6.3. *A day in the life of the Muslim child.*

mulae, appropriate to each situation: Qur'ânic recitation, Muslim greetings, blessings, etc. Daily life becomes textualized, its narrative a sequence of pious texts. The message is clear: the sacred word gives meaning to life as it gives continuity to the narrative. Even the booklet version supports this, since its inserted texts consist mostly of *hadîth*s relevant to the situation.

But iconography is its own language, as is color. In the poster, the frame that reads "he likes sport" shows our young Muslim dressed in a karate outfit yet wearing boxing gloves and working out with a punching bag. With two forms of combat instead of one, its aggressiveness is overcoded. Why not a communal and far more popular sport like soccer? The iconographic contradiction (what Riffaterre would call an ungrammaticality) highlights a semiotic ambiguity.[15] Part of a *hadîth* (not presented as such, but merely in quotes) gives some of the answer: "The strong believer is better and more beloved to God than the weak believer." Juxtaposed with the picture, this would seem to indicate physical strength. The Arabic word *qawî*, however, suggests both mental and physical properties; and al-Nawawî, in his discussion of this *hadîth* in his famous commentary on the *Sahîh* of Muslim, interprets it as psychological and spiritual strength of will, whose manifestations include virtues such as patience, the doing of good deeds, and courage against the enemy in the *jihâd*. Physical fitness is not mentioned. Further, the poster-strip eliminated that part of the *hadîth* which more unequivocally addressed psychological concerns.[16] The frame, therefore, brings together two fields of signification, one purely iconic, the other religio-textual. Their point of contact is the idea of combat. Together, in the syntagm which is the frame, the signification is military struggle on behalf of the community—holy war. And this activity is the closest to play of any in the life of our young Muslim. Is it a coincidence that this frame was one of those omitted in the booklet version, thus depriving it of the potential for fuller *hadîth* citation and commentary? The fuller *hadîth* citation would have rendered more difficult the semiotic shifts which give this poster frame its ideological distinctiveness.

In the boxing frame, the community was present while absent. Something similar transpires in the mosque and prayer frames. Though the poster recounts the daily life of an individual, many frames show his interaction with others; and in most of those, again, the other figures are fully colored in like the hero: his parents, a sick friend. In two frames, however, our young Muslim is shown praying in a mosque with a congregation, once kneeling and once standing. In the kneeling frame, the hero is fully colored in, while the rest of the frame, including the congregation, is done exclusively in a purple-white monochrome. The standing frame displays the same phenomenon, but with the entire background in shades of green. In both cases, also, the boy is drawn with a solid outline, colored in with solid color. The other figures, including those next to him in the row, are shaded in with more indefinite lines. In the frame, they look like ghosts, there and yet not there. Two other frames, one of prayer at school and another a classroom scene, have secondary figures with flesh-tone faces, ghostly white bodies, but polychrome background.

If the presence of others in the hero's background seems occasionally problematic, the mosque scenes are the most provocative. The congregation, in effect the Muslim community, or *umma*, is a ghostly apparition. Perhaps, this poster's iconography suggests, the supportive Muslim community is more an ideal or an echo from the past than a social reality. The family is real, as is the sick friend. But outside this narrow social circle, relationships fade in spirit and in color. Indeed, the sense of collectivity is weak. In thirteen of twenty-one frames, the hero appears alone.

By contrast to such direct prescriptions, most Muslim magazines prefer to wrap their moral messages in narrative, making contemporary moral tales the most ubiquitous Islamic comic-strip form. Such tales follow variations on two basic patterns: either good deeds are rewarded (usually directly, though in unexpected ways) or bad or foolish deeds are punished, generally by their practical consequences. The *al-Firdaws* strip discussed above in which a young girl was rewarded is a good example. Many of these stories include *hadîth*s as justifications (e.g., *Barâ'im*, 1988, no. 156) but others do not (e.g., *Barâ'im*, 1988 no. 158).

The subtleties of *hadîth* citation come out in a strip in *Ahmad* (1988, no. 14). A boy, Muhtadî, comes home angry with his sister, whom he blames for having shamed him in front of a group of other boys, and justifies his criticism with the *hadîth*: "Help your brother, be he a tyrant or a victim of tyranny." Their mother replies that had he finished the *hadîth*, he would have understood that helping your brother when he is a tyrant means helping him to cease his tyranny. The boy now understands and promises never to bully again.

In this case, mother does know best, as the rest of the *hadîth*, never cited in the strip, clearly supports her interpretation.[17] But there are more significant issues here. Muhtadî has understood the *hadîth* as privileging family solidarity over wider social bonds, evoking clan, tribal, and local loyalty networks. These bonds, which the Arabs call ʿasabiyya, have traditionally played a strong role in the region (as in the strip on Saddâm Husayn)[18] and have been the most important competitor to the umma and Islamic values as foci of loyalty. Though the father blesses the whole business at the end, it is the women of the family who uphold correct Islamic values against male bullying; and it is piquant to notice that the girl's name, Salmâ, is also that of the strip's author, Salmâ Badawî (the illustrator is ʿAlî Shams al-Dîn).

Such a gender division of labor forms part of a larger pattern. Girls are more often exemplars of virtuous behavior, boys of improper or simply foolish activity. (Male figures are purveyors of knowledge, but that is another problem.)[19]

"Muhtadî" is one of two Ahmad series which use negative role models. The other is "Fashkûl." If Muhtadî's errors are both moral and practical (as when his overeating is repaid with a stomach ache; 1988, no. 15), those of Fashkûl are almost always practical (as when he fails to prepare his bicycle properly for a race; 1988, no. 14).

Picturing Islam

But what if a hadîth, rather than proving a point, becomes a narrative, the essence of the strip itself? This brings us into the realm of the historico-religious material, strips which tell stories of early Islamic history. Several Firdawsian strips are narrativizations of hadîths. Sometimes the entire formal hadîth follows the strip, duplicating and certifying the story (e.g., Qâdî, pp. 3–5).[20] At other times the strip actually replaces the hadîth, though the young reader is told before and after the story that this was a hadîth from the Prophet (e.g., Sâlim, pp. 6–8).[21]

Putting early Islamic history in strips poses the problem of representation in its acutest form. Like al-Firdaws, al-Muslim al-Saghîr does not shy away from picturing important Islamic personalities or events, though the Prophet himself never appears, being kept carefully out of the frames (e.g., 1983, nos. 13, 16, 17, and 24). Marzûq Hilâl put it to us this way: there are two types of Islam, one backward looking, one forward looking; and images are tools—used for a good purpose they are good, for a bad purpose, bad.[22]

The most conservative stripology is that of Barâʿim al-Imân, whose strips on the early caliphs omit all historical pictorialization (1986, no. 131; 1988, nos. 156 and 157). All we see is a young man narrating the history to male and female colleagues in exclusively verbal balloons. The series' only interest lies in its politics: divisions in the community are blamed on its enemies, "chief among them the Jews," echoing a position of Sayyid Qutb.[23] But even Barâʿim drops this exceedingly dull procedure when it moves to the slightly later, and less sacred, Umayyad period (1988, no. 158).

It is the "official" al-Firdaws which goes farthest in putting Islamic sacred materials in strip form. Two episodes recount events from the lives of pre-Islamic Arabian prophets, Sâlih of the people of Thamûd and Hûd of the people of ʿAd. No sacred reference or source is given in the strips. Both prophetic accounts go back to the Qur'ân (e.g., Sûrat al-Aʿrâf, Sûrat Hûd, Sûrat al-Shuʿarâ'), yet the strips contain im-

6.4. *Halîma with the infant Muhammad.*

portant narrative elements missing from the Qur'ânic versions (though not inconsistent with them). Virtually all the significant material, however, can be found in Qur'ânic commentaries, such as al-Baydâwî's, and the *Anbiyâ'* collections (histories of the prophets).[24] If the Qur'ânic text is understood as including its commentary, then these Firdawsian stories can be seen as narrativized Qur'ân in comic-strip form. This would be particularly provocative, since, as we shall see, a later similar narrativization of the Muslim holy book proved controversial.

The taboo on Prophetic representation was at least partly violated, however, in an earlier *al-Firdaws* (April 1974). Written by ʿAliyya Tawfîq (whom we shall meet again) and drawn by Nabîl al-Ramlî, this strip recounts an episode from the *Sîra*, or biography of the Prophet, by Ibn Hishâm, though no source or reference is given.[25] In no sense a canonical text, the *Sîra* has been for many centuries an extraordinarily popular work, the main source on the life of the Prophet and much venerated by Muslims. In this story, a wet nurse, Halîma, takes on the infant, and orphaned, Muhammad, after which she and her family are blessed with a series of fortunate happenings. Iconographically, the strip takes us into territory heavily exploited in Christian pictorial traditions: a mother figure and holy infant. Not surprisingly, the images have a familiar feeling. Muhammad appears in the woman's arms. We see him only from the back, but his head is surrounded with a brilliant halo (fig. 6.4). Halîma resembles Western representations of the Virgin, in that her head covering exposes the face and even some long tresses,[26] though some of the women in the strip bear more conservative, Islamic-looking veils. Further, while Halîma's companions ride

6.5. Al-Firdaws's *traditional Arabs.*

camels and horses, she and the blessed infant ride a donkey, as in Christian representations of the Flight into Egypt, though this narrative detail was present in the *Sîra*
and not added by the comic strip's authors.[27]

Morality and History: *al-Firdaws*

Al-Firdaws regularly devotes three pages to comic strips, for the last several years
in brilliant colors. The scenarios are by ʿAliyya Tawfîq and drawings by Kamâl Darwîsh. Some of the strips are reused in later issues, and the majority, including virtually all the later ones, have also been collected in two booklets available separately.[28]

The strips themselves recount stories set in the past, the majority in the time of
the Prophet or of the Jâhiliyya. The most modern evoke the Umayyads, the ʿAb-
bâsids, or, in one case, the time of the Crusades. Similarly, the loci of the stories are
either clearly Arabia or an ill-defined Middle East. None of the strips take place in
Egypt. For Egyptian readers, the narratives exist in a time and space not their own.

Space and time are those of the heritage of Islam and of the Arabs, hence the
titles of the collections: Arab and Islamic Stories. Pastoral scenes dominate, camels
and sheep play an important role, and urban life is never clearly evoked. More striking is the physiognomy of the characters. The men (good guys as well as bad guys) are
generally robust if not stout, and majestic, with large almost caricatural noses. This
last trait is reinforced by the tendency of the artist to make the noses of his characters
a bit redder than the rest of their faces (fig. 6.5). These faces neither look Egyptian nor
resemble the customary ways in which Egyptians, or even other Arabs, are drawn in
their own strips. Apparently, a "Semitic" physiognomy is intended. Nevertheless, no
ethnic differentiation is coded visually. The Jewish characters (among whom are both
heroes and villains) are perhaps a bit thinner on the average, but Bilâl, who has traditionally always been considered a black, is not drawn as one (e.g., *Sâlim*, p. 54; *Qâdî*,

pp. 21, 31).[29] Thus the drawings, like the stories, combine a temporal and physical alterity with an Islamic exemplarity. The number of characters represented visually remains small; usually two and rarely more than three per frame, the authors avoiding visual representations of crowds.

This concentration on a small number of individuals in each episode is linked to the way history is understood and exploited in these strips. Unlike *al-Muslim al-Saghîr*, *al-Firdaws* does not treat history as a sequence of events, a diachronic series, the past of the reader and the explanation of his or her present. In the supplement to the *Minbar al-Islâm*, history is sundered from temporal continuities and considered in an essentially synchronic manner. This distant past is a field peopled with exemplary characters whose actions are considered almost uniquely from an ethical perspective. Morality flattens out history into a collection of good and bad actions, a very old form of historical conceptualization.

The system of values expressed revolves around two linked concepts: generosity and exchange, the latter figuring a kind of imminent justice. The first of these is a positive value, the second figures a relationship crucial to a number of the most common morphologies in the comic strips of *al-Firdaws*. In effect, religion centers on practical morality expressed through social relations, themselves conceived in essentially binary terms as the dealings of one individual with another. Generosity is the virtue most prized in the strips of *al-Firdaws*. In a corpus of forty-two comic-strip narratives, fifteen, or more than a third, are almost exclusive celebrations of this value, so traditionally at once Arab and Islamic. Four others relate to the limits and conditions of generosity.

The prominence of generosity and its association with exchange can be seen most clearly in a strip which functions virtually as a perfect generosity anecdote. Two men are lost in the desert and arrive at the camp of a bedouin. The latter decides to kill his last sheep, a ewe, in their honor. His wife protests: what will become of their daughter thus deprived of milk? But her husband goes ahead and kills the animal. After their meal, one of the travelers wants to offer his last five hundred dinars to the generous bedouin. His companion protests: the sheep was worth only five dirhams. The first traveler replies that the bedouin had given all that he had, preferring his guests to his family. After receiving his gift, the bedouin explains to his wife that he can now buy an entire flock of sheep for their daughter (*Sâlim*, pp. 42–44).

All the elements of the systems of generosity and exchange are present in this strip. Much in the scene is classic and evokes the Jâhiliyya. The virtue itself is presented as a social duty, and it is, of course, the hospitality upon which the Arabs have prided themselves from earliest times (and which even the fugitive Saddâm Husayn evoked).[30] Equally manifest is the structure of exchange. The second generous act replies to the first, the gift provoking more than its recompense. This idea of multiplied recompense is quite common in our corpus. Typical also are the two characters who serve as foils, advising against generosity.

It might be tempting to see in the reaction of the bedouin's wife a lesser concern with honor or a greater preoccupation with the material condition of the family, associated with her female role (we seem almost in the presence of a female conspiracy:

the milk of the ewe demanded by the mother for her daughter). Though other women act similarly, in the story in question the same lack of generosity is expressed by the traveler's male companion; in another strip, it is the wife who insists on returning a lost bag of money (*Qâdî*, pp. 45–47). Less equivocal is the relatively mundane treatment of the virtue. Generosity is never justified in religious terms, and though God is invoked in the beginning of the story by the traveler and at the end by the wife, the faith that sustains the generous is present only by implication. When, in her final comments, the bedouin's wife thanks the deity who does not fail to repay those who do good deeds, the young reader would conclude that the repayment is both earthly and material.

The same desert scene, the same exchange of generosity, and the same multiplied recompense characterize another strip appropriately entitled "Sustenance in the Desert." The only missing figure is the nongenerous foil. An element of providence appears with the fact that the guests only find their lost camels (which permits them to repay their host) after having received his hospitality (February 1988).

In *al-Firdaws*, generosity is so important that it can replace, even substitute for, other virtues, always within the structure of exchange. During the Crusades, a young man is charged by his mother with watching over a goat, the only possession left to the family after the depredations of the warriors from Europe. Our young hero himself wishes he were old enough to fight alongside Salâh al-Dîn. Appropriately, a Muslim soldier arrives asking for water for a wounded comrade. Short of water, the young man offers the milk of his goat. The soldiers leave and the boy returns home, only to have his mother blame him for having given away the sole resource of the household. Her son answers that they will have to wait for the nanny to produce more milk, since he could not let a wounded Muslim die of thirst. Several months pass and the Muslims are victorious. One of them brings to the young man an entire flock of goats, explaining to him that it was a gift from the leader whose life he had saved. When our young hero protests that he has done nothing, the soldier answers that, on the contrary, he has without knowing it participated in the victory of the Muslims (*Sâlim*, pp. 33–35). The generosity exchange is as clear as the role of the mother as foil. But generosity here becomes a kind of generic virtue. It permits the young man who dreams of battle to play his part in the war, a stand-in for courage. At the same time, the principle of exchange, equally present in the strip, obviates the need for a hierarchization of values. Evidently, the young man would prefer the glory of battle. But would he be justified in sacrificing the well-being of his family for what could be seen as the greater well-being of the community? The second part of the exchange, clearly defined as a gift and not as booty, occults this political question by reducing the issue to reciprocal generosity.

The connection between generosity and the military virtues appears in other strips as well. In one, a young Muslim wants to fight in the army of the Prophet. His father is rich, but an unbeliever. The solution: the young man's sister gives him money to outfit himself while another Muslim takes him on his horse to the Prophet's army (*Sâlim*, pp. 45–47). In another tale, the caliph ʿUmar ibn al-Khattâb finds work for a man so that he can buy arms, enabling him to go on the *jihâd* (*Qâdî*, pp. 54–56).

Generosity is further glorified by its association with a large number of figures, including the Prophet (*Qâdî*, pp. 24–26 and 33–35), and its presence in a large variety of situations. But exchange, which so often accompanies this Firdawsian virtue, is not limited to the things of this world. In a popular story, apparently often presented to Muslim children[31] and based on a *hadîth*,[32] a man in the desert slakes his thirst at a well. Shortly afterward, he meets a dog who is suffering from thirst but cannot reach the deep well. With great difficulty, our pious hero climbs into the well, fills his babouche with water, and brings it to the dog. Climbing out of the well, he carries the babouche in his mouth. This role reversal between man and animal reinforces the identification of need that motivated the good deed. This equivalence is not complete: it is not the dog who repays the man his kindness but God who pardons him his sins (*Sâlim*, pp. 6–8).

The subtleties of spiritual recompense are developed in another episode. The hero finds a sick man who asks him for a pomegranate. The generous man goes to the village to buy one. Afterward, feeling relieved and spiritually uplifted, he decides to make the pilgrimage. On the way he encounters a lion who miraculously does not attack him. At Mecca he meets up with the sick man, now cured, who explains that his protection from the beast was a divine reward (*al-Firdaws*, December 1987). In effect, there were two rewards: the first psychological and spiritual, the second material.

Trials can come before or after the reward. The latter is the case with the story of the three handicapped individuals: a blind man, a leper, and a bald man (this last infirmity is part of the Arabo-Islamic system of physical marginality).[33] The three men pray to God to cure them, which is done. Only now is their faith tried. An angel, disguised as a beggar, asks alms successively of each of the three in the name of God who gave to each man either his hair, his sight, or his normal skin. Only the blind man proves generous, and the others are repaid with the return of their infirmities (*Qâdî*, pp. 18–20). Here the exchange runs in reverse, though the terms are made clear in the angel's request. In the same terms, generosity can buy off a fault, real or imagined. Hârûn al-Rashîd suddenly gives a large sum of money to the poor when he thinks that he has spent too much on himself (*Qâdî*, pp. 42–44).

Complications and Limits of Exchange

The exchange system easily figured a kind of justice when generosity could be directly repaid, more often by men, sometimes by direct divine agency. But even in the relatively simple society of the Firdawsian strips, the search for the appropriate level of exchange, that is, the harmonization of generosity with reciprocal justice, is not always easy. A man sells his house for the agreed price: a normal commercial exchange. The son of the new owner finds a pot of gold in the new house and exclaims: "Look, my father, here is a treasure that God has sent to us!" But the father will not accept it and insists that the money belongs to the previous owner of the house. The latter refuses it in turn, since he had not known of its existence. The wise judge finds a solution: the son of the one man will marry the daughter of the other and the couple will accept the gold as dowry (*Sâlim*, pp. 3–5). The generosity of the two men provokes the search for a principle of exchange, effectively found by the *qâdî*. By offering the money to the young couple, each man gives and receives at the same time.

But why such a complicated solution based on the narrative pretext of marriageable children of the opposite sex? A simple division of the money would have eliminated generosity, crucial in the transformation of mere exchange into justice. Equally striking is the fact that the *qâdî*, faced with a legal problem, never answers the question and at no time invokes Islamic law. The generosity-as-imminent-justice system effectively precludes positive law, even Islamic law.[34]

The story of the money in the house also implicitly criticizes the idea of treating found objects as gifts of God. The same problematic combines with questions of exchange in the story of a man who goes to the Ka'ba and prays God to provide for his sustenance and the support of his family. After all, as he explains to his wife, all goodness comes from the Lord. During his circuit of the Ka'ba, his foot strikes a sack containing a hundred dinars. Delighted, the man brings the money back to his wife as divine bounty. This time it is the wife who objects, arguing that the money was certainly lost by someone. Her husband accepts her position as a religious duty; returning to the sacred site, he hears a man asking if someone has found a bag of money. The hero identifies himself, but the other insists that he keep the sack and gives him a further thousand dinars. The explanation of the mystery: a believer from Iraq wanted to donate some money but was concerned that the beneficiary be worthy of it (*Qâdî*, pp. 45–47).

The moral is expressed directly in the text: a good Muslim keeps the property of others in trust and returns it to them. But the morality of exchange has been refined. In the beginning, the hero thinks that he is making a deal with the good Lord. He goes to the Ka'ba, he prays, and in return he will receive money. But the terms of the exchange are more complicated than he suspected, and he is obliged to merit the money through his actions. Our hero then turns in his small bag of money for a far larger sum, as in the classical exchange between host and guest already discussed. At the end of the story, we are brought back to the conditions of the first exchange, since the man finds the sustenance he sought at the Ka'ba.

A tension exists within the idea of confidence and divine providence. To receive money directly is to expect too much, but in the end one receives it anyway. Simply, the motivation must be the correct one. The same distinction operates in the strip already cited of the man who was carried on the horse of another to the *jihâd*. In return for the transportation, the zealous young warrior had offered his share of the spoils to his benefactor. The battle over, the other refuses the proffered booty, explaining that this was not his motivation in aiding his Muslim brother. If the exchange becomes too mercantile, it can be refused.

For the authors of *al-Firdaws*, not all exchanges embody an imminent justice. Some are morally superior to others, as in the story, alluded to above, in which a young man asks the believers to help him buy arms so that he can go on a *jihâd*. He is led before the caliph 'Umar ibn al-Khattâb, who finds him work (*Qâdî*, pp. 44–46).

This moral is drawn even more clearly in a narrative entitled "Inciting to Work." A man, wishing to trust in divine providence, is informed by means of a *hadîth* that for a good Muslim the best money is earned through work (*Sâlim*, pp. 21–23). It is better to exchange work for money than to rely on providence.

But there are exchanges, even exchanges of generosity, which are illicit. Knowing that her husband, again the famous caliph ʿUmar ibn al-Khattâb, is going to send a message to the Byzantine emperor Heraclius, Umm Kulthûm seizes the occasion to send a gift to the emperor's wife. The latter answers quite generously with a letter of thanks and gifts of higher value than those sent by Umm Kulthûm. The empress's gifts are intercepted by ʿUmar, who explains to his wife and to the other Muslims that the gifts, as they are brought by the messenger of the community, belong to the community (*Qâdî*, pp. 39–41). Between two men, the exchange might seem perfectly licit. But it is improper because the caliph's wife has meddled in an area in which she has no business, politics. There is, of course, a long tradition in Islam on the impropriety of "first ladies," be they wives of the Prophet, interfering in politics.[35] Noteworthy in this case is the exclusion of women from a male system of reciprocal generosity. Umm Kulthûm's marriage with ʿUmar is not based on reciprocity either. Twice the strip explains that she was an obedient wife who accepted the authority of her husband.

Even between men there are forbidden generosities and improper exchanges. The pious Umayyad caliph ʿUmar ibn ʿAbd al-ʿAzîz refuses a gift of apples. To accept them would have been corruption and the fruit a bribe (*Sâlim*, pp. 48–50). The problem of corruption and of an insufficiently disinterested generosity is evoked as well in the strip entitled "Beware of Corruption" (*Sâlim*, pp. 18–20).

But justice can also be seen as the restitution of an original equal exchange in place of an unequal one. A merchant secretly watered down the milk he was selling by 50 percent. He left the city with his ill-gotten gains, but on the boat a monkey he had just purchased opened his moneybag. The animal threw half the coins in the water and the other half in the boat. The text explains that this is only justice, because the monkey threw overboard the proceeds of the sale of the water and only kept the value of the milk actually sold (*Qâdî*, pp. 3–5). Noteworthy here is the punishment of the cheat, or lack thereof. Instead of making him lose all his money, the monkey restores the legal exchange, but only half of it, since the customers do not get half their money back. The morality of the story consists in the restitution of a parody of exchange, not in a true punishment of the businessman. The same restitution of proper exchange following criminal activity appears in another *al-Firdaws* narrative (*Qâdî*, pp. 48–50).

Binary Justice

The notion of justice as appropriate exchange is reflected in the binary structures dominating this Islamic children's magazine. Even when there are more than two characters, two or rarely three individuals often function narratologically as one. Nor are these conceptions foreign to the visual arrangement of the pages. The most distinctive characteristic of the Firdawsian strips is the horizontal nature of the frames.

The majority of pages are divided uniquely into horizontal registers, each consisting of a single frame. And in almost all the rest of the cases, all but one of the registers are so composed. The result is a visual field far wider than it is high and in which it becomes easiest to arrange figures in profile and from the right to the left of the frame. These profiles, which face each other visually, figure the equivalence of exchange, even when the story does not. They also show the connection of the justice-as-exchange motif to essentially binary social relations.

It is not simply that justice tends to be individualized, linked to the personal virtue of generosity. By being directed to reciprocal relations, justice is severed from overall social organization. And this is hardly an Islamic conception. From the inception of the community, Muslims have always insisted upon the necessity of a just social order, not merely of individually correct behavior.

But, one might object, al-Firdaws is for children, and social justice is a complicated notion. Yet this choice has political implications. The authors have set their stories in earlier, apparently simpler times, certainly in periods for which the dominance of Islamic values is generally assumed. The primary virtue, generosity, though certainly not un-Islamic, is just as clearly pre-Islamic. Thus does this Islamic magazine draw on some of the same Jâhiliyya mystique exploited by the secular Baathist propagandists of Saddâm Husayn.

The Arabism of the Firdawsian faces and settings, already familiar to us, is reinforced by the covers of the booklets in which most of the strips have been reprinted. As Jean-Bruno Renard has shown for French strips, such covers frequently figure iconographic combinations which are not present in the strips themselves and which, as a result, release hidden levels of meaning.[36] The two al-Firdaws covers contain slight variations on a single basic design. In the one shown in fig. 6.6, the four images on the bottom of the diamond are taken from the strips themselves. The two new images are also the two nonvariant ones. Dominating the diamond, a boy reaches out to a sphere, surrounded by an Islamic motto. Normal enough for the circumstances: our young reader reaches out to Islam. More interesting is the other invariant. A bedecked camel with a traditionally dressed Arab rider emerges from outside the visual field, on the right. The level of detail is far greater than that used in the strips themselves. What is this intruder doing? He brings in the Arab heritage, both Jâhiliyya and Islamic, a heritage which the strips use to personify Islamic values. If this Arabism, unlike that of the Iraqi leader, links to religion, they nonetheless share an archaizing backward-looking tendency. It is an Arabism of the past, not a Nasserite pan-Arabism of the present and future.

The exemplary nature of this past is not unproblematic, however. The classical virtue of generosity, the idea of giving all one has to a stranger without leaving resources for the morrow, with its implications of confidence in divine providence, is not exactly modern. Thus is it corrected by another, the superiority of work over passive expectation. One finds an even greater contemporary relevance in the concern with problems of corruption. Does this mean that the old values are no longer valid? After having refused the gift of apples, the pious Umayyad caliph defends his decision before a group of men who object to him that the Prophet always accepted gifts,

6.6. *Islam and Arab tradition on an* al-Firdaws *reprint cover.*

and, could one not add, that the acceptance of gifts is a condition of generosity? But the caliph's response is clear: the Prophet's time is not ours. "At the present time," that is to say, that of the story and that of the reader, accepting gifts becomes corruption. The exemplarity of the distant past has its limits, those of the Firdawsian project itself: the portrayal of Islamic values through a simplified, mythologized social system.

Sacred Biography

If the representation of the Arabo-Islamic past poses the greatest challenges to Islamic comic-strip artists, how much more is this so when in the form of a complete album, rather than selected narratives. *Zuhûr al-Islâm* (The Advent of Islam) is such a historical album, published first in Arabic and then in French translation (*L'Avènement de l'Islam*).[37] The production is actually Euro-Arab, since the drawings are by Clave Florencio, but the whole is under the official caution of Abdel Satar Abou Ghoudda and with the religious visa of the Ministry of Pious Foundations and Islamic Affairs of Kuwait. The work is presented as the first in a series, "The History of Islam in Comic Strips," but in reality it is something else—a comic-strip version of the first part of the *Sîra*, or biography of the Prophet.

Though the album itself begins with a double evocation of the community (through pictures of Muslims praying and circling the Ka'ba) and the Qur'ân (through the *fâtiha*, or opening *sûra*), we soon meet Ibn Ishâq, who, replying to requests from those around him, undertakes to explain the appearance and spread of Islam. Ibn Ishâq was the author of a *sîra*, or biography, of the prophet which has come down to us in the recension of Ibn Hishâm.[38] Though many of the historical appreciations have been effectively modernized, the topics and stories treated in "The Advent of Islam" are essentially those of the medieval Arab scholars.

Thus Ibn Ishâq takes on the familiar role of the *homme-récit*.[39] But he swiftly becomes less *homme* and more *récit*. Even in the frame where his fellows ask him to explain the revelation to Muhammad (p. 4), he alone is entirely in black and white. Every other face bears the flesh tones of living beings. Ibn Ishâq continues to appear as a narrator of sorts—but without speech balloons. Most often his head is in profile, a line drawing in a monochrome frame, with the masculine dignity of an Ottoman sultan painted by Bellini. Though text appears next to his profile, he never "speaks" (his mouth is never open). On only one occasion do we see a finger in a gesture that reminds one of conversation (p. 35). This Ibn Ishâq is not a living narrator, but an icon of a text—of Ibn Ishâq's *sîra*. And this textualization dominates the album. Not only are balloons virtually absent, but the speech of other characters which could easily have gone into speech balloons instead is often subsumed as quotes into the narrative of Ibn Ishâq (e.g., p. 20).

This relentless textualization, which almost turns the album into a text with accompanying illustrations, simplifies the problem of prophetic representation. Neither Muhammad nor any of the pre-Islamic prophets are visualized in any way, not even in profile, in shadow, or as out-of-frame voice. The techniques used in *al-Firdaws*, such as having characters repeat the words of a prophet, are absent. One master narrator has so effectively textualized all the other characters that no further distancing is necessary.

An out-of-frame voice could suggest the numinous, as in the familiar voice from the clouds in a religious film. Since much of "The Advent of Islam" is concerned with the history of the Arab tribes, it is not surprising that like most Islamic strips it avoids the numinous[40]—that is, until the dramatic closing of the album. The last page is a single frame (fig. 6.7). A shaft of light whose point of origin would seem to be the sky outside the frame penetrates the womblike structure of Mount Hîra through a natural opening. A scroll records the event of revelation and the first-revealed verses (Sûrat al-ʿAlaq) in French and in Arabic. The Angel Gabriel, who carries the revelation, and the Prophet Muhammad, who receives it, are equally absent.

The recent Moroccan *History of Islam Series* (*Silsilat Ta'rîkh al-Islâm*), drawn by Muhammad Binmasʿûd with scenario by ʿAbd al-ʿAzîz Ishbâbû, has concentrated largely (at least so far) on the life of the Prophet. Though obviously also relying largely on the *Sîra*, the *Series* does not present itself as a stripification of that work, nor does it employ a personalized, textualizing narrator. The words of the Angel Gabriel to the Prophet Muhammad are shown as huge Kufic characters slicing, balloon-free, through the night sky (e.g. 4/10–11). The words of the Prophet and some of his most important companions are generally transmitted through off-screen voices, rather than reported discourse. The result is to turn some of the frames into confusing collections of speech balloons pointing to no characters (e.g. 4/11, 15).

The Qur'ân in Strips

Problems of representation are only sharper when the text is not a revered biography of the Prophet but the Qur'ân. The sacred text has a centrality in Islam equivalent only to the miracle of the Incarnation in Christianity. Even more, its text is armored with the doctrine of *Iʿjâz al-Qur'ân*. This doctrine, a dogma for virtually all Muslims, states that the Qur'ânic text as the word (and, as Mohammed Arkoun puts it, the wording[41]) of God is perfect in every respect, from the doctrinal to the linguistic and the aesthetic. Hence, whereas *hadîth* and biography are the work of man (and Muslim scholars have long recognized that they are not free from error), the Qur'ân is perfect. When this dogma is added to the highly elusive and figurative nature of much Qur'ânic rhetoric, it is easy to see how many might consider such a project not merely sacrilegious but well-nigh impossible from a practical point of view.

And yet the Tunisian Youssef Seddik has published several volumes of what he considers a comic-strip version of the Qur'ân. As befitting the linguistic situation in Tunisia[42] and in a clear attempt to reach the widest possible audience, Seddik has brought out his sacred strips simultaneously in French and Arabic editions.[43] The scenarios have all been prepared by Youssef Seddik, but the illustration is the work of a number of French artists. While the texts and images of the strips are the same, the

6.7. *Revelation pictured.*

editorial comments introducing and defending the project have been adapted in each case to the differing cultural backgrounds of Francophone and Arabophone readers.

Seddik's strip scripture received prompt condemnation from Islamic authorities both in and out of his own country.[44] The Tunisian writer replied by anticipation, criticizing that school of Muslim thinking which condemns any recourse to images. Nevertheless, he offered the concession of picturing no prophets.[45] He has thus gone no farther than *al-Firdaws*.

Seddik's project attracts controversy because of the breadth of its claim. The French series is labeled *Si le Coran m'était conté* (If the Qur'ân Were Told to Me). The Arabic is more ambiguous: an unattributed quote easily recognized by educated Muslims, verse 3 from Sûrat Yûsuf, the *sûra* of Joseph, "We will tell you the most beautiful of stories, through our revealing to you this Qur'ân, though you were before it one of the heedless."[46]

In his French defense of his project, Seddik criticizes the way the Qur'ân is taught, arguing that it is often without understanding. His insistence on the elliptical and metaphoric qualities of Qur'ânic narrative almost make it seem as if the text needs the clarification of his strips. While the Arabic version is more restrained and respectful, it also suggests that the meaning of Qur'ânic passages will be rendered by the illustrated narrative.[47] Hence, if the artists and scenarists of *al-Firdaws* present to their readers stories from sacred history, Seddik claims to be delivering the Qur'ân. In effect he becomes its interpreter. By the seeming reality of its visualizations, the strip implies a univocal interpretation of the text. This difference in aim between the Tunisian and Egyptian strips may not be unrelated to the fact that while the Egyptians used local artists, the Tunisian (like Abdel Satar Abou Ghoudda of "The Advent of Islam") has relied on Western illustrators.

"If the Qur'ân Were Told to Me" is both more and less than the holy book in strips. It is less because it is only directed to the narrative parts of the Qur'ân, ignoring hortatory, descriptive, legal, and other materials. It is more because Seddik has frequently narrativized the Qur'ânic text by bringing together passages from different locations of the work. (While the Qur'ân contains stories, that of Joseph being the most famous, which appear as seamless narratives, many other events are referred to allusively and in different contexts.) Seddik has further fleshed out the Qur'ânic narratives with material from works on the lives of the prophets, Qur'ânic commentaries, the *Sîra*, etc. This much, of course, is similar to *al-Firdaws*, whose narrative detail also drew from these same sources. The difference is that Seddik goes to great pains both to list his authorities and to indicate in the text when a detail or point of interpretation is derived from one of his sources. These citations, combined with those of Qur'ânic verses, give the strip a para-academic, defensive quality.

Seddik's quest for a narrative easily represented in strip form sometimes leads him to introduce elements (in effect fictions) not found in the tradition. These can be narratologically minor, as in the conversations around the priest in the story of Hûd (*Peuples/Hûd*, p. 11). On occasion they can be narratologically and theologically significant. Based on a remark by al-Qurtubî that Iblîs (Satan in the Islamic tradition) built a siege engine for the tyrant Nimrod in order to hurl Abraham into the fire, Seddik creates a "Satanic personage." This fully drawn character inspires in the tyrant a variety

6.8. *Divine punishment: rapid aging.*

of challenges to the God of Abraham. One of them involves a complicated story in which this "devil" raises and trains vultures, eventually accompanying Nimrod on a mad voyage into space to challenge the deity (*Abraham/Ibrâhîm*, pp. 21, 27–37). By contrast, Seddik chooses not to illustrate the Angel of Shadow who, his text tells us, protects Abraham in the fire. Seddik had explained that he would pictorialize neither prophets nor angels (and the angelic nature of Iblîs is a disputed issue in the Islamic tradition).[48]

Hence, while the force for divine mercy is not represented, that of evil takes human form. This personification of temptation depsychologizes the Qur'ânic text. Perhaps more noteworthy, it runs counter to the trend found in some recent comic-strip versions of the New Testament in which the temptations of Christ (traditionally rendered with a personified Satan) are turned into internal psychological phenomena.[49]

Sometimes Seddik's interpretations effectively substitute new sets of events for the traditional ones. The people of Thamûd are punished by God. The Qur'ân in Sûrat al-Aʿrâf (verse 78) says they were destroyed by an earthquake. The passage in question occupies a frame at the end of the story in the Arabic version, while the French text quotes from Sûrat Hûd, which does not mention the quake. The visual frames are ambiguous on the matter at best (*Peuples/Hûd*, p. 33). Seddik cites al-Qurtubî to the effect that before this, the faces of the people of Thamûd became yellow on the first day, red on the second, black on the third, and on the fourth they were destroyed (pp. 30–32).[50] In the strip itself, however, something else entirely occurs. The people of Thamûd age suddenly, and their faces fill with wrinkles (fig. 6.8). Seddik has introduced a visually compelling set of events that is common in contemporary science fiction and horror literature but seems without foundation in the traditional sources.[51]

The nonrepresentation of prophets is a familiar enough challenge in Islamic strips. Some of Seddik's solutions are equally familiar, such as reported discourse. Unlike his predecessors, however, he also often puts prophets into the frame, representing them with a kind of burst bubble, from which can even emanate speech bal-

6.9. *The Prophet Abraham as a burst bubble.*

loons (fig. 6.9). This absence then becomes a semiotic presence signifying the numinous, not unlike bursts of light replacing the faces of sacred characters in some traditional Islamic iconography. Prophetic humanity is invisible, its divine connection visually manifest.

Prophetic nonrepresentation can open a path to the visualization of other religious themes. Eight frames illustrate verses 75–79 of Sûrat al-Anʿâm in which Abraham, rejecting the false deities of the sky for their impermanence, deduces monotheism. The descriptive parts of the verses are in explanatory bands, while Abraham's words are in balloons emanating from a series of landscapes, almost as if their speaker were hidden behind a rock or a bush (fig. 6.10). The "speaking" landscape becomes

6.10. *Abrahamic monotheism as a landscape.*

an argument from design, at once illustrating and commenting the Qur'ânic argument. Similarly, the impact of the Qur'ânic verse "We said, 'O fire, be coolness and safety for Abraham!' " is magnified by the fiery full-page frame which surrounds it.[52]

Such pages are the exception, however. The albums devote most of their space to more dramatic storytelling. Paradoxically, the avoidance of the prophetic figures when combined with the incidents chosen for narrative elaboration has the effect of emphasizing God's wrath over his bounty. The Abraham album concentrates less on that prophet than on his struggle with Nimrod and the latter's mad battle with the God of Abraham. As it has been argued that Satan is the hero of *Paradise Lost*, so in a way is the Mesopotamian tyrant the anti-hero of the Abraham album. Similarly, the punishments of the peoples of ʿAd and Thamûd take visual precedence over the prophets Hûd and Sâlih, just as Nimrod's vulture-led flight received maximum elaboration. Divine punishments, whether personal (against Nimrod) or collective (against the peoples of ʿAd and Thamûd, or the Ethiopian army attacking the Kaʿba), are narratively elaborated and richly illustrated (fig. 6.11).

6.11. *Divine wrath narrativized: the destruction
of the men of the elephant.*

Each of the European illustrators brings his own Western-inspired visual style. Gioux, who did "The Men of the Elephant," draws in the style of "the Belgian school" of Hergé and Jacobs; Teulat's illustrations of Hûd and Sâlih are clearly inspired by U.S. adventure and horror strips. *Newsweek* printed the charge that Seddik's strips visually stereotype Arabs (negatively is implied).[53] With the series' multiple artists, this would be difficult. Nothing resembling a racial stereotype (even a mild or positive one) exists in *Peuples/Hûd* or *Ashâb al-Fîl*. The forms of faces are instead taken from the average physical types of the comic-strip school to which the artist belongs, with the concession to realism that these Near Easterners are not blond, except when the story makes them so. Many of the figures in *Abraham/Ibrâhîm* have what, in a Western context, are ethnically marked Near Eastern faces. But probably the clearest in this regard, Abraham's father, is drawn with the dignity that belies caricature. In either case, no one in this album is an Arab. The image held up by *Newsweek* of a supposed Arab king imposing religious uniformity on his people (fig. 6.12) is just a "Belgian school" render-

6.12. *An Arabian tyrant persecutes the Christians.*

ing of a hysterical individual who in the strip is (a) a Jew and (b) an evil figure in the story. In either case, compared to the treatment of *al-Firdaws*'s Arabs, Seddik's heroes and villains are virtually North European in physiognomy.

Not surprisingly, Occidental images wink at us from the pages of Seddik's strips. The city of Iram with its Qur'ânic tall pillars becomes in some frames, and quite inappropriately, Stonehenge (fig. 6.13). The devil in the Nimrod sequence has the waxed mustache of a Gounod Mephistopheles (fig. 6.14) and the face and red headgear of a modern Satan.

In effect, the decision to largely ignore the existing (though marginal) Islamic iconographic tradition and turn to Western illustrators has given Seddik's Qur'ânic albums some of the shape of the Western comic-strip container into which he has poured his Islamic contents. Avoiding the prophets while concentrating on more easily represented dramatic episodes has only increased this tendency. The challenge is not the same for comic-strip versions of the Bible because the West has a long iconographic tradition, which grew up in symbiosis with its own religious interpretations. The artists and scenarists of *al-Firdaws* avoided this problem through their fragmentary approach. "The Advent of Islam" ducked the difficulties through the familiar technique of the *homme-récit* responsible for narrative continuity. By accepting the full

6.13. *Stonehenge in Arabia.*

6.14. *Personifying the Satan of the Qur'ân.*

challenge of putting the Qur'ân into comic-strip form while respecting at least some Islamic taboos, Seddik's albums bring to their clearest point the tensions implicit in stripifying the word of Islam.

7

Syria: The Party-State and Its Strips

During the Gulf War, Americans were bombarded with images of the Iraqi tyrant, his dictatorial control over party, security forces, and army. Television viewers could see the visual signs of his cult of personality. Only the more perspicacious would have noted any references to Saddâm Husayn's fellow-yet-enemy Baath ruler in neighboring Syria, which backed the U.S. side in the Gulf War. With the same pan-Arab secular ideology, the Syrian Baath regime has been the rival of its Iraqi cousin since 1966; and since 1970 it has been in the firm grip of its own strongman, Hâfiz al-Asad.

Though the Syrians cannot match the resources of their oil-rich neighbor, in some ways they provide the most perfect example of state- and party-dominated comic strips. For Syria, virtually alone among major Arab states, blocks the entry of other Arab strips, creating its own monopoly of images. Foreign publications do leak in. Copies of *Mîkî* sometimes turn up in the bazaar. The Soviet children's publication *Misha* is available in English (Soviet materials have a considerable impact on children's mass media in Syria).[1] But nowhere in the Arab world does a government so effectively control the comic strip as in the Syrian Arab Republic.

Al-Talî'î

Syria has two children's magazines; both regularly include comic strips, and both are official publications of the regime. One, *al-Talî'î*, is produced by the youth organization of the Baath party, Talâ'i⁽ al-Ba⁽th, the Baath Vanguards, or more loosely translated, the Baath Pioneers.[2] Since 1984, *al-Talî⁽î* has been appearing monthly. Its fifty-thousand print run is distributed in the schools.[3]

Al-Talî⁽î regularly provides a variety of strip genres: historico-political narratives, adventure, science fiction, and humor. What most distinguishes *al-Talî⁽î's* strips is the general subordination of narrative to pedagogy and politics. Islamic strips also carry a message, but their narratives are more internally coherent and, especially, directed to issues of personal development. Perhaps more significant, where the Islamic strips stress the importance of the family, *al-Talî⁽î* substitutes the state. The preeminent values presented by this party magazine are those of the regime: Arab nationalism and Syrian patriotism, militarism, secularism and the worship of science, and productivism.

Some strips show the young Pioneers in their scout-type uniforms. One such "story," however, is merely a dull discussion of the requirements of Arab nationalism and socialism (1986, no. 2). Nationalism and patriotism are more effectively portrayed in a series of strips devoted to anti-French resistance between the world wars, written by ⁽Adil Abû Shanab and illustrated by Mumtâz al-Bahra. Martyrs die for Syrian independence, always taking a maximum number of Frenchmen with them. The French are treacherous, their officers hysterical, their soldiers cowardly. The connection between these early resisters (the strips call them revolutionaries) and the current regime is shown toward the end of the series "Hasan Muqabba⁽a, Hero of the Ghûta" (1986, no. 6). As the martyr dies, he sees in a vision the future success of the Syrian revolution, which just happens to be, iconographically, the triumph of the Baath and its Talâ'i⁽ (see fig. 7.1).

Another series is based on the French capture of yet another hero, Mahmûd al-Hindî. But its title is "The Siege of al-Mîdân," referring to the al-Mîdân quarter in Damascus, where the hero carries on his house-to-house battle. Only at the end is it made clear how the French have attacked this entire neighborhood (1987, nos. 11, 12, 1, and 2).[4] The sense of violent penetration and invasion is graphically displayed through a series of phallic images, associating the French colonel's outstretched finger, the barrel of a tank, and that same officer's saber threatening a venerable old man (fig. 7.2). A bit more historical contextualization is provided in the series "The Revolution of Shaykh Sâlih al-⁽Alî," which recounts resistance in the Tartûs region to the French invasion of 1918–20 (1987, nos. 6, 7, 8, and 9).

Lessons of nationalism and anti-imperialism are not confined to historical strips but are relentlessly crammed into all the departments of the magazine. In a series on the alphabet, *alif* is for imperialism (*ambiryâliyya*), *bâ'* for bourgeoisie (*al-burjuwâziyya*) (1986, nos. 5 and 6).

Images of fighters, of weapons, are legion. The young Pioneer, whether male or female, is armed. A large painting shows a girl holding an assault rifle while her male companion bears the Syrian flag (1986, no. 7). Behind them a map of the Arab world reminds the reader of the Baath's pan-Arab ambitions. The presence of armed females should not surprise us. Syria has probably gone further than any other Arab state in vocally pushing women's liberation. Young women soldiers strut down the streets of Damascus in combat gear while their grandmothers can still be seen with their faces

7.1. *Left: The hero dreams of the triumph of the revolution.*

7.2. *Below: Visualizing the French as threatening invaders.*

hidden behind black veils. Indeed, wherever possible, *al-Talî'î*, in picture and story, mixes boy and girl Pioneers together.

Secularism for *al-Talî'î* means a virtual occultation of Islam. It is difficult to think of an Arab magazine where religion is more absent. The Friday of the model girl is a school holiday and she dons her Friday best. But of mosque, prayer, or Muslim sabbath there is not a word—a situation which would be inconceivable, for example, in an Egyptian context (1986, no. 7).

In the place of religion, *al-Talî'î* gives science. A series on a scientific utopia, written by Dr. Tâlib 'Imrân and illustrated by Surûr 'Alwânî, is entitled "Madînat al-Hikma" (The City of Wisdom). In a plot reminiscent of Jules Verne, its characters all bear Arabic names but are drawn like turn-of-the-century Europeans. The scientific advances are inspired by the present day. The rocket ship, for example, is a recognizable space shuttle.

The title carries other resonances. The Bayt al-Hikma (House of Wisdom) was a ninth-century institute for translation and scientific study in Baghdad, founded by the caliph al-Ma'mûn.[5] As such, it has remained a preeminent symbol of scientific (as opposed to religious) research in the classical Islamic world. In "Madînat al-Hikma," science ('ilm) is the one god. As one of the scientists puts it to the man being initiated into this magical world, "Everything is easy for science as long one thinks correctly" (1986, no. 2).

At its conclusion the story takes an Arab turn. For now, the city of science will remain secret. But its members plan for the future: "The coming generations will renew this dream, O Sâmî . . . and will build cities of wisdom in our Arab fatherland." To which Sâmî replies: "By science alone . . . and by love of the land . . . it is possible to make miracles," finally exhorting his friends to "study and struggle" to build Arab "Cities of Wisdom" in their countries (1986, no. 6).

With science comes productivism. This is pushed in *al-Talî'î* less through lessons in science and technology, as it is in many Muslim strips, than through the ubiquitous visual icon of the factory. Sets of belching smokestacks are frequent background elements in *al-Talî'î* illustrations (e.g., cover of 1986, no. 9). Modern buildings are far more common than traditional ones. In an arresting image (fig. 7.3) which capsules Baath attitudes to modernity, a girl stands behind a boy with a wrench in her uplifted arm. Above her head, two stacks emit a cloud of smoke which becomes the Syrian flag, except that in place of the flag's two stars are green flowers. Flowers also grow from the roof of the factory. Linking the power of the nation to industrialization is commonplace in Arab nationalism.[6] More striking is that this smoke, rather than snuffing out flowers, seems to bring them to life. Hardly environmentalist, the image is also a projection, since Syria is a predominantly agricultural country. The illustration, by Anwar Diyâb, accompanies an ode to work.

The choice of the modern and technological becomes especially clear when traditional elements are in play. In late 1986 and 1987, an adventure series appeared entitled "Secrets of the Brass Statues," written by Târiq Harîb and drawn by Lujayna al-Asîl.[7] The series is unavowedly inspired by a story from *The Thousand and One Nights*, "The City of Brass."[8] The tale is appropriate for a Syrian magazine. The medieval story begins in Damascus, set in motion by the actions of the Umayyad caliph 'Abd al-Malik ibn Marwân. The caliph sends a group of men to bring back jars in which

الع‍ـــــمـل

شعر وليد مشوح

هيّا نعمل هيّا هيّا نعمل
فالحقلُ لنا وكَذا المعملْ
هيّا نعمل هيّا هيّا نعمل
الحقلُ تُنادي أزهارُهْ
والمعملُ تعلو أسوارُهْ
هيّا نعمل هيّا هيّا

* * *

فلنمضِ نَحو الغابات
ولنْرفعْ هَذي الرايّات
هيّا نعمل هيّا هيّا

* * *

الكادح سمة للوطنْ
والخامل منبوذ مهمل
هيّا نعملْ هيّا هيّا
هيّا نعملْ هيّا هيّا
الحقلُ لنا وكَذا المعملْ
هيّا نعمل هيّا هيّا

7.3. *Flowers from the factory.*

Solomon had imprisoned jinn. On their way, the Arab group discovers a City of Brass, all of whose inhabitants are dead, as the story continues to work in references to the brevity of life and inevitability of death. The visitors may take anything they wish except the garments of the embalmed queen. One of the men, who violates this taboo, is killed.

The "Secrets of the Brass Statues" is also a quest: a group of adolescents hunting for some lost brass statues. As in "The City of Brass," the way is pointed by a statue, though the modern one is of stone, not metal. The youngsters discover a fabulous ancient city. They touch nothing of the riches in it. One of their number, who had been separated from them earlier, emerges to explain that the real treasure of the city is behind a set of doors: "a very large lake whose waters will reach our city through canals. Then our land will become green and we will all be prosperous" (1987, no. 10).

"Secrets" invokes the past in two ways: through *The Thousand and One Nights* subtext and through the ancient city itself, symbol of the bygone glory of the Arabs. But this past is of no use. In place of the spiritual message of the medieval tale, the comic strip places modernity and productivism.[9] Instead of archaeology, there is irrigation. The water behind the doors reminds one irresistibly of the Euphrates behind the Dayr al-Zûr dam.

The Father-Leader

One regular feature of *al-Talî'î* seems free of ideological baggage, the short humorous strips which grace a great number of back covers. Many of these have little or no text and are clearly designed to be "read" by younger children. *Schadenfreude* seems the dominant mode of humor in these strips, most of which involve the misadventures of the child protagonist. But unlike the unfortunate heroes in Islamic strips, there rarely seems to be any moral lesson. In a typical example, drawn by Anwar Diyâb, Yâsir, who is walking a tightrope, falls because a bird has alighted on his balancing rod (1987, no. 11).

On the rare occasion when the cleverness of the child is rewarded, this is outside any moral context (1986, no. 5). Equally absent from these strips is any real evocation of family. The closest these strips come to a parental relationship is when a little girl, wishing to surprise her mother, tries to bake but only succeeds in destroying the kitchen in the process. The strip ends with this image of chaos. No parental forgiving or familial resolution is offered.

Deemphasis of the family characterizes *al-Talî'î* as a whole. Pioneers are shown with their peers, other Pioneers. To some degree, this is normal, given that the youth group is the vehicle of socialization which the magazine is dedicated to serve. But when a family member is evoked it is generally the mother. The father is replaced. Hâfiz al-Asad is the "Father-Leader" (*al-ab al-qâ'id*). He is so referred to in the introductory remarks on the first page of, apparently, every issue of *al-Talî'î*. We also see him wearing a white suit and the *talâ'i'î* scarf surrounded by children on every inside cover (fig. 7.4). Since the Father-Leader also graces many covers, his is the adult fig-

من فكر الحزب

كان قيام الحركة التصحيحية المباركة مطلباً جماهيرياً ملحاً وضرورة قومية فرضتها إرادة شعبنا وقواعد حزبنا من أجل تصحيح مسيرة الحزب والثورة ودفعها خطوات متقدمة إلى الأمام .

من أقوال الأب القائد .

إن الأجيال التي ترعرعت وتربت في كنف الثورة قد اقتبست من مبادئ حزب البعث العربي الاشتراكي ومن القيم الروحية والتراث التاريخي لأمتنا العربية فتبلورت الشخصية الوطنية والقومية لأبناء هذه الأجيال .

من أهداف المنظمة :

تربية جيل المدرسة الابتدائية وبناؤه وتكوينه ليكون قومياً اشتراكياً .

7.4. *The Father-Leader.*

ure, by far, most often associated with the children who are the subject and the audience of *al-Talî'î*. The ruler as father is, of course, a traditional notion. But having him
replace rather than reinforce the *pater familias* bespeaks a more modern political ambition. If the clear emphasis on the family in Islamic strips celebrates that civil society
which has been the organizational basis of Islamist power, then its deemphasis by the
Syrian Baath magnifies the all-powerful state and party, which are the vehicles of election of that regime.

On the inside cover, Hâfiz al-Asad is linked to the children by flowers, flowers
they collect and flowers that simply fill the air. We have seen these flowers before: in
the smoke from the factory stacks (fig. 7.3). Flowers are also associated with war. In
one story, a young boy who goes out to gather flowers for his mother runs into Israeli
soldiers. The Arab fighters who help capture the enemy then also help him collect his
blossoms (1986, no. 7).

In all these contexts—the industrial, the military, and the political—flowers figure the carefree joys of childhood. But in this system they become an alibi for the contradiction between such a view of childhood and the paramilitary *talâ'i'î* ideal. If one
looks again at the children on the inside cover (fig. 7.4), those in the foreground with
the flowers are gamboling about, an image of freedom. In the background, however,
they are little soldiers, arms raised in salute. Linking the two groups is a child with a
floral crown, destined for the Father-Leader who towers over them.

Usâma

Al-Talî'î's party line represents only one pole of the Syrian government strip. Since
1969 the Ministry of Culture has produced its own children's magazine, *Usâma*.[10] The
name evokes Usâma ibn Munqidh, the twelfth-century Syrian nobleman who fought the
Crusaders and whose autobiographical *al-I'tibâr* is a classic of Arabic letters, the perfect
combination of culture and patriotism.[11] Some involved with the birth of the journal insist that no such reference was intended, but it is difficult to eliminate the association.[12]

The children's magazine appeared almost twice a month, in runs up to fifty
thousand,[13] until the middle 1980s, when its periodicity declined, apparently for lack
of funds. Though always politically conformist (it is a government publication), *Usâma*
included a larger variety of comic-strip materials—and viewpoints. Morality was
clearer, parent-child relations were not occulted, the Baath party and its organizations
not foregrounded. The magazine has remained, throughout its history, secularist,
progressive, and Arab nationalist. For a few years, however, *Usâma* took on a special
tone, imparted to it by an unusual director, Zakariyyâ Tâmir.

Zakariyyâ Tâmir

One of the Arab world's leading short-story writers and arguably Syria's best author
of the century, Zakariyyâ Tâmir has also written a number of children's books. Filled with

7.5. *Absurdist visual humor.*

political allegory, these are sometimes quite critical of the Arab establishment. One such allegory, for example, blames the failures of Arab society for the loss of Palestine.[14]

Tâmir took over *Usâma* as editor-in-chief in 1975, leaving the journal two years later, in October 1977.[15] His impact on *Usâma* came less from his own direct contributions than from the brilliant team he was able to assemble, including some of the Arab world's leading talents: the artists Nadhîr Nabʿa and ʿAdlî Rizq Allâh, the cartoonist ʿAlî Farzât, the Palestinian writer Liyâna Badr, etc.

Tâmir's *Usâma* included a variety of materials: morality stories, adventures, animal fables. What most distinguished Tâmir's period, however, was a special kind of humor. Never innocent, this humor was derisive, occasionally subversive, and very adult in orientation and appeal. Much of it reminds one more of the newspaper editorial cartoon than of the children's comic strip. A series, "Cheerful Stories without Words," by Mâhir Farîd, uses adult characters to play a series of absurdist visual games. We see a man pouring water into a flowerpot from which sprouts forth some kind of tree whose branches end in flowerpots (fig. 7.5). The same man watches the sun on television. As it sets, it slips below the horizon/bottom of the television screen to emerge in his living room (1977, nos. 198–99).

Television watching becomes more subversive in "A Man Watches Television" by Fâʾiz al-Sharqî. A series of registers shows the reactions of an adult male viewer to different kinds of programs (1977, no. 195). A melodrama reduces him to tears, a surgical program turns him green with nausea. But as the man watches the news, he becomes increasingly tense, pulls a pistol from his pocket, and shoots himself in the head (fig. 7.6), a caustic attack on the officially optimistic, propaganda-drenched news program so common to the region.

7.6. *Watching the news broadcast.*

Sometimes it is old and not new wisdom that is subverted. In one strip belonging to a series called "Caricatures" from the pen of Jamîl, proverbs in a framed text are ridiculed by cartoon vignettes beneath them (1977, no. 202). Under "Cleanliness Is Part of Faith," we see two bears about to eat what looks like a forest ranger, while the parent bear lectures his child on the importance of washing before meals. Under "If Speech Is of Silver, Then Silence Is of Gold," a teacher berates a tight-lipped student who cannot tell him what two plus two equals. Under "Do Not Put Off Today's Work

7.7. *Ibn Battûta mocked.*

until Tomorrow," a surgeon standing over the operating table says: "If the patient does not arrive, I will perform the operation without him."

Ibn Battûta

The fourteenth-century traveler Ibn Battûta is an Arab culture hero and a staple of Arab strips. His usual presentation is heroic; this is the man whose famous travel account goes from Morocco to China.[16] This is how, for example, he is presented in a version prepared by the Lebanese children's magazine, *Bisât al-Rîh*, and in another which appeared in the United Arab Emirates' *Mâjid*.[17]

Quite different is the vision of ʿAlî Farzât in the *Usâma* strip he wrote and illustrated, "The Travels of Ibn Battûta" (1977, no. 196). His Ibn Battûta is a comic icon. His oversized spherical turban, a caricature of an Ottoman headpiece, doubles as an image of the globe, mocking the world travels of its bearer (fig. 7.7). Farzât's strip begins with a simultaneous deheroization of the medieval Arab and humorous bisociation of present with past. Ibn Battûta starts not with who he is but with who he is not. He is not the boxer "Muhammad Ali Clay," nor the actor Omar Sharif, nor the singer ʿAbd al-Halîm Hâfiz. To keep the comparisons silly, we see each of these contemporary celebrities inappropriately garbed in the same spherical turban, while either boxing (Ali), embracing a leading lady (Sharif), or singing into a microphone (the pop star ʿAbd al-Halîm Hâfiz).

Against a background of traditional scenes, Ibn Battûta explains his travels and his authorship of the famous travel book. Accompanying this last point we see the old writer buried under a mess of sheets of paper while ink spills from an overturned bottle. So much for the *turâth*, or literary tradition. Ibn Battûta explains that, reborn into the modern world, he will travel and report on the strange and wondrous things to be found there. All he finds, however, is trouble. Confused by the traffic signs, Ibn Battûta is run over and ends up in the hospital, his trademark turban now made of bandages.

The comic comedown from explorer to traffic victim is strengthened by creative page arrangements. Each of the four pages is surmounted by a single horizontal frame which is both in and outside the continuing narrative. The first carries the title. The second shows Ibn Battûta pulling a reluctant, braying donkey, which illustrates the difficult move from past to present (fig. 7.8). The same donkey appears on the cover of the issue, comically decked out with rear-view mirror and brake lights. In the third,

7.8. Pulling the donkey into the modern world.

7.9. The great traveler lost in the modern city.

we see a reduced Ibn Battûta, confused by large traffic signs, clearly foreshadowing the accident on that page (fig. 7.9). The last of these visual commentaries is the most clearly allegorical. A diminutive Ibn Battûta (he gets progressively smaller as the registers follow one another) is almost completely obscured by a monstrously large turban which is coming unwound. More than the replacement of his traditional turban with the new one of bandages, this image suggests the unraveling of tradition. Not only does this brilliant strip poke fun at a famous medieval Arab (albeit a Moroccan, not a Syrian) but, like "Ramsîs in Paris",[18] it argues for the incompatibility of traditional values with the contemporary world.

The gap between tradition and modernity also figures in a humorous series called "Adventures of a Ghost," written by Sharîf Bahbûh and illustrated by Jaroslawa Batuszewska. The introductions to several of the episodes explain that if in old stories ghosts frightened people, these stories would be of ghosts in our time (e.g., 1977, no. 200). The ghosts are cute, almost childlike figures, bemused if not lost in the modern world, who rarely frighten anyone. In one story the swirl emerging from the ghost's head becomes the basis for a contemporary hairdo (1977, no. 201). The choice of coiffure in a Middle Eastern environment is not innocent. The last frame shows a conservatively veiled woman staring at the "modern" females with their new swirl hairdos.

Secularizing Tradition

Zakariyyâ Tâmir insists that he left *Usâma* in 1977 for reasons of personal health alone.[19] Whatever the explanation, the magazine, taken over by Dalâl Hâtim, began to change as many of the older collaborators gradually fell away. Within a few years the number of strips per issue declined from five or more to one or two.

The shift in tone was gradual but marked. As the quasi-subversive, more adult humor disappeared, *Usâma* became, partly by default, partly by choice, more respectful of tradition, more clearly reflective of political orthodoxies. The new direction was signaled by a letter to the editor in the November 1977 issue, Dalâl Hâtim's second (1977, nos. 211–12). Bearing the uncharacteristic title "I Am Angry with *Usâma*," this letter embodies a penetrating critique of ʿAlî Farzât's "Ibn Battûta." This famous traveler and writer was not Abû Nuwâs or Juhâ, the reader notes. The point is apt. Abû Nuwâs and especially Juhâ are traditional figures of fun and buffoonery in Arab culture. As we shall see later, Juhâ has been transposed to the modern world in other magazines.[20] Giving Ibn Battûta such a treatment undercuts his cultural achievement. The young reader (so much perspicacity suggests adult assistance) also zeroed in on the turban of bandages. Indeed, this image climaxes Farzât's mockery of the turban, a symbol of tradition. The editor's response was half defensive, half confused, but subsequent issues carried a prose series devoted to the glories of Arabic letters from the usual respectful point of view.

History is a major topic of the later *Usâma*, even becoming a character in a series called "ʿIsâ the Swimmer," by Usâma Daʿbûl and Mumtâz al-Bahra (1978, nos. 223–28). *Usâma*'s Clio is a venerable old man with a flowing white beard and quill pen. He writes the book of history, which lies open in front of him. From its pages rush forward Crusaders, as they land on the beaches of the Holy Land, swords outstretched and pointing threateningly forward (fig. 7.10), as in the artist's similar work for *al-Talîʿî*.

This figure is even more secular than his iconic cousin, "The Visiting Philosopher," of *al-Muslim al-Saghîr*.[21] So is his vision of history. Mr. History is accompanied by a mural-like visual composite. The scenes it evokes all come from the history of the eastern Mediterranean. But there is little that is Islamic or even Arab about them. We see cavemen, a Pharaonic temple, a Mesopotamian stele, the winged victory of Samothrace. Greek scrolls lie next to a Roman portrait head (fig. 7.11). In terms of soldiers, a Greek cavalryman rides in front of what look vaguely like Mongols. The Arabian warrior fighting a Roman or Byzantine soldier behind the right shoulder of History (fig. 7.10) is the only suggestion of an essentially Islamic or Arab history. Except that the Crusaders are bad guys, this two-page spread could easily serve as cover art for a traditional Western civilization textbook (part one, that is).

"ʿIsâ the Swimmer" is organized as an adventure story. Its hero sinks Crusader ships, meets Salâh al-Dîn in Damascus, and dies as a martyr. ʿIsâ, Arabic for Jesus, is a very common name among Arab Christians, though it is also a possible name for Muslims. The medieval account by Ibn Shaddâd on which this strip apparently is based clearly identifies ʿIsâ as a Muslim.[22] In the strip, however, the hero's apparent religious allegiance is shown by the tattooed cross ʿIsâ bears on his muscular arm and whose continued exposure is guaranteed by his frequent representation bare-chested. The text of the strip takes no position on the matter, so that the Christian symbol re-

7.10. *The Syrian Mr. History.*

7.11. *The history of civilization.*

mains uncontradicted. A Muslim hero has been transformed into an apparently non-Muslim Arab one. In this magazine, the Crusades are not a Holy War, more an anti-imperialist one. The personified narrator does not refer to *mujâhidûn*, as did *al-Muslim al-Saghîr*, speaking instead of *fidâ'* (1979, no. 228), a term which despite its original religious denotation is now largely secularized.

A later series, "Zenobia Queen of the East," omits Mr. History, telling the story of the state based on Syrian Palmyra during the Roman Empire's third-century period of troubles. Pan-Arab solidarity is vaguely foreshadowed when Zenobia tries to help the Egyptians in their revolt against the empire from the West. More bluntly, when Palmyra finally falls to the Romans, we are told that the Arab fatherland remains the grave of invaders and imperialists (1983, no. 349; 1984, no. 367).

An even more pregnant (though slightly less anachronistic) link was made at the end of "'Isâ the Swimmer." Our white-bearded History explained that Acre was retaken and, after the victorious battle of Hattîn, the invaders were repulsed and Arab lands purified of "occupiers." The two place-names are in the modern state of Israel. But even were they not, the evocation of the Palestinian problem is automatic in any contemporary Arab discussion of the Crusades, so often has this self-flattering comparison linked the two "invasions." Similar associations are present in the story series "The Caravan" (1984, no. 368; 1985, no. 383). There a group of youngsters led their own guerrilla attacks on the Frankish occupiers.

Not surprisingly, this vision of Arabs versus imperialists dominates the strips which relate the contemporary struggle against Israel. The Israeli invasion of Lebanon in 1982 inspired a spate of strips (neighboring Lebanon is a security concern of the Syrian state, whose troops were already in that country). One series, "Zayn," started in November 1982 (1982, nos. 331–32; 1983, no. 337), while a second, "The Cheetah," overlapped it, running from December 1982 through July of the following year (1982, no. 334; 1983, nos. 347–48). "Zayn," by 'Adil Abû Shanab and Anwar Diyâb, tells of a Palestinian orphan girl who heroically helps the *fidâ'iyyûn*. "The Cheetah," by Dalâl Hâtim and Ghassân al-Sibâ'î, recounts the story of a group of adolescents from the Râshidiyya refugee camp in southern Lebanon who help adults to fight Israelis. One of their heroes is known as the Cheetah (the title of the strip is written in thick characters with a cheetah's spots), and when the Israelis capture him, the officer cannot believe that the legendary cheetah is but a boy.

A journalist who has been accompanying the Israelis questions our young hero (he had to bribe the officer to get the interview):

> —Are you a Palestinian or a Lebanese?
> —Neither one nor the other.
> —A Syrian then?
> —Not that either. I am an Arab, and all the lands of the Arabs are a fatherland to me.
> (1983, nos. 345–46)

The journalist, clearly won over to the truth of the Arab cause, declares that he will present this truth to the world. Thus he echoes the journalist from *al-Muslim al-Saghîr* who certified the authenticity of the *intifâda*.[23] Though the identity of the journalist is not specified, he is probably Western—he could not be an Arab with the Israeli army. As an outsider, he adds an element of credibility that an Arab spokesman apparently would not have had, suggesting a sense among the Syrian authors of the strip that Arabs themselves are not believed by world opinion.

Whatever time period is evoked, modern ("Zayn", "The Cheetah"), medieval ("The Caravan," "ʿIsâ the Swimmer"), or ancient ("Zenobia"), the historical vision remains the same. Through Arab nationalism, all ethnic groups in all periods are assimilated to the Arabs (Salâh al-Din was a Kurd, his troops largely Turkish). Secularism replaces a Christian-Muslim dichotomy with one between Western invaders and local inhabitants of various religions. One of the ironies of the historical anachronies played out here is that the Christians of the Orient, many of whom joined forces with the Crusaders, are enlisted on the Arab side. The Jews, who made no such choice and who suffered from the Crusaders, are tactfully glossed over.

Laughing with the *Turâth*

The young reader who objected to the ridicule of Ibn Battûta pointed out that there were established classical Arabic clowns to whom the magazine could have turned. As if responding to the reader's suggestion, the later *Usâma* published strips of Juhâ, whom the letter had mentioned, as well as of Ashʿab and of stories from *The Book of Misers* by al-Jâhiz (d. 868–69).

Along with his aliases, Nasr al-Dîn Khôja and Mollâ Nasr al-Dîn, Juhâ is a virtually universal comic figure in the Middle East. He figures at times the wise fool, at others a model of stupidity. Though Juhâ is classical in origin, his place in Arabic tradition is more folkloric than literary. *Usâma*'s Juhâ is clever in some stories (1985, nos. 412, 413, and 414) and gullible or foolish in others (1985, nos. 415 and 416). He also sports a large turban, which is, however, traditional in his iconography.

Ashʿab is an equally classical but somewhat more literary figure, playing a major role in classical Arabic anecdotal collections. The greatest associations of this multitalented individual are with greed and wit. One of the *Usâma* stories is entitled "Ashʿab, Father of *Tufaylîs*" (1980, no. 274); the other chronicles attempts to become the leader of such people (1980, no. 275). The *tufaylîs*, loosely translated as party crashers or uninvited guests, are a well-known comic group in medieval Arabic literature. Though some characterizations and a few anecdotes overlap, the *tufaylî* and Ashʿab corpora are essentially distinct.[24] The plots of the strips themselves are not typical of the *tufaylî* corpus.

The Book of Misers, too, is a famous source of humor, but it is also one of the masterpieces of al-Jâhiz, the ninth-century littérateur generally considered the finest prose writer in the Arabic language.[25] The strips are written by Dalâl Hâtim and illustrated by Ghassân al-Sibâʿî. The first does not give the name al-Jâhiz, only saying that the stories are "From the stories of the Misers" (1984, nos. 376, 377, and 378). But the often brief anecdotes from the famous book have been narratively extended. A narrator appears, readily identifiable as al-Jâhiz himself—he has bulging eyes (fig. 7.12) (al-Jâhiz means "the goggle-eyed") and a character calls him Abû ʿUthmân (al-Jâhiz's

7.12. *Al-Jâhiz narrates his* Bukhalâ'.

kunya).[26] The second two strips attribute the stories directly to *The Book of Misers* of al-Jâhiz.

In the first tale, some guests come upon al-Jâhiz as he is finishing up some writing. He explains, in answer to their query, that he has just penned some anecdotes about the misers of Merv. His two guests ask him for some stories, and he gives one. While traveling in Merv, he alighted at a hotel and found a group of travelers eating dinner. One of them was blindfolded, it turns out, because he had refused to pay his share of the money for a new candle. The narrating al-Jâhiz then explains the misers' actions. The original anecdote is far shorter; al-Jâhiz has no place as witness or narrator.[27] Nor is there any explanation of the misers' ruse, such narratively superfluous explanations being generally avoided in al-Jâhiz's book. The second and third strips work the same way, except that no explanations are appended, as al-Jâhiz recounts other anecdotes ostensibly about Marwazî misers.

Merv is a city in Khurâsân whose Persian-speaking inhabitants receive a special chapter in *The Book of Misers*. But of the three stories told in *Usâma*, only the first is in that chapter and has Khurâsânians as its misers.[28] *Usâma* has taken misers from across the Middle East and placed them in the category of Marwazîs, who are non-Arabs. Al-Jâhiz's work includes noted Arab misers; the *Usâma* selections do not, thus effectively reviving an old canard about Persians not sharing the proverbial generosity of the Arabs.[29]

A great many of the anecdotes in the ninth-century work revolve around hospitality, and especially attempts by misers to deny it to their guests.[30] None of the three stories chosen by Dalâl Hâtim does so, however. But hospitality figures in another way. It is al-Jâhiz who is always giving hospitality to his guests when he relates the stories. He makes a point of asking his guests if they have eaten enough, the opposite of the behavior of misers in his book. Hence the Arab virtue of hospitality, which we saw exploited in the saga of Saddâm Husayn,[31] is carried in these strips by the ninth-century author. This is mildly ironic because, while al-Jâhiz is a hero of Arab culture, he is not ethnically labeled as an Arab, considered at least partly of African descent and appropriately colored with dark skin in the *Usâma* strips.[32]

Educational Narratives

Usâma, of course, includes many other types of strips: animal stories, fairy tales from around the world, Sindibâd, etc. Standard moral principles are inculcated: being wary of strangers and the importance of work, learning, and study, though with a marked productivist, modernizing flavor. One of the more distinctive features, and one which began even before Dalâl Hâtim assumed the leadership of the magazine, is a creative type of educational narrative. These strips, rather than having human beings explain scientific or other information (as we saw in the Muslim magazines[33]), turn the scientific elements into characters themselves. For example, in one strip, by Nâsir Na'sânî, hydrogen meets oxygen, who falls in love with hydrogen's sister, thus producing water (1977, no. 195). In another strip by the same author, atoms are characters (1978, no. 222).

Perhaps the best example is a series entitled "Adventure in a Soap Bubble," written by Dalâl Hâtim and illustrated by Lujayna al-Asîl (1980, no. 286; 1981, no. 296). A little girl, Rîma, is carried in a magical bubble by a "Princess of Cleanliness" to worlds where she learns different subjects. In the rainbow, she learns about the spectrum. The most elaborate world, however, is that of the *hamza*. An Arabic consonant (signifying the glottal stop), the *hamza* poses considerable problems in spelling. Rîma had lost credit in a dictation over her *hamza*s, so the Princess takes her to the Kingdom of Hamzas, a fairy-tale world where buildings, signs, and uniforms bear the form of the *hamza*, the "c"-like curl with a tail pointing to the left, similar to the French cedilla (fig. 7.13). The traditional Middle Eastern dome is hollowed out from the right to give it the form of this consonant. With the aid of orthographically defined *hamza* battalions, the Queen explains the rules for the correct spelling of words with *hamza*s.

The *hamza* and spelling: these may seem small points. But they are part of the correct writing of the Arabic language. And the Arabic language for the editors and writers of *Usâma* is part of an Arab heritage to be cherished and an Arab nationalism to be defended.

7.13. *The City of Hamzas.*

8

Tradition Viewed from the
Maghrib: Tunisia

The Syrian party-state, despite its modernizing productivism, uses history and tradition to define its role in the modern world. So too do the strips of that other modernizing, yet generally pro-Western state, Tunisia. In the case of the North African country, however, the contexts and perspectives reflect a different history and different choices.

For a small country, rich in neither oil nor population, Tunisia plays an enormous role in Arab comic strips. Its children's magazines have an influence second only to that of the magazines of Egypt, the most populous Arab state and the traditional leader in mass culture. Tunisia is, in addition, the leading source of children's magazines for all of North Africa.

Tunisia's preeminence results from a unique cultural position. The Arabization of North Africa was historically less thorough than that of the eastern Arab lands (significant Berber-speaking populations have survived), and French colonialism was especially effective in promoting the Gallic tongue and culture. Tunisians are particularly receptive to modern French culture (the country is virtually bilingual), including comic strips. In Algeria, where the French impress was greater and the de-Arabization more severe, most of those attracted to the comic-strip medium have not traditionally been comfortable with written Arabic.[1] Tunisian culture is modern and secular enough (unlike Morocco's) to make it unusually receptive to a Western-developed medium like comic strips but Arab enough to write its strips in Arabic.[2] Unlike the Tunisian adult press, which is fully bilingual, children's magazines are reserved to Arabic. French only appears in Tunisian children's periodicals as occasional, pedagogically inspired foreign-language lessons.[3] Ironically, this Western medium is part of the country's project of Arabization. Tunisian comic-strip authors and publishers take their responsibilities as purveyors of the Arabic language very seriously, some even using fully vocalized Arabic writing, a choice rare outside the North African state.[4]

The comics of Tunis range from the party strip through the semiofficial magazine to the purely independent publication. ʿIrfân, the granddaddy of Tunisian children's magazines, is one of the oldest, most influential children's periodicals in the Arab world. Begun in 1966, this monthly apparently has sold in the area of fifty thousand copies per issue. Distributed in the schools and sold in kiosks, ʿIrfân is aimed at young teenagers.[5] A publication of the ruling Neo-Destour party, ʿIrfân is supported by the Tunisian government.[6] For younger readers (aged five to eight), the party, in March 1984, began another magazine, Shahlûl, which sells twenty-five to thirty-thousand copies per issue.[7]

Though they are party publications, ʿIrfân and Shahlûl are not, like al-Talîʿî, associated with a specific youth group. Much of the paramilitary feel of al-Talîʿî is missing from them as a result. Certainly the official line is well represented. President Bourguiba's picture appeared often during his rule and was as regularly replaced by Zayn al-ʿAbidîn Ben ʿAlî when the latter took over in 1987. Nevertheless, the cult of personality is less insistent in these Tunisian strips than in their Syrian and Iraqi equivalents.

There results also a lighter tone. ʿIrfân is a typical Tunisian boy whose face sometimes ornaments the cover and who occasionally surfaces as a character in the strips (e.g., January 1987, April 1975). A more memorable figure and one whose striking icon is in some respects more visible on the covers than that of ʿIrfân is Bû Tartûra.[8] Tartûra refers to the high red hat worn by this buffoonlike character whose potbelly echoes his penchant for silliness and minor scrapes (see fig. 8.1). Though his position might seem like that of the ʿAbduh of the Syrian Usâma or the Kaslân of the United Arab Emirates' Mâjid,[9] his iconic ubiquity makes him function virtually as a symbol of the magazine. The artists of ʿIrfân have recognized this in a design used regularly for the back covers of the annual collected volumes of the magazine (fig. 8.2). A father offers a copy of the publication to his son, while a mother, in a nurturing gesture, presents a magazine to her daughter.[10] Behind the boy's outstretched arms is the shadow of Bû Tartûra, the child's unexpressed alter ego. The insertion of ʿIrfân into this idyllic domestic scene is in sharp contrast with al-Talîʿî, where the "Father-Leader" replaces the pater familias.

The monthly al-Riyâd, begun in January 1981, is published by the semiofficial National Childhood Organization of Tunisia. This nonprofit association, founded by a group of primary and secondary schoolteachers, receives subventions from the minister of youth and sports. The first goal of this organization was the creation of summer camps for Tunisian children of modest means. The organizational infrastructure has facilitated the distribution of the magazine. Al-Riyâd is sold in schools, using a system that has permitted it to outsell the official party comic strips: a part of the proceeds of every issue is kicked back to the local schools, providing their administrators

8.1. *Left: Bû Tartûra.*

8.2. *Below: Only the shadow knows:*
Tunisian boy as Bû Tartûra.

with valuable unrestricted funds. Combining this system with distribution through the summer camps and in cooperation with local governorates has given this magazine sales of over sixty thousand per issue. *Al-Riyâd* is directed to children between the ages of eight and fifteen. Five percent of the copies of each issue are distributed free to the poorest children.[11]

'Irfân, *Shahlûl*, and *al-Riyâd* are all dependent, directly or indirectly, upon government largess. *Qaws Quzah*, which means "rainbow," prides itself on its financial independence. Proceeds from the sale of thirty thousand copies per issue cover most of the costs of publication. The editors resisted accepting advertisements as long as they could but were finally obliged to take them from economic necessity. The magazine, which has been a monthly since its inception in February 1984, aims at children from ten to fourteen. Perhaps because of its production by a private company and consequent need to compete in an open market, *Qaws Quzah* is printed on better stock, with far superior color and overall graphics than any other Tunisian children's magazine or the overwhelming majority of Arab comic strips. It makes considerable use of free-lance writers and artists, many from Algeria. This practice has not been without problems, since the Algerian artists, conceiving their work in French, arranged the frames in the Western order, from left to right. Reversing the page before dropping in the Arabic text has the disadvantage of confusing the left and right of characters, a particularly damaging switch when representing sports events. As a result, the editors now try to get their contributors to plan their strips in Arabic order from the start.[12]

Local color appears in a variety of ways. For its young readers, *Shahlûl* has created two vegetable characters, Falfûl and Tamtûma. The first is a pepper (from *fulful/filfil*), the second a tomato. The forms of the names give gender: Falfûl is masculine, Tamtûma feminine (fig. 8.3). While these plants are hardly unique to Tunisia, they are unusually important in the national cuisine and can stand in for the country. They also stand in for children. As the editor, Kamâl al-'Askarî, explains, child psychology teaches that it is less threatening to have nonhuman characters. In this way the young readers can maintain a sufficient psychological distance from the sometimes dangerous situations in which these characters are involved.[13]

Turâth and Women

Tunisia has gone further from Islamic law and tradition in its family codes than any other Arab state. Bourguiba's code, with its prohibition of polygamy, is well known in this respect. Under his rule, modernization and Westernization went hand in hand, especially in regard to the legal and social status of women.

Thus the Tunisian evocation of the *turâth* poses special problems. What would be done with the very different situation of women in traditional Arabo-Islamic society? Could this society be held up as a model for young Tunisians if it were at variance with modern Western conceptions of women's role? In different ways this problem of women's role in the *turâth* appears in a version of a story cycle from *The Thousand and*

8.3. *Vegetables as national symbols: Falfûl and Tamtûma.*

One Nights in *Qaws Quzah*, a comic-strip version of a medieval Islamic philosophical classic in *al-Riyâd*, and a fictionalized piece of medieval Arab history in *'Irfân*.

The Nights Bowdlerized

From February to December 1984, *Qaws Quzah* published a series entitled "Jâbir and the Amazing Fish," by Bilkhâmisa al-Shâdhilî, a founder and frequent contributor to the magazine as well as one of Tunisia's leading political cartoonists. The series, also published separately as an album,[14] is based on a story cycle from *The Thousand and One Nights* usually called "The Fisherman and the Jinni."

A fisherman finds a jug in his net. When he unseals it, an enormous jinn emerges, explaining that he had been imprisoned by the Prophet Solomon and threatening to kill the fisherman. The clever mortal tricks the jinn back into the jug and reseals it. After further dialogue between fisherman and jinn (illustrated by exemplary tales),[15] the demonic creature swears to reward the human if he liberates him a second time.

The fisherman's reward is the occasion for further wonders. Before departing, the jinn tells the poor man to fish from a lake on the other side of the hill. There the fisherman catches four extraordinary fish, one red, one white, one yellow, one blue, which he sells at a high price to the royal palace. To the amazement of the palace cook, then the vizier, then the king, the fish refuse to be cooked and are miraculously saved each time from the frying pan. The king then has the fisherman show him where these miraculous fish came from and, after seeing the lake, decides to investigate and find the source of this mystery. On his own now, the king comes upon a palace in which is a young man whose top half is live but whose lower half is stone. The young man tells the king his own story.

He too was a king but was betrayed by his wife, who, in an echo of the frame-story of *The Nights*, snuck out every night to consort with a "decrepit black man." The jealous husband tried to kill his wife's lover but only succeeded in leaving the man seriously injured. His wife continued to tend her helpless paramour and eventually, being a witch, wreaked vengeance on her husband by turning his lower half to stone and by whipping his upper half on a daily basis. The first king, hearing this story, decides to liberate his colleague. He tricks the witch into freeing first her husband and then the townspeople who had been turned into fish, one color for each of the religious communities: Christian, Jewish, Zoroastrian, and Muslim. Finally he slays her. The two men go off happily together and the fisherman is covered with riches.[16]

Bilkhâmisa's version is well drawn in dramatic colors, reminiscent of the best fantasy productions from the United States and of Corben and Strnad's *The Last Voyage of Sindbad*.[17] His frames are cinematic in spirit, combining partial shots and closeups, like those of the Italian Guido Crépax. The fearsomeness of the jinn is magnified by having him fill an entire single-page frame. In an unusual move, two smaller frames, which show the fisherman, are inset within this large one (fig. 8.4).

The Tunisian version follows the original tale, but only up to a point. In the

8.4. *The fisherman and the jinn.*

comic, the king, the vizier, and the fisherman go out to the lake, from which five large crystalline cylinders thrust themselves upward. The three take a raft, approach one of the cylinders, and enter it. Inside they find a gold statue in somewhat modernized Pharaonic form (fig. 8.5). His ancient Egyptian identity is further strengthened by his name, Râ the Fifth, a reference to either the Egyptian Sun God or the Pharaonic name derived from it, Ramsîs. He explains that his people had made great scientific achievements, going even to the stars, but their science had turned against them in the form of a robot. The speaker had been turned into a statue, his people into fish. The evil robot enters and fixes his eyes on the fisherman, who finds himself in the water, fearing that he will be turned into a fish. He awakens on the shore, but it is not the shore we saw before. It is a beach. Behind it lies a resort, like those that grace present-day

8.5. *Tradition and science fiction:
the updated Pharaoh.*

8.6. *Awakening from the dream: Tunisians
work for the tourists.*

Hammâmât and Jerba (fig. 8.6). A colleague greets him and invites him to help clean the beach before the tourists arrive.

The collusion of Pharaohs and space travel echoes ''Mickey and Red Cat, Adventure on Mars,'' but without the happy ending.[18] Nor does the replacement of traditional fantasy with science fiction provide the modernizing optimism of the Syrian strips.[19] This is a dystopian, not a utopian, view of science. But even that view of modernity has a tragic grandeur compared to the story's ultimate denouement. The world of *The Nights* is only a dream. Our poor fisherman does not become a wealthy man, whose sons marry the daughters of kings. He is but a poor Tunisian, relegated to cleaning up for the benefit of European tourists, and his last words are ''Yes, sir. Yes, sir.'' This is the real contemporary Tunisia, the *Qaws Quzah* version suggests.

Equally important is what Bilkhâmisa has left out: the story of the evil wife, her adultery, and her vengeance upon her husband. After all, in *The Nights* cycle it was her behavior which set the entire sequence of enchantment and mystery into motion (as did the royal adultery in that same work's frame). The Tunisian author may have decided that this story was inappropriate for his young readers. Certainly, the text of *The Thousand and One Nights*, with its frank discussions of sexuality, is too daring for the official censors of contemporary Arab society. Even the famous Bûlâq edition cannot be republished openly in its native Egypt but circulates secretly, like cultural contraband. An illustrated verse version in the Emirates' magazine *Mâjid* solved this problem by simply ending the narrative after the fisherman has talked the jinn back into the bottle.[20]

Yet Bilkhâmisa removed more than sex. He eliminated a sharply negative image of woman. Indeed, where the Nights had the feminine, he has placed the masculine: technology run amuck and phallic columns rising from the surface of the lake. *The Thousand and One Nights* is not a misogynist work, but it introduces misogynist strains well established in medieval Arabo-Islamic culture in order to recuperate them and defend womankind in a nonfeminist, essentially conservative manner.[21] Removing the evil woman is part of the adaptation of the *turâth* to modern sensibilities.

In the process, the religious diversity of the classical Islamic world, represented by the different-colored fish, has also been occulted. Though this point is less central to the original story, its elimination is still convenient, since religious diversity and minority cultures are topics most Arab strips prefer to avoid.

Hayy ibn Yaqzân

Similar effects are achieved in the comic-strip adaptation of the medieval Arabic philosophical text, *Hayy ibn Yaqzân*. This transformation by Tawfîq Bûghadîr, Abû Inâs, and ʿAbd al-Jabbâr al-ʿAmmârî was serialized in *al-Riyâd* in 1981 and 1982 (nos. 1–15 and 19–20).

The narrative of the famous twelfth-century writer, physician, and philosopher, Ibn Tufayl, whether or not one considers it a precursor of Defoe's *Robinson Crusoe* (opinions are divided), remains an Arabic literary and philosophical masterpiece. By its purely literary qualities it plays a unique role in the Arabic and even Islamic narrative corpus. The literary aspects of *Hayy ibn Yaqzân* are not foreign to the philosophical richness of the text, its multiple levels of signification, or the subtleties of meaning which have spawned discussions down to our own day.[22] From a Tunisian point of view, this text is part of the most clearly defined cultural patrimony: Ibn Tufayl hailed from al-Andalus. While from a contemporary viewpoint this might seem an annexation (Spain is neither North African, Arab, nor Muslim), in terms of history and collective *mentalités* it is altogether appropriate. Until the completion of the Reconquista, Muslim Spain was an integral part of the Maghrib in terms of politics, culture, and economics.

Ibn Tufayl's text distinguishes itself quite clearly in spirit and in organization from the more Oriental productions of the Perso-Arabic writers Ibn Sînâ (Avicenna)

and al-Suhrawardî. It would be difficult to conceive of a text which more clearly illustrates the difference between a Maghribian and an Eastern approach to the same
philosophical territory.[23] More concrete than the other works of the same title, Ibn
Tufayl's narrative, while keeping its allegorical level of meaning, inserts itself more
directly into the material lives of human beings.

Briefly, *Hayy ibn Yaqzân* tells the story of a male child who grows up alone on a
deserted island where he discovers, using only his natural reason, philosophy and
religion. Later our hero, Hayy, meets a kindred spirit, Asâl, and after a few adventures the two men decide to spend the rest of their days in a life of contemplation on
Hayy's island.

One of the principal philosophical burdens of Ibn Tufayl's work is the compati-
bility, even harmony, of science or rational knowledge and religion. In a modern context, the *Hayy ibn Yaqzân* of Ibn Tufayl and that of *al-Riyâd* function as joint defenses of
both science and religion. In this way the strip is closer to the Islamic strips of Egypt
than the party strips of Syria.

The hero's discovery of the natural world becomes both a science lesson and an
argument from design. After the gazelle who has mothered our young hero dies,
Hayy dissects her, discovering her heart, its functioning, and its role in her body
(1982, no. 11). The page in question is divided into frames that evoke the chambers of
the heart (fig. 8.7).

In addition to its philosophical and religious positions, the *Hayy ibn Yaqzân* of Ibn
Tufayl presents a problematic which, though linked in the last analysis to its philosophical conclusions, operates on a terrain that could be described as extraphilosoph-
ical. The terrain is that of psychology, the problematic, that of woman.[24] To write a
novel, even a philosophical novel, is to create characters imitating those of flesh and
blood. The decision to narrate the life of Hayy and the circumstances of his birth have
obliged the narrator to deal with certain problems.

The formal aspect of the work itself directs us toward the same gender problematic. The attentive reader is quickly struck by an "ungrammaticality" (in Riffaterre's
terms) in the text.[25] This violation of discursive rules is the presence of two variants,
between which the narrator never really chooses, for the birth of Hayy. Variants, of
course, are not foreign to classical Arabic literature. But it is precisely in this that the
discourse of Ibn Tufayl's *Hayy ibn Yaqzân* differs from the prose texts of *adab* works,
tabaqât and biographical dictionaries, and chronicles. The Tufaylian narrative (this
case excepted) unfolds seamlessly, as Léon Gauthier has correctly noted.[26] The variants thus signal a troubled zone on the level of narrative significations.

What are the variants? In one, the simplest, Hayy is born by spontaneous generation on the island of al-Waqwâq.[27] The other version is more complicated. Our
hero is the fruit of a secret marriage. The king of a prosperous island is jealous of his
beautiful sister and rejects all offers for her hand. She then marries one of her relatives, Yaqzân, in secret. Having become a mother, to hide her shame the woman puts
her infant child in a box and casts it out on the sea. Through good fortune the child
lands on the island of al-Waqwâq where he grows up without knowledge of other
human beings, as in the spontaneous-generation version.

8.7. *Creative stripology: frames as chambers of the heart.*

Thus the two versions (each in its own way) underline a problematic of woman and sexuality. In the version which one could call biological because the child is born of a real father and a real mother, his abandonment results from sexual jealousy, from the unconscious desire of a brother for his sister. They make a problematic couple. The other story, that of spontaneous generation, is the dream of birth without a mother, without woman. It is a land where children appear without parents.

Hayy grows up essentially without sexuality. He learns asceticism, and though he later meets normal humanity, he never takes a wife (a rather extraordinary situation in the Islamic tradition). By contrast, Hayy meets Asâl, his alter ego, and the two men eventually decide to retire to the island of al-Waqwâq to devote the rest of their days, alone, to meditation. They form a couple that is male, peaceful, devoid of sexuality, and without women.

From several points of view, therefore, the *Hayy ibn Yaqzân* of Ibn Tufayl raises problems of sexuality and relations between men and women. Its conclusions could be qualified as antisexual, if not misogynist.

With its novelistic nature, its linear and continuous narrative, Ibn Tufayl's *Hayy ibn Yaqzân* seems, of all classical Islamic philosophical texts, the one best adapted for treatment as a comic strip. There remains, of course, this formal problem of the variants and the greater challenge of the antifeminist potential of the work, ill adapted to the integration of women in modern society. The adaptation in *al-Riyâd* is lively, well drawn, and effectively innovative.

To begin, the authors of the comic strip *Hayy* simplified their task by eliminating without further ado one of the two variants—that of spontaneous generation. Only the biological-birth version remains. But this story itself is so completely reworked that its sexual politics are totally transformed.

What first strikes a reader familiar with the *Hayy ibn Yaqzân* of Ibn Tufayl is the difference in relative length. The biological version took a bit less than 2 percent of the text, 4 percent if one adds the spontaneous-generation version. In the comic strip, the story of Hayy's birth fills seven of the seventeen episodes, more than a third of the text. This elongation not only gives more importance to these events, but it permits the authors to weave an entire story around the threatened birth of our young hero.

More than a story of jealousy, the story becomes that of two lovers fighting against the interest of the state. The strip begins by explaining to us that the king of the island of al-Waqwâq had a sister to marry off. The island has thus changed place. In the original text, al-Waqwâq was the deserted island where Hayy grew up and not the populated island of his mother and father. In the Arab geographical tradition, al-Waqwâq is a place where the normal rules of sexuality are suspended.[28] This appellation therefore does not at all fit the island of the king and his sister, where men and women behave normally. It signals a change of importance. The island of the king, of so little importance in Ibn Tufayl's text that it remained nameless, becomes in the strip the main scene of the action.

Yaqzân wants to marry the sister of the king, but the ruler refuses the match. In this modern adaptation, however, the monarch acts from political duty. Concerned with the weakness of his kingdom and army before menacing enemies, he is looking for allies and wishes to use matrimonial politics to create ties with other kings and countries. His sister herself wants to wed Yaqzân, who is drawn as a very good-looking young man (fig. 8.8). She complains that her brother takes no account of her hap-

8.8. *Philosophic narrative in strips: Yaqzân and the mother of Hayy.*

piness. But is the king to blame? One could say that he is but doing his duty and should be praised for preferring the welfare of his kingdom to the happiness of his family. Instead of hidden desire, one finds a noble, almost Cornélien conflict between love and duty.

Yaqzân himself, in contrast with his role in the Tufaylian narrative, is very active. One might even say he is a *dhakî*, or trickster, in the Arabic tradition.[29] He succeeds in fooling both the king and his vizier.

The king decides to offer his sister's hand to the son of King Nâtûs, since the latter's hostility is apparently motivated by an earlier matrimonial refusal. Yaqzân, who is a friend of the vizier, succeeds in getting himself named part of the delegation to King Nâtûs. Once arrived, Yaqzân, without the vizier's knowledge, explains to one of King Nâtûs's ministers that the lady in question suffers from leprosy but that no blame attached to the king of al-Waqwâq, who was not aware of this fact. The vizier of al-Waqwâq is then quite surprised by the actions of King Nâtûs, who politely refuses his colleague's sister and sends the delegation back to al-Waqwâq loaded with presents. The vizier (completely in the dark over Yaqzân's maneuvers) explains to the surprised king of al-Waqwâq that King Nâtûs must not have been angry since he sent gifts. All this was to block the ruler's projects and permit the secret marriage of Yaqzân and his beloved.

Yaqzân's activities are not limited to politics. When his wife becomes pregnant, it is he who invents ruses to keep this fact secret, just as it is he who insists on getting rid of their child. Instead of the almost monstrous mother in Ibn Tufayl, the comic-strip mother is pressured, full of tears, by her husband; and it is Yaqzân who throws the child into the sea, while in Ibn Tufayl it was Hayy's mother, in the complete absence of her husband, who took care of the dirty business.

Much has changed in the sexual politics of *Hayy ibn Yaqzân*. An entire dimension of troubled sexuality has been eliminated—the royal brother's jealousy of his beautiful sister. At first sight this change seems positive, since it eliminates (when combined with the elimination of the spontaneous-generation version) those elements susceptible to antisexual or misogynist interpretation. This tendency is reinforced by the much more passive role played by the mother in the abandonment of her child. Does not a less unworthy mother mean a more worthy image of womankind? But the relative merit of the *al-Riyâd* mother is purchased at the price of an essentially passive role throughout the story. Apparently one has only replaced a troubled vision of the woman with the traditional image of feminine passivity. This is so much the case that the story ceases to be that of the mother to become that of the father, that is, Yaqzân. He is the real hero of this prologue swollen to become virtually half the narrative. Instead of one story almost entirely about Hayy, we have two linked stories, one of Hayy and one of Yaqzân.

The Tufaylian *Hayy ibn Yaqzân* was a flight from a world of problematic sexuality to a world without women. The *Hayy* of *al-Riyâd* is also a flight, but from a world filled with court intrigue, in a word, a world of politics. There are many things in the story of Hayy ibn Yaqzân: a celebration of natural reason, an explanation of mystical knowledge. But all this is wrapped in a renunciation of the world. The most important difference between the medieval text and the modern comic-strip version is the description of this element of trouble, of confusion, of chaos in the world. For the Andalusian philosopher, the principle of trouble was the flesh and woman. The modern *Hayy* has placed the problems of male-female relations and sexuality in the larger category of politics. The conflict comes from the tension between love, family, and state interests. To see that the problems of sexuality do not stem from the nature of the sexual object (woman) but are part of the more general choices of a society, to see woman's role as a political question, is to be effectively feminist, with or without slogans.

The Model Tunisian

Both *Qaws Quzah*'s revision of *The Nights* and *al-Riyâd*'s presentation of *Hayy ibn Yaqzân* promote by omission, by removing elements discordant with contemporary values. *Irfân* provides a positive heroine in a romanticized historical account, the adventures of a model Tunisian girl, heroine of Islam and of her nation, "Jamîla al-Qayrawâniyya." This text of twelve episodes, by Muhammad Salâm and Hasanayn ibn ʿAmmu, appeared in 1982.

Our story takes place at the end of the fifteenth century. The Spanish Reconquista is triumphing with the defeat of the last Muslim ruler, in Granada. A girl from al-Qayrawân leaves her hometown to fight alongside the last Muslim warriors in Spain. She dies a martyr for her faith.

Jamîla (that is her name) is a symbol of patriotism, even nationalism. But what is her homeland? Her nation? We have already seen that such questions are not always simple in Arab strips. Nor is it in the case of Jamîla. At first glance she is Tunisian—

her connection to the city of al-Qayrawân is stressed in the title itself, just as her presence in the party magazine reinforces her identification with the Tunisian state. But the homeland of Jamîla is not limited to Tunisia. This homeland merges into three others: the Maghrib, that is, North Africa; the Arab world; and the Muslim world.

The Maghrib is the geographic locus of the story. The unity of the story is based on a close connection between Tunisia and Muslim Spain. Jamîla's journey from al-Qayrawân to Granada is not presented as a crossing of frontiers but rather as a movement from the center of a territory to a threatened borderland. The inhabitants of one country (Tunisia or Spain) do not consider those of the other as foreigners. Conceptually, Spain is part of a larger Maghribian homeland, as it was for *al-Riyâd*'s *Hayy*.

The strip itself notes that the artisans of Spain were forced to flee Christian tyranny and had settled "in the countries of the Maghrib" (1982, no. 173). The settlement of Andalusian refugees is more than a historical anecdote to most Tunisians. The mosques of the Spanish settlers stand out visibly today, with their octagonal minarets so different from the square towers of the original North African inhabitants. As we shall see, this Maghribian space, like the problem of refugees, opens other possibilities of identification.

Of the two last points of identification, Arabism and Islam, it is the first which is the more clearly expressed in "Jamîla al-Qayrawâniyya." The heroine defines herself often, almost exclusively, as Arab, never as Tunisian or Maghribian. As a prisoner of the king of France, Jamîla explains that he will never win her heart because she is an Arab and a Muslim. To another person she explains that wisdom for her is to keep her religion, her honor, and her Arabism (1982, no. 182). In this strip the world of Islam functions as a direct parallel to the Arab nation, the two being virtually coessential. The *"jihâd"* is presented as a struggle for the Arab nation (1982, no. 173), as if the worlds of Islam and the Arabs were the same.

This contrast with the exclusive Arabism of *Usâma* is not primarily due to a lesser secularism, though this is one of its effects. In the Eastern Arab lands, of which Syria is a prime example, nationalism developed as an alternative to an Islamic identification, and it encompassed the frequently substantial Christian Arab minorities. The Baath is an excellent example, its leading ideologue Michel ʿAflaq being a Christian. In the lands of the Maghrib, however, no significant Christian minorities survived. Virtually the sole opponent of local nationalism was French colonialism, and nationalism and Islam were considered one and the same. The presence of larger Berber, though Muslim, minorities also strengthened the value of religion as a point of national identification.

This multiplicity of potential allegiances permits some interesting games of identification and contrast. At the end of the story, the execution of Jamîla by the French is described as a crime comparable to the killing of Joan of Arc by the English; like Joan, Jamîla is burned at the stake (1982, no. 183). This assimilation to the maid of Orleans opens a number of perspectives. It is a clever attack on France, turning the heroine of French nationalism (and the indignation associated with her execution) against her own country. This double-edged sword is a weapon particularly appropriate to Tunisian nationalism, a nationalism at once anti-French from the necessities of the struggle for independence and infused with French civilization by the facts of colonization.

But the identification goes further. Speaking of Joan of Arc suggests another Jamîla, Jamîla Bouhayrid, called during the Algerian Revolution the Algerian Joan of Arc.[30] Associating the two Jamîlas strengthens the Maghribian identification. Moreover, the linkage of the Tunisian Jamîla with her Algerian sister through a French saint underlines the shared history of Gallic imperialism.

Paralleling this reference to the Algerian Revolution is another, to the Palestinian tragedy. Though it is never mentioned explicitly in the text, Palestine remains part of the subtext, if only for reasons of intertextuality. The year's worth of ʿIrfâns carrying the episodes of "Jamîla al-Qayrawâniyya" is full of references to events in Palestine. After June 1982 the cadres of the Palestine Liberation Organization took refuge in Tunisia, as had many Andalusians centuries earlier. Even if this event came after the composition of most, perhaps all, of "Jamîla al-Qayrawâniyya," it formed part of the world in which the strip was read. The situation in which Jamîla found herself resembles, in many ways, that of Palestine. Her war was a defeat for the Arabs and Muslims, who were driven from their land, in this like the history of Palestine but in contrast to the Algerian Revolution, which was crowned with success, though after a long and bloody struggle.

There are other, more precise, allusions. The defeat in Spain is called the "*nakba*" (disaster) (1982, no. 172), a term commonly used today to refer to the Arab defeat in the first Arab-Israeli War and its consequences for the Palestinians. The phrase "*al-jihâd hattâ al-nasr* (Jihâd until Victory)" (1982, no. 176) evokes the familiar Palestinian slogan *al-thawra hattâ al-nasr* (Revolution until Victory). Even the conditions of Jamîla's struggle suggest those of our century. The people want to go on fighting, and it is only the corrupt leaders who surrender through cowardice and greed (1982, no. 181). This vision expresses equally well the interpretations given by the Arab Left and the Palestinian movement of the Arab defeats and compromises in the struggle with Israel.

These multiple associations do more than simply anchor Tunisia in the Maghribian and Arab contexts. The Algerian and Palestinian examples are particularly valorizing. Though Tunisian independence was not won without struggle, and though there was armed resistance and bloodshed, this was without common measure with the enormous cost paid by the Algerian people, on one hand, and still being paid by the Palestinians, on the other. Insofar as the combat of the Tunisian Jamîla is comparable to the more recent struggles of her Arab sisters and brothers, she and her nation become more heroic.

But there is still more in the Palestinianizing or Algerianizing of our heroine. The fact of a Muslim woman playing an important role in a medieval Islamic war is an eye opener, to say the least. If the Syrians of *al-Talîʿî* and *Usâma* suggest feminine participation in contemporary struggles, their heroines never took arms in actual combat, nor was such female militarism projected back into the Middle Ages.[31] The positions of the Egyptian *al-Firdaws* were even more conservative. Many stories effectively posed the problem of the direct participation of women and children in the *jihâd*. The answer was clear: women and children should remain in the rear, take care of the wounded, or pay for the equipment of regular soldiers (*Sâlim*, pp. 12–14, 33–35, 45–47).

The revolutionary and feminist implications of the Tunisian story stand out all the more clearly. In an Arab context the Algerian and Palestinian cases form the clearest counterexamples to the conservatism of *al-Firdaws*. In both these struggles, women have played important and highly visible roles. For the Palestinian conflict, many women have participated in acts of armed struggle, such as airplane hijackings. Leila Khaled echoes Jamîla al-Qayrawâniyya, if not the reverse.[32] In the Algerian War, women fought in the *maquis* alongside their male compatriots; and in the more famous cases of the "carriers of fire" (as they were called by Assia Djebar), they planted bombs.[33] The allusions to more recent revolutions respond to the principal problem in the story of Jamîla: the role of the woman, of an exemplary woman, in the masculine world of war.

As warrior, Jamîla is an exceptional woman. Our own Occidental societies are still not comfortable with this idea. In an Arabo-Muslim context, a woman in combat (despite a few early and controversial exceptions) risks impropriety.[34] Thus the strip introduces this problematic behavior very gradually.

At the beginning of the story we meet Jamîla, the only child of a father who is a professional arms-maker. Since there are no boys in the house, it is she who aids her father in the workshop, learning the trade. Reasonable enough, but Jamîla has crossed a line, that which separates masculine occupations from the more domestic responsibilities of women. Her "liberation" proceeds by stages. With the death of her father, Jamîla becomes a master arms-maker. It is then that the soldiers from Spain explain to her their lack of weapons and craftsmen to manufacture them. Jamîla decides to accompany them—not as a soldier but as an artisan.

It is only in the war zone itself that the transformation from young woman to warrior is completed, a transformation which takes place by degrees and apparently as a function of circumstance. Immediately after they disembark, a Christian attacks one of Jamîla's companions from behind. The Tunisian warns her Muslim brother, who kills the Spaniard (1982, nos. 174 and 175). Arriving in the Muslim camp, Jamîla is presented as an artisan, come to manufacture weapons. But she corrects the speaker by adding "*mujâhida*," holy warrior.[35]

From this moment forward, Jamîla is a combatant. Although she immediately organizes the manufacture and repair of weapons, she becomes the leader of a group of volunteer women fighters, and as such she plays an important part in the fighting around Granada.

More striking, this war becomes a fight between women. Jamîla is the soul of the Muslim resistance. On the other side, the most important personality is Queen Isabella. The Catholic monarch even becomes the prize of the battle when the Muslims, led by Jamîla, try to capture her. Instead it is Jamîla who is taken prisoner. One has the impression that in this war the men cannot match the women and that were it only up to Jamîla and her women warriors the Muslims would have been victorious. From this point of view, Jamîla and her sisters are associated with the people as a reservoir of national energy. One is reminded of the famous phrase of Chateaubriand on the loss of Muslim Spain. In *L'Aventure du dernier Abencérage*, the queen mother says to her royal son, who is crying over the country he has just lost: "Cry now like a woman over a kingdom that you were not able to defend like a man."[36] The sexual politics are so similar that one wonders if the comic-strip author of "Jamîla al-Qay-rawâniyya" was not influenced by the French writer, unless, of course, the two drew their inspiration from the same source.

In either case, the reversal of normal gender roles, an augury of catastrophe, is only the final product of a series of transformations that have made of a girl of al-Qayrawân the leader of an army. Jamîla can become a man, but only in an exceptional situation where all roles are called into question.

This masculinization at once occults and underlines sexual differences. In her workshop in al-Qayrawân, Jamîla goes into a room alone with a male customer as if this were the most natural thing in the world (fig. 8.9) (1982, no. 173). On the boat,

8.9. *Jamîla alone in her shop with a man.*

she shares the space freely with the men (1982, no. 174). People act as if there were no need to pay heed to the oft-quoted *hadîth*: when a man and a woman are together, the devil is the third.[37] The body language of Jamîla is that of a man. She is desexualized, liberated from the constraints traditionally associated with the modesty of women. But this liberation also accentuates certain feminine qualities. When she goes into battle, Jamîla loses her veil and leaves her hair flowing freely over her shoulders (fig. 8.10) (e.g., October 1982). Modest with the men, she becomes an amazon with the warrior women.

This corporal liberation signals a danger that becomes real with Jamîla's capture.

8.10. *Jamîla as war leader.*

While the Tunisian girl is a prisoner of the Spanish, the king of France hears of the beautiful captive and wants to have her for himself. This is the first time that anyone speaks of the beauty of Jamîla. Before this, among the Arabs, her charms went unnoticed, or at least remained uncommented. With her liberty, she loses her relatively masculine status, becoming woman and sexual object. Captured by the king of France, she is brought to his palace, where he tries to win her favors. When she refuses, she is sent to the kitchen to do domestic chores, the first time that we see her in a traditional female role. Jamîla escapes and is captured and executed. It is only with the king of France that she is treated as a woman and punished when she rebels.

Certainly this tragic ending for a liberated woman serves to criticize the French, whose behavior is less moral than that of the Arabs. It is also a clever reversal of the standard Occidental critique of the Muslims as antifemale, as well as a demonstration of Jamîla's virtues. But more profoundly, the end of Jamîla (as much the heroine as her story) calls into question the entire project of the strip. As in the story of the women who went on the *jihâd* in *al-Firdaws* (*Sâlim*, pp. 12–14), if it is not the Muslims who bring women back to their proper role, it is the others, the Christians in this case, who underline the vulnerability of the female. Yes, she can be brave, strong, bold—up to the point at which she passes into the hands of the enemy. There she risks what men do not.

The story of Jamîla of al-Qayrawân is that of a woman at once exemplary and exceptional. The model woman, the female Tunisian of tomorrow, is a patriot, certainly. But military action for a woman is more exceptional and more risky.

Women have traditionally been more visible in the history of the Maghrib. In its comic-strip series on the Islamic conquest of North Africa, 'Irfân repeats the well-known story of the Berber priestess-queen who led resistance to the Arabs and was finally defeated. Despite her position as enemy of Islam, her treatment in the strip is not unsympathetic, making the queen function as both national representative and witness to the Islamization of the region (1984, nos. 196–98).

Should we see Jamîla and the elimination of much traditional misogyny as an echo of more matriarchial Berber origins? Perhaps. But the Tunisian strips are engaged in a more traditional ideological function: the smoothing of potential contradictions between a *turâth* held dear and a social project that includes some most untraditional values.

9

Arabian Success Story: *Mâjid*

Abu Dhabi is a city that oil made—the capital of the United Arab Emirates, a young small country rich in oil but almost empty of water and, until recently, of population. In this city is produced the most successful and the most pan-Arab of comic-strip magazines, *Mâjid*. Oil wealth has something to do with this, but more important are the quality of the periodical's collaborators, its blending of local and regional foci, and its integration of common children's magazine materials into an integrated vision of the Arab child.

With a certified circulation of 150,000 to 175,000, *Mâjid* is probably the most widely read children's magazine in the region, delighting readers in every Arab state, with the sole exception of Syria. And its presence has been reported in the occupied territories.

In Cairo copies at the newsstands are snatched up the day they are put on sale. If Egyptian demand is not saturated, it is because *Mâjid*'s editor, Ahmad ʿUmar, prices his magazine lower in poorer and more populous states such as Egypt than in the richer countries around the Gulf (which until recently included Iraq). Since the Egyptian prices do not cover costs, they are effectively subsidized by profits from the richer petroleum states. Thus Ahmad ʿUmar sells as many *Mâjid*s in Egypt as he can afford to.[1] In this way, *Mâjid* has remained self-supporting and has appeared weekly from 1979 to the present. By its geographic diffusion, its print run, and its frequency of publication, *Mâjid* is the Arab world's most influential purveyor of comic strips.[2]

If one of *Mâjid*'s feet stands on the shores of the Gulf, the other is planted in the Nile Valley. In different ways, *Mâjid* is both Emiratian and Egyptian. Administratively, *Mâjid* depends on the newspaper *al-Ittihâd* and thus on the Ministry of Information of the United Arab Emirates. It is published in Abu Dhabi. But as an artistic and journalistic achievement it is the work of an Egyptian, Ahmad ʿUmar. A Nasserite journalist, Ahmad ʿUmar left his native Egypt upon the death of his hero and the accession of Sadat. His concern for the future of Arab children and discussions held during the Year of the Child (1979) led him to found *Mâjid*. In addition to his activities as editor-in-chief and commercial director of the magazine, Ahmad ʿUmar composes the majority of the scenarios. Behind Ahmad ʿUmar is a largely Egyptian team of whom the most important is the Egyptian cartoonist Ahmad Hijâzî (who remains in Cairo).[3] He illustrates the majority of stories, writes a few of the scenarios, coordinates the expedition of materials from Egypt to Abu Dhabi, and is the true artistic second in command of the magazine. The two noted Egyptian cartoonists Bahjat ʿUthmân and Muhyî al-Dîn al-Labbâd are also regular contributors, joined in more recent years by the Egyptian painter, sculptor, and political cartoonist Georges Bahgory, who lives in Paris.[4] Ahmad ʿUmar, Hijâzî, and their compatriots have introduced a number of very Egyptian elements into their magazine, and ʿUmar's Nasserism, as much an attachment to the personality of the great Egyptian as an ideological position, finds frequent expression in the pages of *Mâjid*.

None of this keeps *Mâjid* from also being linked to the Emirates and the Arabian peninsula as a whole. The magazine is named after Ahmad ibn Mâjid, a famous fifteenth-century navigator and scholar, expert in the geography of the Red and Arabian seas and the Indian Ocean who was apparently instrumental in helping Vasco da Gama reach India.[5] The magazine's hero and namesake, Mâjid, wears the familiar national costume, and the weekly celebrates the national holidays of the Emirates. The head of state, Shaykh Zâ'id, makes discreet appearances, and many of the stories take their inspiration from realities specific to the Gulf.

But rather than allowing itself to be torn between two competing provincialisms, *Mâjid* tries to assume the totality of the Arab heritage and to serve a pan-Arabism conceived in both political and cultural terms. Over the years, *Mâjid* has featured the work of the best and brightest in the Arab world, from the Egyptian ʿAdlî Rizq Allâh to the Syrian ʿAlî Farzât. This pan-Arab project is all the easier, given that Ahmad ʿUmar's magazine contains an enormous quantity of general information on the world, politics, and the relations between different civilizations.

Its artists help give *Mâjid* a visual aesthetic and a consistently high quality of artwork that places it above competing magazines. There is certainly more than one type of drawing in *Mâjid*. Ihâb's art is quite different from that of Farzât or al-Labbâd. But the considerable visual presence of Hijâzî, especially when combined with that of Bahjat and Muhammad Bayram, whose styles are so similar to his, produces something resembling a dominant *Mâjid* visual style or look. This is essentially flat, makes heavy use of rhythmic repetitions and geometric forms, and is brightly colored. The effect is reminiscent of much of the region's folk art, especially textiles, or the tribal carpets that one finds from Arabia to Morocco (see fig. 9.1). In addition, strips tend to be longer in *Mâjid*, often six to eight pages, unlike the common two-page selections in other periodicals. The result is often more sophisticated narrative development.

The *Mâjid* Family

Contributing to *Mâjid*'s appeal are several series and their associated characters, which have followed the magazine over the years. One of the most popular figures, Kaslân (Lazy), will be discussed below. A set of crime narratives, "Captain Khalfân and Adjutant Fahmân," are drawn by Muhammad Bayram but have been composed by a number of authors, including Ahmad ʿUmar (writing under the pseudonym Hissa ʿUbayd) and the noted Egyptian short-story writer Muhammad al-Mansî Qindîl.[6] The two policemen carry on investigations in this detective series. Adding a sense of continuity, the same characters sometimes appear in spinoff series, such as "The Gang of Five . . . and the Maharaja," written by Jamâl Salîm and illustrated by Hijâzî.[7]

More unusual in Arab strips is the "Shamsa and Dâna" series by Samîra Shafîq (the text) and Ihâb (the illustrations). The two lead characters live on an island by themselves, from which they make occasional forays into the civilized world. But unlike the island of *Hayy ibn Yaqzân* (and *Robinson Crusoe*), this is a female land. Shamsa and Dâna are girls. Shamsa is the fairer of the two, with long black hair; Dâna is darker, with short kinky hair and broader lips (in later years, the difference in complexion between the two virtually disappears). Though they are the same age, Dâna is the more childish, Shamsa the more mature and responsible, of the two. Such a psychological division is a common device. Much less common is the female nature of the story as a whole. In most children's strips in the Arab world (as in the West), the casts of characters are either all male or mixed male and female, with the latter often in the minority. The twin heroines of this series tend to redress the balance, giving a more female presence in *Mâjid* than in any other Arab children's magazine.

Shamsa and Dâna share their island with animals: a goat, a giant tortoise (who provides transportation to and from the mainland), and an eagle (fig. 9.2). The tortoise and goat have female names. The eagle, Mansûr, is the lone male presence. The eagle's gender is perhaps not insignificant since this bird is the national symbol of the United Arab Emirates (as of so many other Arab—and non-Arab—states). The animals are fully sentient and speak as equals with the two girls; an ecological, proanimal subtext permeates the adventures of this human and animal group (e.g., 1984, no. 290).

Local color combines with family themes in one of the oldest series, "al-Dalla wal-Finjân." Though this series, written by Ahmad ʿUmar (under pseudonyms), began with the first issue of the magazine (1979, no. 1), it went through a number of variations until it found its best pen in 1986 at the hands of Bahjat ʿUthmân. Dalla and Finjân are coffee pot and cup, but not just any coffee pot and cup. This pot with strong spout and matching metal handleless cup have become symbols of the Emirates and of bedouin hospitality. They represent the authentic Arabian culture of the country before petrodollars buried it under imported luxury and foreign labor. The symbolism is pervasive: one of the chief landmarks of Abu Dhabi is an enormous *dalla* and *finjân* sculpture-fountain. A similar one graces downtown al-ʿAyn and, of course, the souvenirs sell like miniature Eiffel Towers.

9.2. *Shamsa, Dâna, and their animal friends.*

Like *Shahlûl's* vegetables,[8] Dalla and Finjân stand in for characters. Dalla is larger, clearly the adult, Finjân the child. In many ways Dalla acts like a mother—after all, such a pot pours liquid into the open mouth of a cup.[9] Though gender indications are not consistent in the series, Dalla takes a protective, nurturing attitude to Finjân, allowing the young reader to react to the parent-and-child scenarios while apparently laughing over the adventures of a national symbol.

The series also draws humor (and an irresistible cuteness) from the bisociation of the human and object characteristics of the protagonists. In one episode, when a male coffee drinker tries to put out his cigarette in poor Finjân, Dalla chastises him loudly. The pot and cup, who are round bottomed when handled by their human owners, can take on feet and arms when speaking between themselves (1986, nos. 369 and 389) (fig. 9.3).

Which Tradition?

Mâjid, too, puts the *turâth* in strips. It does so, however, both creatively and in ways that speak to the special problems of children. Stories from classical Arabic anecdotal collections, such as the *Akhbâr al-Adhkiyâ'* (Stories of the Clever) of Ibn al-Jawzî, have graced the pages of the magazine (e.g., 1982, no. 166),[10] as have Juhâ anecdotes (e.g., 1981, no. 121).

But Juhâ is also modernized in a series from the pen of Bahjat ʿUthmân (text by Ahmad ʿUmar under the pseudonym Ahmad Muhammad), entitled "Juhâ 2." This Juhâ, who joined the *Mâjid* family in 1987, is not a traditional figure lost in the modern world but a completely up-to-date fool whose donkey has been replaced by a motorcycle and his turban by a motorcycle helmet (fig. 9.4).

9.3. *Coffee pot and cup as national symbols:*
Dalla and Finjân.

All these examples derive from the familiar Arab bag of traditional materials. As such, they fit as well with the Emirates as with any other Arab state. Not so, however, with a comic-strip rendition by Jamâl Salîm and Ahmad Hijâzî of the ancient Egyptian classic "The Eloquent Peasant" (1982, no. 182). This Middle Kingdom tale weaves together the search for justice with a meditation on the creation of text and art. Briefly, it tells the story of an oasis dweller who was robbed by a local notable. When he goes to the provincial governor for redress, the official is so impressed with his eloquence that he informs the Pharaoh and delays the administration of justice so that he can draw from the peasant all the eloquence that is within him. After the peasant has delivered beautiful speeches on justice and its role in the human and divine orders, the mystery of his apparent injustice is revealed to him. His family has been taken care of all this time, his property is more than restored, and his eloquence has been recorded for posterity.[11]

We are in the Egyptian cultural realm here, not the Arab. With its powerful cries for justice, "The Eloquent Peasant" has probably been the Pharaonic story which has

9.4. *The up-to-date fool: Juhâ 2.*

appealed most to modern Egyptian intellectuals. Though it has received a number of Arabic adaptations, it has been most central to intellectuals, such as the filmmaker Shâdî ʿAbd al-Salâm, who seek to elevate the Egyptian and Pharaonic over the Arab and Islamic elements in that country's cultural heritage.[12]

Aside from the necessary abbreviation of the peasant's eloquence, there is only one major change in the comic-strip version. Though we are reminded (as in the original) that the peasant has a wife and children, Hijâzî has drawn him shorter in stature and with childlike features. In this way, a story of justice is adapted to the world of children, so that in place of the divisions of class and social hierarchy in the original we have that between the world of adults and that of children. As we have seen, the assimilation of these two types of hierarchies is characteristic of much of Hijâzî's work.[13]

The Politics of Little Girls

Like its Syrian and Tunisian cousins, *Mâjid* raises political issues with its young readers—indeed, more explicitly than even the party magazines. But it does so in distinctive ways: by integrating local and regional issues in a view of the world and by relating adult politics to the realities of children's lives. It is not just that Shaykh Zâ'id is less ubiquitous than either Hâfiz al-Asad or Bourguiba. A photo of a group of children looking at a picture of the Shaykh graces one of the magazine's covers. Shaykh Zâ'id is not in majesty but at play—billiards, in fact. Behind the children stands the real Shaykh benevolently watching the whole scene (1986, no. 389). The ruler is a father but also a child who likes his play, a derogation that perhaps only a traditional ruler such as an Arabian *shaykh* could permit himself.

Politics appears in other parts of the magazine, as in the frequent coloring pages which function almost as political cartoons (e.g., 1986, no. 384). But the most common location for politics in *Mâjid* is a regular series entitled "Zakiyya al-Dhakiyya" (Zakiyya the Clever), written by Ahmad ʿUmar and illustrated by Hijâzî. Dhakiyya refers to cleverness but also to a classical Arabic tradition of clever and witty individuals.[14] The name Zakiyya signifies moral purity but also cleverness. Hence, beyond the homonymy, our heroine is twice clever.

Zakiyya is a mine of information. And she introduces her colleagues (and her young readers) to issues of politics, science, general information, even religion, playing the role in *Mâjid* that the Visiting Philosopher does in *al-Muslim al-Saghîr*.[15] Making an authority both female *and* juvenile is revolutionary in an Arab context (indeed, in a Western one as well). We have already seen that some knowledge purveyors were adolescent males and that young women could be models, but of moral behavior more than of science. Zakiyya's expertise, by contrast, even extends to the masculine realms of politics and war.

Ahmad ʿUmar was well aware of the gender implications of his choice. He thought that picking a girl would encourage his female readers while challenging the boys to do at least as well.[16] One strip develops this issue when Zakiyya helps a girl's team in an academic competition. The girls thank her for leading them to a tie with the boys' team, since they did not want the boys to say that they were smarter than they (I, pp. 30–31).[17] Similarly, after Zakiyya provides a masterful (and elogious) discussion of Indira Gandhi, the other school girls are pleased that the boys should know that girls are as good as they are since a great leader has come from their ranks (I, pp. 100-101). On yet another occasion, the girls visit Zakiyya in her study to express their gratitude and we clearly see a book on the shelf labeled *Madame Curie* (I, pp. 32–33). Zakiyya is a central part of the strong female presence in *Mâjid*.

Zakiyya wears glasses and looks like a female Arab Dilton Doiley (fig. 9.5). Ahmad ʿUmar, who discussed her image with Hijâzî, was afraid that giving her beauty as well as intelligence might create jealousy in his female readers.[18] His decision, of course, reinforces the zero-sum view that opposes intelligence and beauty, especially in women. Zakiyya, the eldest child in her family, provides information to a younger brother and sister. Her father's activities often raise the subject, but it is rarely he or another adult who supplies the information. Adult males are knowledgeable, but they rarely compete with Zakiyya in her role as spokesperson. Zakiyya's mother, more traditional, listens patiently, occasionally asking questions, bringing her intel-

9.5. *The little girl as brain: Zakiyya.*

lectual role closer to that of the other children. "Zakiyya al-Dhakiyya," rather than seeing this as a species of the eternal feminine, treats it as a generational difference: the traditional Arab woman on one hand, the modern one on the other. In one story, Zakiyya is bringing in drinks to a male guest. This is one of the classic ways in contemporary Arab culture in which a girl is presented as a potential marriage prospect. The guest complements Zakiyya, calling her a "bride," a flattering way of saying that a girl is entering the flower of womanhood. In the course of discussion, he expresses surprise at the level of her learning (II, pp. 10–11). In a similar situation in another story (II, pp. 122–23), a male guest states that he wishes his son would marry a "refined and cultured" girl like Zakiyya. Her father objects that Zakiyya is still young and that in any case she has expressed her desire not to marry until she has completed her university studies.

On two occasions when her brother is sick, Zakiyya takes a more aggressive stance, insisting on calling a doctor, while her mother thinks only to propose, for example, a glass of warm milk (I, pp. 22–23, 114–15). The two females of Abu Dhabi are acting out a variant on a classic scenario. The traditional mother eschewing the physician in favor of folk remedies is almost a topos in the contemporary Arab and Third World.[19] The new element is the younger female as bearer of science and progress.

Ahmad ʿUmar regularly surveys his readers to find out what they like and dislike in his magazine. Zakiyya is one of the most popular characters in the *Mâjid* family, coming in second only to Kaslân (whom we will meet again below).[20] This popularity is extraordinary, since it is normally so easy to tire of the continual presentation of information, if not to resent this infallible know-it-all. Ahmad ʿUmar appeases such impatience by sometimes expressing it through other characters, girls who claim they knew the answers but forgot to raise their hands or who make use of Zakiyya's information to shine in class themselves. Humor here makes an effective psychological safety valve.

The series also avoids organizational repetition by narrativizing Zakiyya's speeches as much as possible and in a variety of ways. The audiences vary; they are either her young siblings and the family group, her female classmates (in or out of school), or even a television audience when she is interviewed through that medium. In some of the later strips, Zakiyya appears with other *Mâjid* stars: Mâjid himself, Kaslân, Captain Khalfân and Adjutant Fahmân, etc. Sometimes Zakiyya responds to a question from her siblings or classmates. At other times the subject is introduced from the television or newspaper, with Zakiyya completing the information. A discussion of Israeli atrocities is instigated when Zakiyya meets a new classmate from Kuwait. Zakiyya notes that the new girl's accent is not Kuwaiti, upon which the girl explains her Palestinian origin (II, pp. 46–47). On another occasion Zakiyya receives a letter from a Palestinian penpal from southern Lebanon (I, pp. 86–87). Zakiyya is more than a neutral *femme-récit*. She becomes emotionally involved, tearing up a letter to the United Nations in frustration and crying over the atomic destruction of Hiroshima (I, pp. 50–51, 58–59).

Perhaps even more important for the appeal of the series is the way in which international politics are intercalated with domestic ones. When Zakiyya's brother bullies her, she calls him a dictator, explaining only later the meaning of the term (I, pp. 10–11). The squabbling of her younger brother and sister reminds our learned heroine of the conflict between NATO and the Warsaw Pact (I, pp. 96–97). Such comparisons deride unacceptable forms of political behavior and always lead to a reconciliation within the family. The unfairness of the veto system in the U.N. Security Council is shown when Zakiyya tries to veto family plans (I, pp. 46–47). Some conflicts are taken more seriously. A discussion of Palestine is framed in a story of the desire of Zakiyya's younger brother for a new toy. The frame closes with the boy's selection of a toy gun over more peaceful playthings (I, pp. 20–21). Yet in another strip Zakiyya calls her brother's toy gun a noxious plaything and uses it as an *entrée en matière* for a discussion of the wastefulness of the international arms race (II, pp. 34–35).

The World according to Zakiyya

The world of Zakiyya thus is not without contradictions. It is organized around a number of geopolitical-ideological constructs. The series explains the world system as a competition between blocs, usually operating at the expense of smaller countries, some of whom have organized as the nonaligned movement.

But the planet is also divided between rich and poor, North and South. The developing nations remain poor because they lack the money to build industrial infrastructure, because they are only offered loans at exorbitant rates, and because many of them waste their money on consumer goods instead of investing it wisely (I, pp. 66–67). The fundamental injustice of the world situation is effectively intimated.

Superimposed on this dichotomy is another one, of East and West; not the United States versus the Soviet Union but the Occident versus the Orient—in contemporary terms, the imperialists versus the colonized. The entire Arab world, including even the Gulf states, fits easily within this second group. While the general *tiers-mondisme* of *Mâjid* would wish to identify the two exploited groups, the poor and the colonized, such a system would break down if applied to the United Arab Emirates. The *Mâjid* family is not poor. Zakiyya's notebook, for instance, is returned from a fellow student late—by the young girl's driver (I, pp. 40–41). Zakiyya's family takes vacations in Europe (II, pp. 86–87). The United Arab Emirates is treated as a developed country (at least implicitly), and Zakiyya forcefully urges her classmates to contribute money to African famine relief (I, pp. 126–27; II, pp. 110–11). Pan-Arabism, stretching from the rich states of the Gulf to the poorer central Arab lands, effects the union between the two dichotomies of East and West, on one hand, and of rich and poor, on the other.

In addition to general and scientific information, Zakiyya presents background information on Arab culture, often with an Arabian slant. We read about the famous pre-Islamic *Mu'allaqât*, or hanging odes, and the market of 'Ukâz, where poets recited their texts, but also about the Qur'ân (I, pp. 38–39, 60–61; II, pp. 90–91, 112–13). As this last example shows, Zakiyya presents information on Islam. In a story that has also circulated among Muslims in the United States, the series explains how the astronaut Neil Armstrong converted to Islam after discovering, during trips to Morocco and Egypt, that the words he had heard uncomprehendingly on the moon were the Muslim call to prayer (I, pp. 120–21).

The modern history of the Arabs is conceptualized in "Zakiyya al-Dhakiyya" essentially as resistance first to imperialism and then to Zionism. With imperialism, the Arabs have been successful, with Zionism, not yet so. Zakiyya explains the Italian invasion of Libya in 1911–12 and the unsuccessful resistance of ʿUmar al-Mukhtâr. Rather than ending on a note of defeat, however, she explains that the Libyan revolution eventually freed the country of the Italian occupiers (II, pp. 50–51). No mention is made of the role in this of the Second World War or the actions of the Allies. Similarly, the discussion of the Suez War of 1956 argues that it was Egyptian resistance on the ground that forced the withdrawal of the French, British, and Israeli forces (I, pp. 76–77). Again the actions of the Great Powers, like the compromises accepted by Nasser's government, are glossed over. *Mâjid* presents a uniform pattern: native resistance produces imperial evacuation. This historical mythification (Ahmad ʿUmar understands the relations between international and local forces) has more behind it than simply stimulating patriotic pride. Its implications for Palestine are clear. Even Nasser's military defeats are turned into eventual victories. After the 1967 defeat, the Egyptian leader was able to so strengthen his country's army as to make possible the 1973 victory (I, pp. 16–17). Thus does Ahmad ʿUmar move the credit for the October War from the ledger of his enemy Sadat to that of his hero Nasser.

As anti-imperialists, the Arabs are not alone. Zakiyya takes a swipe at racist-inspired prejudices in a strip on the Mau Mau rebellion. Her younger brother frightens her by running around accoutered as a naked savage—a brief skirt, a spear, and a large mask—while shouting "Mau Mau." He then explains that his schoolmates told him that the Mau Mau were cannibals. Zakiyya explains that they were courageous fighters against British imperialism and that the first president of the independent state of Kenya, Jomo Kenyatta, was one of them (I, pp. 36–37).

Imperialism includes Zionism. Zakiyya's survey of the Israel-Palestine issue reflects standard Arab views. Palestine was an Arab land in which Jews, Christians, and Muslims lived together in peace until the Zionists colonized it after the 1917 Balfour Declaration (I, pp. 20–21). Only toward the end of the strip are the occupiers of Palestine referred to as Jews. The basis of the Zionists' historical claim and their reason for choosing Palestine are left unmentioned. Nor does the second argument for the legitimacy of the state of Israel (and the one most commonly used in the West), the Holocaust, receive any support from Zakiyya. On the contrary, the horrors of Nazism become a weapon against the Jewish state. Zakiyya explains that what Menachem Begin has done to the Palestinians in camps in southern Lebanon is exactly the same as what Hitler had done in his concentration camps years before. What were these camps? They were places where Hitler imprisoned his political opponents and where he killed many with machine guns and poison gas. After the war, hundreds of thousands of bodies were found (I, pp. 86–87). In a discussion about Rudolf Hess, Zakiyya's father declares that the Nazi deserves his imprisonment. Zakiyya agrees but insists that there are others who deserve it too, the terrorists Ariel Sharon and Begin, who also caused thousands of deaths (II, pp. 92–93). Israeli crimes are liberally denounced: the siege of Beirut, the burning of al-Aqsâ Mosque, the destruction of Arab villages and the murder of their inhabitants. After a story on the Mafia which discusses its activities in Italy and the United States, Zakiyya notes that there is a gang in the Middle East of two million people who occupy land, invade Lebanon, etc. — Israel, the biggest gang in history (II, pp. 68–69).

Camp David is never mentioned (under the circumstances a courtesy to the Egyptian government) but Zakiyya's position on negotiations is clear. What was taken by force can only be recovered by force (II, pp. 16–17). The weakness of the Arabs lies in their disunity, and the need for Arab unity is a topos in "Zakiyya al-Dhakiyya." In one story, Zakiyya adds up the numbers of men and machines on both sides to show that the Arabs would win if they could ever come together. Look how well they did in 1973 with the cooperation of only Egypt and Syria, she argues, forgetting the dismal results of 1967, when three Arab governments were directly involved (II, pp. 120–21). One senses a mounting frustration and anger as the 1980s advance, perhaps due in part to the Israeli incursion into Lebanon. The fighting in Lebanon, like that between Iran and Iraq, benefits only Israel, Zakiyya explains (II, pp. 54–55).

Zakiyya's view of the United States is scarcely more positive, though her attention to the gap between image and reality puts a distinctive spin on it. It is also a recognition, particularly appropriate in a comic strip, of U.S. dominance in the international market of images. An episode explaining how the Native Americans were unfairly deprived of their land begins with the children watching a movie western in which the Indians are bought off with trinkets (I, pp. 18–19). Zakiyya's discussion of the Oscars ends with the opinion that the United States would never give one to an Arab artist (I, pp. 56–57). (No mention is made of Omar Sharif's success in the U.S. cinema.) The United States is also the land of racism, and one strip is even devoted to the Ku Klux Klan (I, pp. 62–63; II, pp. 38–39). The relation between *Mâjid*'s anti-Americanism and Middle Eastern realities shows through in a strip entitled "The Politics of Deceit and Treachery." As Zakiyya is explaining the meaning of the term *Machiavellism* on television, her father is reading the newspaper at home. The headline reads: "America seeks to establish peace in the Middle East" (I, pp. 30–31).

Illustrating Zakiyya: Icon and Hieroglyph

Zakiyya's words are often angry. But they are not her only weapon. The series makes frequent use of photographs. These are chosen by Ahmad ʿUmar, largely from the *Ittihâd* archives, and inserted directly into the strips.[21] Though this mixed-media procedure is not unique to "Zakiyya al-Dhakiyya" or *Mâjid*, no other comic strip uses it as extensively or with such clear ideological intent.

Photographs stand out visually and break the code of the comic strip. The drawn figures, the speech balloons, the explanatory texts are, of course, fictions. The reader accepts that they represent people and conversations. It is perfectly possible to introduce photographs within this fiction, as is done, for example, in some French historical strips. In a biography of Charles de Gaulle, the father-narrator makes his point by showing "photos" to his sons. But the text shows these "photos" as drawn images.[22] The "photo" comes from and stays within the fictional world of the strips. Not so with Zakiyya. Her photos come from the "real" world outside the strip. Their ideological function is to establish a second level of proof. Words can lie. Drawn images need not represent reality. But the dominant fiction of the photograph is its self-evident truth.

In a discussion of the Falasha Jews of Ethiopia, Zakiyya brandishes a photo which becomes its own frame (II, pp. 124–25). It is proof, she says, that the Israelis are lying. They say the Falashas are starving. One can see from the photo that they are not (fig. 9.6).

9.6. Zakiyya uses photographs: the Falashas.

Semiotically, the photo is an icon, since the signifier is an image of its signified. But these photos become icons in another sense: as manifestations, virtual incarnations, of truth and as visual and ideological foci of the strips. Their placement or arrangement can carry its own message. The charge that Begin's actions are as bad as those of Hitler is illustrated by a striking diptych: similar photos of Begin and Hitler next to one another (I, pp. 86–87). Visual juxtaposition equals ideological juxtaposition.

Most of the time, Zakiyya does not bring the photographs herself. They simply illustrate her words, doubling the linguistic with an iconic message, as in the pictures of Begin and Hitler. Nevertheless, having introduced the photo as an insertion from the "real" world (the world of national and international politics) into the fictional world of Zakiyya, the authors of the strip then turn around and relink the two worlds by visually combining the photographic-external with the drawn-internal. The strip on the pan-Islamicist anti-imperialist Jamâl al-Dîn al-Afghânî includes portrait-photos of the famous man, as one would expect. But there is also a drawn frame, green with black lines, showing Egyptian intellectuals at a café. Al-Afghânî's head is pink, like the pink of the photo in the register above and with a form copied from that photo and distinct from the stylized representations of the other figures. The historical al-Afghânî of the photo is inserted into the drawn al-Afghânî of the strip, uniting the two (I, pp. 110–11). Such a device seeks to occult the distance between referent and sign inherent in all representation.[23] In the same strip, al-Afghânî's call to Egyptian peasants to revolt is illustrated through a speech balloon that extends from the mouth of a photo to the preceding frame, a drawing of an Egyptian peasant tilling the soil (fig. 9.7).

9.7. *Photos and drawings combined: al-Afghânî calls on Egyptian peasants to revolt.*

The photos often reach out to touch the private world of Zakiyya herself. U.S. hypocrisy is illustrated by a double-frame montage (I, pp. 64–65). The right frame contains two photos of African Americans, abused or in tears. On the left, Zakiyya describes the situation. A cut-out photo of the Statue of Liberty is superimposed on the two frames with its arm thrust into the frame of Zakiyya and a classmate (fig. 9.8).

9.8. *Comic strip and montage: race relations in the U.S.*

The ultimate involvement of our young heroine comes in a strip on the atomic bomb (I, p. 51). A frame comprises a photo of a mushroom cloud, next to which Zakiyya has been drawn in, over the photo. Her figure is left in outline, so that the photo shows through her. She is frightened and seems to be trying to run away. The text had been explaining that hundreds of thousands were killed in the bombings of Hiroshima and Nagasaki, and the little girl from the United Arab Emirates, becomes, at least potentially, one of the victims (fig. 9.9).

9.9. *Photo and drawing: Zakiyya threatened by the atomic bomb.*

But the importance of a subject for the Arab collective memory does not necessarily dictate the availability of photographs. Zakiyya's rendition of the Dinshawây incident, in which Egyptians and British authorities clashed over the deaths of a peasant woman and a British soldier, uses no photos. Instead, Hijâzî has provided sketches of the main events (I, pp. 116–17). The Egyptian artist uses a similar technique in the discussion of the Ku Klux Klan (II, pp. 38–39). A black man wishes to marry a white woman, Zakiyya explains, introducing the subject. The rest of the story is told with drawings alone. In four eloquent frames, we see first an interracial wedding, then a hooded Klansman holding a rifle, then the rifle firing, and last, the white bride bending over her black groom as blood spurts from his chest and the wedding flowers are scattered on the ground (fig. 9.10). "And the wedding became a funeral," Zakiyya concludes in her own frame. Relating this crime without the use of words adds to its dramatic force, as in the cinematic technique of suddenly cutting the sound behind a powerful visual scene.

In this series there are three main types of drawn frames: (1) those which imitate the detail and the monochrome of photographs, whose authenticity they are attempting to imitate; (2) the colored line drawings of Zakiyya and her world; and (3) the colored line drawings of historical incidents or other subjects evoked by Zakiyya. These last are more crowded than the drawings of Zakiyya and her friends. The details, used to signify historical or geographical context as well as action, suggest a more

9.10. *Without words: the Ku Klux Klan in action.*

complicated political world, in contrast with the simpler world of Zakiyya, her friends, family, and schoolmates (fig. 9.11).

Some of Hijâzî's illustrative drawings become true hieroglyphs. Rather than picturing a scene more or less naively, Hijâzî draws on his cartoonist repertoire to create constructed images that signify an idea. The notion of Zionists coming from around the world to Palestine is shown in two frames. In one, a group of men are superimposed below a map of the world. In another, a boat is filled with a pyramid of European men, each shown by a head and black hat. The idea of dictatorship as a denial of the rights of free expression accompanies a rhythmic, virtually geometric frame. Eight repeated images show the head and shoulders of an unhappy man with his hand over his mouth in a gesture of silence (fig. 9.12). The repetition functions visually like those in many a Warhol design. Even more abstract is a pictorialization of racial injustice: two groups of round faces, the white ones all smiling, the black all frowning (I, p. 63).

Such cartoons do more than bring complicated political ideas down to a concrete level where they can be understood by children. By avoiding individual representation, they show politics as an affair of masses, in line, of course, with Hijâzî's leftist views. Since Hijâzî, unlike Georges Bahgory for example, is not highly skilled as a portraitist, his simplified interchangeable figures turn a potential weakness into a strength.

A more traditional political image graces a discussion of the Statue of Liberty (I,

9.11. *Zakiyya narrates history: British soldiers kill an Egyptian woman in the Dinshawây incident.*

9.12. *A hieroglyph for dictatorship.*

pp. 64–65). Zakiyya's teacher had asked the class to draw this famous symbol. But Zakiyya rejects the traditional iconography — the United States is a land that supports the Israelis in southern Lebanon and oppresses its own blacks. She draws her own version of the statue: blindfolded and carrying a large studded club (fig. 9.13). In the

9.13. *The Statue of Liberty as seen by Zakiyya.*

discussion of the Falasha (II, pp. 124–25), when Zakiyya explains that the Israelis train these new immigrants to hate the Arabs, Hijâzî's drawing shows a young black boy being led to a punching bag by an adult Israeli. On the punching bag is the image of an Arab with stereotypical headdress (fig. 9.14). The association of punching bag and holy war, implicit in the poster day-in-the-life-of-a-young-Muslim,[24] is here made explicit.

Image and Reciprocity: Travel

''Zakiyya'' raises the issue of the gap between image (especially politically inter-

9.14. *Falasha children taught to hate the Arabs.*

ested image) and reality, but only as regards Western images of non-Western peoples. This is of course familiar ground to contemporary scholarship, both in and out of the Arab world. And travel narratives have played a central role as purveyors of Western images of the world and as the loci for the exposure or criticism of such images.[25]

Mâjid, in its own way, does the reverse. Probably more than any other Arab children's magazine, *Mâjid* uses travel narratives as a way of acquainting its readers with the world. The voyages of the Mâjidian personalities are fiction. Another specificity: designed specifically for children, they speak as much to their special preoccupations as they do of the world and its diversity. Perhaps most important, the travel narratives of *Mâjid* take the problem of the image of the Other farther than does "Zakiyya al-Dhakiyya." Her photos are the final word, the guarantors of truth. The travel stories, by contrast, open into another world, the world of reciprocity, in which the problem of images and prejudices can cut in both directions.

A Camel Abroad

One of the earliest travel narratives to appear in the magazine is that of the trip of Sâbir the camel (*sâbir* means "patient") and his master to London. Sâbir and his friend are the heroes of a series of stories in which two thematics are interwoven. In the first, Sâbir is the child. The second evokes the phenomenon that one can call "Badawiyya fî Rômâ," after the series of Muhammad Salmân films starring Samîra Tawfîq in which a daughter of the desert is lost in the modern city.[26] This thematic, dear to many contemporary Arab authors, permits a psychological negotiation between tradition and modernity.[27]

Travel poses many problems for our Arabian camel. Aboard ship, he gets seasick, and in England he falls ill from the cold, to which he is so unaccustomed (1979, nos. 19 and 24). Arriving in London, the two Arabians run into a dishonest taxi driver who demands the then enormous price of fifty pounds (in English in the text) to take them into town (1979, no. 23). In the British capital, Sâbir, who turns out to be strong-willed, refuses the classic tourist itinerary and only shows an interest in things connected to his native country. He speaks to the camels in the zoo and wants to visit the British Museum to consult documents on the history of Arabia (1979, no. 28). While these actions show an exclusive concern with the self, they also carry a flavor of post-imperial resentment. The camels are locked in the zoo and the history of Arabia is enclosed in the British Museum.

As a camel, Sâbir is a wonderful symbol, linking the Arab with the Arabian. In a separate story, Sâbir knocks down the sign of a new supermarket (intrusive modernity). When he is tried for his crimes, our camel is acquitted because the sign was in English, not in Arabic as it should have been (1986, no. 362).

More clearly pedagogical is the series of trips undertaken by Mâjid, Sindibâd, and a bird, Yasmîna, with the aid of a magic carpet. Of this trio, it is Yasmîna who asks the questions like a curious child, Mâjid who provides information on the modern world, and Sindibâd who, appropriately enough, represents the classical tradition (e.g., 1979, nos. 18–19; 1980, no. 49).

The three fly around the Arab world noting the cultural or geographical virtues of the lands they visit. Their journeys also provide the opportunity for an apology of Islam. We are treated, for example, to an explicit defense of the practice of cutting off the hands of thieves. But one senses that the subject is a troublesome one. The thief in question is pardoned by his victim and is spared the Qur'ânic punishment (1979, no. 18). This is certainly not reciprocity, but behind the apology lurks the Other's vision.

Kaslân Jiddan

The most sophisticated travel narrative is without doubt that of Kaslân Jiddan, the favorite personality among the readers of *Mâjid* whose name means "very lazy."[28] Kaslân's popularity stems from his character, created by Ahmad ʿUmar and drawn by Mustafâ Rahma. A bit lazy but gay and enthusiastic, Kaslân regularly encounters problems as the price of his ill-conceived efforts. He is a child clumsily trying to play the adult.

Kaslân wins his trip on a televised game show. He visits India, Bali, Hong Kong, Japan, New York, and London. The choice of locations is interesting: no Arab countries and only one Muslim country, which is not treated as such. The countries themselves divide into two groups: those of the non-Arab East and those of the Anglophone West.

This division permits us to redefine our idea of the Other, since, as we shall see, there are two zones of alterity which receive different treatment and which can be called the Orient and the Occident, East and West. Such a binarism dissolves the classic division between East and West by putting the Arab world in the center between these two antipodes. By the same token, the Arab world remains available as a reference for normality or nonalterity.

Kaslân in the East

From India to Japan what Kaslân finds is a land of exoticism. With the exception of a small quantity of information transmitted in writing, all we see is a rather traditional Asia where people dress and eat differently. In effect, cuisine and clothing dominate the adventures of our hero in the Orient.

Arriving in Bombay, his first spot, Kaslân discovers that the airline has lost his baggage; it is a rather banal episode, but one which provides the occasion for a game of disguise and identity. Without his personal effects, Kaslân tells himself that he must buy the clothing of the country. His voyage begins with a lack which provokes a change, if not a loss, of identity.

Kaslân dresses, thus, as an Indian, but not as a typical Indian, that is, not like the ordinary Indians that one sees in the strip. Instead, Kaslân becomes the stereo-type Indian, donning the robes and turban of a maharajah. In each new country, Kaslân wears a new costume, always more stereotypical than truly typical. The process is perhaps clearest in the United States. Our hero arrives in clothing that we could classify as neutral or Western: ordinary pants and shirt. But the first thing he does is to go straight to his hotel, change his clothing, and show himself in the streets of New York outfitted like a cowboy from a movie western.

This choice of stereotyped uniforms has curious effects. The first, almost para-doxical, is to distinguish Kaslân from his environment. The inhabitants of the coun-tries he visits are always dressed in a manner that is appropriate but less singular or glaring. In Japan, for example, Kaslân wears a kimono while the other Japanese males appear in Western dress. (The women, on the other hand, are drawn in kimonos, but we know that women are often made to fill the role of symbolic representation.) In-dians are shown in a realistic variety of outfits, but never, of course, in the outfit of a maharajah. Thus Kaslân never really adopts the dress of the countries he frequents; he does not take on the local identity. His position is an intermediate one, represent-ing not the reality of the country but its symbol or exotic manifestation.

The representation of exoticism becomes almost conscious in a frame that takes place in India. With a group of tourists (who look rather Western), Kaslân takes a guided tour. Like the others, he looks, he takes photographs. But all at once the po-sitions are reversed (p. 10). The crowd of tourists stares at Kaslân, who is charming snakes with a horn (fig. 9.15). With his mahajarah's costume, Kaslân is able to replace

9.15. *Kaslân as snake charmer.*

the Indian as a touristic representation of exoticism. The reader may also remember that some Arab countries have their own snake charmers.

Certainly Kaslân's vestimentary singularization strengthens a bit the good-na-tured mockery inherent in his character. (These costumes call to mind the humorously glaring disguises of Dupond and Dupont in *Tintin*.)[29] But our hero's situation can also be understood as a commentary on the impossibility of completely assuming the identity of the Other, or even as an ironic allusion to the famous European travelers of past centuries who disguised themselves as Arabs or Muslims. This recognition of a certain opacity of the Other is the beginning of reciprocity.

But Kaslân's problems are not merely vestimentary. Exotic cuisines (and table manners) provide their own challenges. In India, with his typical childish enthusiasm, Kaslân throws himself on a cake, only to discover to his great surprise that it is filled with hot pepper. He screams and drinks enormous quantities of water. The Indian apologizes, explaining that it is the custom of his country to put red pepper in cakes. In Hong Kong the Arab child tries to eat with chopsticks. The result: a piece of food flies off his plate and breaks a lamp on the ceiling. On the plane from Japan to New York he has to refuse a meal containing pork.

Kaslân has other misadventures in the East, but they are equally physical. In Hong Kong he insists on rowing in place of a lady but only gets himself knocked overboard. In Japan, to be polite, he bows so often that he gets a backache.

Kaslân in the West

When Kaslân leaves Japan for the United States, he crosses a crucial frontier. The nature of his trip changes, dominated now by the ideas of consciousness and reciprocity. The transformation begins during the flight itself (pp. 20–21). A young American boy (whose mother wears a low-cut dress) is surprised by Kaslân's refusal to eat a meal containing pork and asks our hero why he will not eat that meat. Kaslân replies that he is a Muslim and that pork is forbidden because it comes from an animal that eats garbage and whose organs carry parasitic worms.

This is a key discussion. To begin with, it is the first time that Kaslân acts as a Muslim. In neither India nor Indonesia did he visit mosques. And in other countries, the problem of *halâl*, or ritually proper, food never arose. When Kaslân enters the realm of the West, his identity as a Muslim (and, as we shall see, as an Arab as well) comes to the fore.

But the frame in question opens a process that is none other than that of the discovery of reciprocity. Thus, too, it has an unusual form (fig. 9.16). Each of the two speech balloons is placed above the heads of one of the children— not above the child who speaks it, but above the other, forcing the tails of the balloons to cross over the heads of the two speakers. Needless to say, there is no visual necessity in such an arrangement. It would have been far easier to place each balloon over the head of its appropriate speaker. This crossing is the visual sign of the relationship which is going to develop between the two children.

The American mother asks Kaslân where he comes from. When he answers, "The Emirates, in the Arab Gulf," the other little boy exclaims that that is the land of oil and asks if everyone there rides camels. "So that's the way you imagine the Arabs," replies Kaslân, "only oil and camels." He goes on to explain that his country is

9.16. *Reciprocity: Kaslân and
the American child
discover one another.*

beautiful and modern and that camels are only used for races. The idea of stereotypes, never clearly expressed when Asians were involved, is introduced with the Western image of the Arabs.

But the process continues. The film shown on the plane turns out to be a western, and Kaslân asks if all Americans dress like cowboys. "Oh, no," answers the other child, "only in films." "I know, I know," protests Kaslân, adding that when he was small, he thought that all Americans wore cowboy suits.

Reciprocity is now complete. An exchange of prejudices has led to an exchange of knowledge. Everyone understands that alterity and the prejudices it generates are inversible.[30] However, a hint of anti-American criticism remains. Kaslân observes, without being contradicted, that the hero of the western has already killed at least a hundred people.

In the West, reciprocity, child of the Western vision of the Arab world, is accompanied by the presence of the self (that is, of the Arab) within the Other, a presence which did not exist in South and East Asia. In New York, Kaslân hears people speaking Arabic in the street. His new American friend explains to him that there are Arabs in New York and that they live in Brooklyn (p. 23). In London, Kaslân visits a wax museum (p. 25). A frame shows him standing alone in front of a statue of Nasser, while hearts emanate from the head of the young man, an emotional identification with the Egyptian leader in the British capital. The possibility of an identification between person and statue is underlined by the mistake of a young Arab girl who takes Kaslân for his own wax figure.

Kaslân's Geography

Like Sâbir the camel, Kaslân finds the Arab world inside the West. Of course, he finds other things as well: Hyde Park, skyscrapers, the Statue of Liberty. But there is a consistency between these two travel narratives. It is only in the West that the Arab becomes the object of another person's vision. In the countries of non-Arab Asia, the "Orient" of Kaslân, exoticism is univocal and unidirectional. India and Japan become loci of strangeness and foreignness. Is Kaslân's vision truthful? The question is not even posed. Still less are we told the vision which the inhabitants of these countries might have of the native land of our young traveler. Asia remains the land of an exoticism without complexes. Reciprocity only appears in the West. Why? Most probably because the power of Western civilization gives an importance to its image of the Arabs. This would explain the choice of countries. Great Britain is the former colonial power of both the Egypt of Ahmad ʿUmar and the Emirates of Kaslân. The United States is the new hegemonic power in the region.

Reciprocity thus is real, as is the praiseworthy attack on prejudice. But both remain defensive, directed toward the West and imperfectly integrated into the visions of South and East Asia. One could argue that this difference is linked to the *tiers-mondisme* of the magazine. Since there are no conflicts between the Arabs and their Asian brothers, there is no place for cultural misunderstanding. But the comical misadventures of Kaslân in the East, which are not repeated either in London or in New York, where our traveler displays a complete mastery of circumstances, tell us otherwise. The Orient is quite certainly the Other, but an Other where the game of exoticism can be played without real risk. *Mâjid*'s world only hints at universality. Its true locus is Arabism.

10

Bilingual Politics:
The Algerian Strip

Algeria has a vigorous comic-strip literature: talented and experienced artists and scenarists, cultural openness to the comic-strip form, a thriving publishing industry. But Algerian strips are almost invisible in the rest of the Arab world (though some show up in Tunisia and Morocco). The reason? Algeria's production, Arab though it is, is dominated by French. There are Arabic Algerian comic-strip magazines, but the most significant children's periodicals have been in the language of the colonial master. In addition, as in France, the comic-strip album (with its focus on youthful and even young adult audiences) has tended to be more important than the children's magazine. In neighboring Tunisia, by contrast, it was children's magazines (and in Arabic) that held pride of place. Most of the increasingly available Algerian Arabic-language comic-strip albums are translated from Francophone originals.

French forms accompany the French language. By their visual styles and to a considerable degree their stripological sophistication, Algerian comics are far closer to European (especially French) comic-strip styles than any of their cousins in other Arab countries.

Algeria's history has given a high charge to linguistic issues. Though the Arabization of precolonial Algeria was modest compared with the countries of the Mashriq, Arabic was the unique language of literacy. French colonialism actively disrupted the Arabic-based indigenous educational institutions while teaching French to a tiny native elite. French was also the language of administration and of the substantial Pied Noir (or European-origin) minority. The result: except for a small group trained in the religious sciences (who usually had to go to Tunisia to study), literate Arab Algerians read and wrote in French while speaking their native Algerian dialect of Arabic. Berbers, whether or not they knew French, frequently had no knowledge of Arabic at all.

The war of liberation was fought in the name of Arabism and Islam. And the Algerian government has, since independence in 1962, pushed the increasing Arabization of the educational system; but this has been most effective at the lower, and hence nonelite, levels. In recent years the burgeoning Islamist movement, one of the most vigorous in the region, has demanded the replacement of French by Arabic. Partly forced and partly as preemption, the government of Chadli Benjedid pushed its own more modest, but still controversial, Arabization program.

By setting comics in French (or less often in Arabic), the Algerian artist or scenarist makes a potent choice, whether or not he or she admits its consequences, in terms of audience and cultural identification. (A similar situation obtains with the largely Francophone Algerian novel.) In Tunisia, comics are a major force for secular Arabization. In Algeria, they are both linguistic battlefield and bastion of Francophonia.

Between French and Arabic

There are Algerian Arabic-language comic-strip periodicals. In 1985 the National Union of Algerian Youth, acting under the authority of the FLN—the Front de Libération Nationale, till recently the official party of this one-party state—began an Arabic-language children's periodical very similar to those published in other Arab states. Entitled *Riyâd* (sometimes vocalized as Rayyâd), the magazine serves the government's scouting program and pushes an appropriate ideology.

If the scouts in *Riyâd* have strong similarities with their Syrian cousins of *al-Talî'î*, the Algerian magazine's treatment of the Arabic language is quite distinctive. *Riyâd*'s strips are either fully or very heavily vocalized, which would fit a pedagogical model designed to introduce proper Arabic to children. Yet, while some stories are in *fushâ*, others are in Algerian dialect and still others in a mixture of the two. A lack of ease with written Arabic also becomes visible. In early numbers the Arabic was written after the frames and balloons had been drawn, producing ill-designed and sometimes barely readable balloons (see fig. 10.1). In later numbers the Arabic text was typed and inserted, with somewhat more satisfactory results. The Arabic versions of otherwise visually sophisticated albums often contain half-empty speech balloons (fig. 10.2).[1] Such difficulties are virtually unknown in the strips of other Arab lands.

Francophone magazines are both older and more plentiful. *Jeunesse-Action*, with its offshoots, *M'Cid* and *Djeha*, is a product of the national secretariat of the FLN youth organization. *Tarik*, also in French, begun in 1979, was published by the Musée National du Moudjahid. Arabic for "one who participates in a holy war," the term *moudjahid* is especially used in Algeria to refer to the combatants of the war of national liberation.[2]

Jeunesse-Action advertises itself as the first comic-strip periodical (*illustré*) printed in Algeria and as a "political" magazine. Not surprisingly, the political line is clear.

10.1. *Above: Balloons and lettering that do not match in an animal story for children.*

10.2. *Left: Balloons and lettering that do not match in a historical strip for young adults.*

The United States, Britain, Israel, South Africa, and a few other countries (but not France) are listed among "Les Douze Salopards" (1971, no. 4). Since this is the phrase by which the Hollywood movie *The Dirty Dozen* was translated into French, the reference both exploits and mocks the cultural power of U.S. media.

Probably the most famous of Algerian children's magazines has been an unofficial one, *M'Quidèch*, which ran from 1969 to 1973 (and irregularly after 1978)[3] and acted as an artistic nursery for many of Algeria's most talented artists and scenarists. Along with the brief *Tarik* (which shared many of its artists), *M'Quidèch* featured a high level of verbal wit along with social characterizations bordering frequently on satire. Strips and characters which started in these two magazines often became the bases of later albums.[4]

The language of most Francophone strips is an Algerian French, spiced with words or phrases in Algerian Arabic. When added to the tendency of many Arabic-language strips to hesitate between dialect and literary, this creates a typically Algerian linguistic instability—and corresponding room for semiotic play. In an adventure album by Ramzi Rafik, the Algerian secret-agent hero finds himself in Jordan being questioned by a Palestinian fighter.[5] Up till this point everyone in the album has spoken in French, with the few Arabic words in Roman characters (Hebrew is suggested by using characters imitating the block print of formal printed Hebrew). But the Arab freedom fighter speaks Arabic. More important, he uses Arabic characters (fig. 10.3). He switches quickly to French,

10.3. *Arabic letters in a French language environment: the Palestinian questions the Algerian secret agent.*

but the Arabic letters become a sign of arrival in an exotic locale—like the use of Arabic or Chinese characters in a Western series such as *Tintin*.[6] The Palestinian's Arabic question could have been rendered in Roman characters. Arabic script indicates that this is the Mashriq, where Arabic is written (and read) as well as just spoken.

French in an Arabo-Islamic environment also permits bilingual puns and play on Arabic names of a kind usually associated with Western strips. In *Tarik* (1979, no. 1), a story by Rachid Taibi features an animal character named Ali Gator.[7] The two most important evil characters in Malek's witty and sophisticated *La Route du Sel*, are the Qadi (or judge) Bou F'tou, and the governor Ben Efis. Bou F'tou is *bouffe-tout* (eats all), and Ben Efis is *bénéfice* (profit)—comical commentaries on the venality of the two personnages.[8]

Commerce and Its Tricks

The adolescent or young adult focus of so many of Algeria's strips goes with large doses of social humor and verbal games. In a story by Lamine with drawings by Rahmoun, the young hero, M'Quidèch, foils a "charlatan," a kind of Algerian itinerant snake-oil salesman (fig. 10.4). The trickster distributes a laughing potion to gull-

10.4. *M'Quidèch and the laughing potion.*

ible villagers so that his men can rob them while they are disabled by hysterical laughter. The text is full of wisecracks and puns on laughter and hard times (1971, no. 17).

For *Tarik* and later in an album called *Histoires pour rire*, Mahfoud Aïder created the character of Kalitousse Lazhar.[9] This greedy unlucky trickster, with the girth and fez of a member of the merchant class, is always trying to con money out of his gullible fellow citizens (fig. 10.5). The story's end finds our hero either robbed, beaten, or arrested. Lazhar's most frequent con is fortune-telling, a racket he got into when he accidentally found himself in the empty chapel of a *marabout*. A *marabout* is a Sûfî saint, popularly considered to have miraculous powers and a major figure in the religious landscape of the Maghrib. In one story, Kalitousse impersonates the *marabout* whose chapel he has occupied. In another, he competes with an existing divine, Si Djaoui (*Histoires*, pp. 3–19). As in the story of M'Quidèch and the charlatan, popular

10.5. *The merchant as trickster: Kalitousse Lazhar.*

healers, magicians, and the like are cast in negative terms, reflecting the modernizing ideology both of most strips and of the FLN.

There is more to Mr. Lazhar than folk religion. His cheerful greed draws less from the traditional miser portrayed in the Syrian *Usâma* than from images of mercantile capitalism. In a brief set of strips, our hero speaks in the name "du Pèze, du Flousse et du Saint Bénéfice" (*Tarik* 1979, no. 1). *Pèze* is French slang for money, dough; *flousse* is Arabic for money; and the *saint-bénéfice* is the holy profit. The triad is also a play on *le Père, le Fils et le Saint Esprit* (Father, Son, and Holy Spirit), a joke which presupposes a knowledge not just of French but also of Christianity, something much more rare in Algeria. Equally Western is the title of an episode, "Autant en emporte le vent," the French translation of *Gone with the Wind* (*Histoires*, p. 5).

Swipes at the black market and profiteering are common in Mahfoud Aïder's and other series. A speculator wants to know if he can raise his prices. *"Pénuriste"* (one who exploits shortages) is flung as an insult (*Histoires*, p. 11). The trickster anti-hero of ʿAbd al-Halîm Riyâd's *Mukhâtarât Muhtâl* (Risks of a Scoundrel) tries to sell bananas on the black market. His schemes, like those of Lazhar, eventually turn against him.[10] A Kalitousse Lazhar story is entitled "Hubbak Nâr Yâ Dînâr" (loosely, Love of Money is the Root of All Evil). A socialist hostility to the market joins with an attack on religious hypocrisy, since this was the story in which Lazhar competed with a local *shaykh*. The world of mercantile corruption is familiar to us from the work of the Egyptian Hijâzî.[11] Its evocation is more common, however, in Algerian strips than in those of any other Arab state.

War and the Hero

War and heroism are frequent topics in the strips of many Arab countries. In Algeria they take on a special color. Heroes are more singularized as individuals. They are also less frequently children, more often adults. This is partly due to the older audiences targeted by Algeria's comic-strip artists, but partly also to the Algerian emphasis on the war of national liberation and the struggle against French colonialism.

Algeria has also created an Arab superhero. A specialty of U.S. comic strips, the superhero is relatively rare in European production, as in that of the Arab world. The Algerian "Super Dabza" is the creation of ʿAbd al-Karîm Qâdirî (*Riyâd*, 1986, no. 5). This young hero fights a villain worthy of Superman: a mad scientist bent on taking over the world. Our hero flies by putting on a magical burnoose (fig. 10.6). This cloak-like outer garment is a family heirloom given to Dabza's ancestor by an angel to allow him to make the pilgrimage to Mecca. The magic of the burnoose, a traditional garment, is that of traditional religion, an attitude which contrasts with the attacks on popular credulity in other strips.

But our superhero also contains an unmistakable element of parody. The burnoose looks more like Superman's cape on the issue's cover. One is reminded just a bit of Lob, Gotlib, and Alexis's Superdupont, except that Super Dabza maintains his heroic status while Superdupont provides the occasion for a biting satire of French politics and society.[12]

A similar blend of satire and parody operates in two adventures of "Maachou, the Algerian Superman" (fig. 10.7) by the prolific artist and scenarist known as Slim (on whom more below). In one episode, a criminal lets fall a sack full of sheep parasites and rotten sardines which will poison thousands. Suspense builds as the superhero hesitates between catching the falling bag and going to buy a set of electric trains which have just been put on sale. We are treated to two endings. "The official version": Maachou catches the sack, saving the people; the "grapevine version": he buys

10.6. *Algerian superhero: Super Dabza.*

10.7. *Algerian superman: heroic or selfish.*

the trains.[13] In another story, Super Maachou is busy catching an Algerian about to eat during the Ramadân fast while a businessman is making sinister deals with foreign industrialists.[14]

Revolutionary *Turâth*

The bloody eight-year war through which Algeria wrested its independence from a reluctant France plays an outsized role in the strips of that North African country. It receives more attention than any historical event in the strips of other Arab countries. The war of liberation has been the principal legitimizing force of the FLN governments of independent Algeria. It was, after all, the FLN which started the war, rose to dominance during it, and carried it to a successful conclusion.

The commemoration of the war and its heroes takes up much of the space occupied by the cult of personality in other Arab states. The war (and a limited number of other episodes conceptually tied to it) virtually monopolizes the vision of history transmitted by Algerian comic strips and largely replaces the evocation of Arab historical and cultural heroes that we find in the strips of other countries. *Riyâd* describes a series of war stories with the telling phrase: "From the Revolutionary *Turâth*" (1985, no. 0).

Most distinctive in the Algerian war stories is their tendency to kill off the hero or leading protagonists. Mustapha Tenani's *Les Hommes du Djebel* (The Men of the Mountain) consists of three stories, in each of which the hero does not survive. In the first, he refuses to accept the help of his fellows in arms and dies fighting his French pursuers. In another, the hero who has assassinated a French policeman is executed after torture. In the third, the lone survivor of an attack on an FLN hideout is killed by French soldiers while engaged in a fistfight with the Algerian who betrayed his compatriots.[15]

In the *M'Cid* series, we see a Fellagha (the term used by both the French and the Arabs for the FLN fighters) captured and tortured to death when the neighborhood where he was hiding is surrounded by the French, thanks to a tip by an Algerian informer. In the stories in Guerroui's *Abnâ' al-Hurriyya* (The Sons of Liberty), either many troops or the heroes of the narratives themselves meet their deaths.[16]

Part of this can be chalked up to historical verisimilitude. The Arabs call the Algerian War the "Revolution of the Million Martyrs"[17] because of the heavy losses sustained by the local population.[18] But the dead also bear a message. They speak frequently of "sacrifice."[19] Their gestures will permit a free Algeria, the one enjoyed by the readers of the strips. This sacrifice remains essentially secular; the term *martyrdom* is rarely evoked.

This is not to say that other countries' strips do not speak of Arab deaths. They are a commonplace in the denunciation of Israeli atrocities in "Zakiyya," for example,[20] and various military heroes, from the Tunisian Jamîla to the Syrian ʿIsâ the Swimmer, met heroic deaths.[21] But in the war stories of other countries, Arab heroes are far more successful, at least taken individually. That is partly because many of them are children. The Algerian hero is almost always a man, even when the strips are clearly aimed at a juvenile audience. M'Cid, for example, is a child, but rather than being the hero in his series, he is more of a witness to the frequently fatal activities of his elders (*Jeunesse-Action*, 1971, no. 4; *M'Cid*).

History as Resistance

The war of liberation against the French, rather than being treated as an isolated episode, serves as a paradigm through which the rest of Algerian history is projected. The armed resistance of the Algerian people against French invasion and colonization is the leitmotif of the overwhelming majority of historical strips. From the battles of 1830 and the campaigns of ʿAbd al-Qâdir (national leader of resistance to the French invasion) through the revolts of the late nineteenth century and the social bandits of the 1930s,[22] a unified picture of modern Algerian history is drawn, one emphasizing the continuity and popular basis of resistance to foreign occupation of the national soil. This vision is an obvious counterhistory to the official Gallic version of Algeria as part of France and the 1954 revolt as a recent stirring of Arab nationalism.

Even individual albums set their episodes in the context of the long struggle. *Malhamat al-Shaykh Bû ʿImâma*, for example, traces the history of revolts from 1830 to 1879, when its story begins (pp. 9–13). Other albums provide extensive historical contextualization and interpretation. For Tenani, for example, Algeria in 1830 was a progressing society in the process of forming a national state (*Le Fusil chargé*, p. 7). In *La Ballade du proscrit*, Bouslah interrupts his strip text with long quotes from histories of modern Algeria, early nationalist newspapers, poems, etc. These passages both provide a broader political and economic context for the actions of his bandit-hero and serve as evidence for the verisimilitude of fictional incidents (e.g., pp. 22, 61).[23]

The model of national resistance is even extended to the struggles of Berber Numidia against Rome. The national soil is evoked, Roman settlement colonies are criticized, and local traitors are excoriated in terms that fit perfectly the war of 1954–62. One ancient nationalist even insists on the union of Mauritania, Numidia, and Africa, the ancient equivalents of Morocco, Algeria, and Tunisia (*M'Quidèch*, 1971, no. 17; *Jeunesse-Action*, 1971, no. 4; *M'Cid*). It goes without saying that this model of national resistance is used against European invaders from the north, not Arabs from the east.

This Algerian political line is all the clearer when compared with a comic-strip biography of the Roman client king, Juba II, prepared in French by the students of a French school in Meknes, Morocco. In this strikingly pro-Imperialist account, the monarch-hero happily serves the Romans, and his greatest concern seems to be to put down anti-Roman Berber revolts. The influence of the school's French faculty may have been decisive here, since the Moroccan guides at the nearby Roman ruins of Volubilis (the clear inspiration for the album) deal more harshly with the Roman occupation, speaking of the Berber "slaves" who served the Romans. No such relationships are hinted at in the comic strip.[24]

The Algerian pattern of anti-imperialist resistance invades other genres. Hankour's *Soloeïs* looks like a typical European fantasy album.[25] Local color is limited to the clothing of the hero and heroine. He wears traditional Arab garb. Her outfit, though it possesses the corporal explicitness normal for the genre, is bedecked with North African folkloric elements, such as the hand of Fâtima (fig. 10.8). These two figures (with the help of a local resistance group) liberate an island under the thumb of an evil machine and mercenaries controlled from "the super continent." As the album ends, the heroes prepare to liberate other oppressed peoples.

Heroes and Heroines

Soloeïs is unusual in its inclusion of a female protagonist who, while she is guided by her wiser male companion, plays an active role in destroying the evil machine. More typical in the strips of resistance and revolution is a male camaraderie of the sort exploited in Mohamed Lakhdar Hamîna's famous 1975 film of Algerian revolt, *Chronicle of the Years of Embers.*[26] Kenza and Christiane Achour justly complain of the limited role women play in these strips; in a large number they are absent, in others mere decor.[27] The two critics also provide a brief but trenchant critique of Amouri's *al-Durûb al-Wa'ra* (The Rugged Mountain Passes).[28] They note that the seemingly liberated female commando remains nameless, unlike her male counterparts, and that she disappears from view when the real fighting starts.[29] They could have added that her chief action in the story is to be saved from a land mine by a wiser male soldier (fig. 10.9) (*al-Durûb*, pp. 5–6).

There are stories of heroines, like one of a little girl who courageously brings medicine to the fighters (*Riyâd*, 1985, no. 8). But Kenza and Christiane Achour are right to stress the absence of the female in Algerian war strips. They are particularly indignant because they see this as contrary to the sociological reality of important female participation in the fight for national liberation. The critics close their discussion with a quote from Frantz Fanon.[30] Fanon was the FLN spokesman and anti-imperialist theoretician famous for, among other things, explaining how the participation by Algerian women in the national liberation struggle rescued them and their society from the traditional and patriarchal oppression of women.[31]

Even among male Algerians there are those who have found the postindependence reality far from the revolutionary promise. The Algerian cartoonist and comic-strip writer Kaci satirized this development in four wordless yet eloquent frames (fig. 10.10).[32] The first picture shows a girl in pigtails; the second, a slightly older school girl, her hair modestly veiled. The third image is that of the woman fighter with short hair and cap like the woman warrior of *al-Durûb al-Wa'ra*. The final picture, like the others framed and mounted on a wall, shows a mother and child. But the mother is completely swaddled in a traditional *haïk*, which hides her body, hair, and face. The woman as framed social object is allowed but a brief military vacation between the socially controlled roles of school girl and mother.

But how could this come about? Did not women's heroic activities fit them for more public roles in the new society?[33] The answer is provided in a pair of albums describing more recent struggles against international imperialism. *SM-15: Halte au*

10.8. Soloeïs: *science-fiction fantasy and North African tradition.*

10.9. *The woman soldier saved by her male comrade.*

"Plan" Terreur and *SM-15: Echec au "Plan Terreur"* by Ramzi Rafik[34] tell the story of a secret agent, Mourad Saber, who foils an Israeli plot to import U.S. ballistic missiles and upset the military balance of power in the region. Though the story is contemporary not historical, enough references are made to tie this adventure with the great war of liberation. An Israeli calls Mourad a *raton*, or little rat. This was a common term of abuse for Arabs used by the French in Algeria, and our hero grimly notes its familiarity (*Halte*, p. 33). On another occasion the secret agent explains that the uselessness of torture for those who believe in their cause was demonstrated by his compatriots in their struggle for liberation (*Echec*, p. 59).

10.10. *The life of the Algerian woman according to Kaci.*

SM-15 conforms to most of the rules of the secret-agent genre. The hero is intelligent and athletic and continually defies death. The villains (Israelis and their allies) laugh demonically when they think they have an Arab in their power. But a James Bond (or Malko Linge) should also be irresistably sexy.[35] Yet in the traditional wisdom of Islamic societies, such sexuality risks the creation of *fitna*, a kind of social chaos produced by the unbridled play of emotion.[36] This is exactly what happens in *SM-15*. A young woman virtually throws herself on the handsome Mourad. He rebuffs her advances, but not before the scene is misinterpreted by one of our hero's local allies who is enamoured of the girl. The jealous young man then turns the Arabs in to the local Zionist agents. Mourad manages to avoid the trap. He rescues everyone, and all returns to normal. Mourad forgives the woman and the man with a phrase encapsuling traditional attitudes: "Since the beginning of time, whenever a man has done something stupid, it has been because of a woman" (*Echec*, pp. 19–50).

The young woman, Asmaa, shows an un-Islamic cleavage (fig. 10.11), but it is

10.11. *The secret agent and the temptress.*

her dialogue with Mourad that is most revealing. The talk begins respectably enough when Asmaa tells Mourad that any woman would be honored to marry him. When Mourad argues that his life-style is hardly compatible with marriage, Asmaa notes that many women possess the courage necessary for such a life.

> Mourad: I know! I knew remarkable ones in my country during our war of liberation! But those were exceptional circumstances. In normal times it is woman's nature to fulfill herself in the bosom of the home among her children!
> Asmaa: How old-fashioned you are, Mourad! Ha! Ha! Ha! Ha!
> Mourad: If you call being old-fashioned to want everyone in society to occupy the place

that is destined for him, then, yes, I am old-fashioned! It is man's job to protect and feed his family. Thank God this has not yet gone out of fashion!

It is at this point that the temptress makes her move. He asks her to take her hands off him.

> Asmaa: Oh! Mourad . . . we are no longer in the Middle Ages. What about the liberation of the Muslim woman?
> Mourad: Aren't you confusing liberation and license?

With the argument comes the demonstration. Asmaa kisses Mourad passionately, validating traditional wisdom on the separation of men's and women's roles (*Echec*, pp. 19–20).

Slim

These issues are writ larger in the work of Algeria's best-known comic-strip artist, Menouar Merabtene, known as Slim. The author of numerous albums which circulate in Algeria, France, and even some circles in the United States, Slim writes humorous but political strips for an adult audience. Much of his work consists of barely narrativized sets of five to sixteen frames which function almost as political cartoons, often like those of the American Jules Feiffer. These strips paint a picture of a corrupt society beset by shortages (especially in housing), served by arrogant bureaucrats and a mendacious press.[37]

But Slim is best known for his fictional character Bouzid, whose adventures have been collected in three volumes under the label *Zid Ya Bouzid*.[38] Bouzid, from the village of Oued Bèsbès, is a handsome young peasant accompanied by his fiancé, Zina, and a black cat (fig. 10.12).

Multilingual/Intertextual

Despite their rustic setting, the Bouzid strips are immensely sophisticated linguistically, referentially, and stripologically. Like Malek, Slim turns Arabic names into character descriptions (e.g., Ben Fric, *fric* being French slang for money) (*Zid I & II*, p. 90), but he makes far greater use of bilingual puns (e.g., "Oued Side Story" or "A l'Oued, gentille à l'Oued, Je te plumerai babek . . .") (*Zid I & II*, pp. 7, 35). References extend beyond English and French to German. A rich man talks of a gift from "Abdelhimmler IV"; a frame shows Hitler (without naming him) in front of the gates of Auschwitz with its Arbeit Macht Frei! (*Zid I & II*, pp. 34, 47). The references to Nazi Germany are meant to be politically disobliging, but Abdelhimmler burlesques a familiar Arabic name pattern: ʿAbd plus one of the names of God (e.g., ʿAbd Allâh or ʿAbd al-Rahmân, servant of the Merciful). Substituting Himmler for a divine name is a most un-Islamic, potentially blasphemous form of play. Though this anti-Islamic im-

10.12. *The Algerian peasant as positive hero: Bouzid, his girl, and his cat.*

10.13. *Aping a Hollywood movie poster.*

plication is neither supported nor repeated in the text, it represents a taking of liberties and a secularization of discouse that would be unthinkable in an Egyptian, or even a Tunisian, comic strip.

In virtually all cases, the puns are between a European language and Arabic, rather than between French and English or one of these two and German. Indeed, any "foreign" language becomes available for puns with Arabic provided that the elements taken from it have become part of the common currency of the international media. One of the Slim stories is entitled "Taoura! Taoura! Taoura!" *Taoura* is Algerian dialect for *thawra*, revolution, but the tripartite title apes the movie on the Japanese attack on Pearl Harbor, *Tora! Tora! Tora!* The cover page of the strip (*Zid 3*, p. 5) even copies the monumental block characters of movie posters (the film appeared in 1970,[39] the strip in 1972) (fig. 10.13). Algerian Arabic thus functions as a kind of semiconscious local color, perennially available for humoristic play. French is the dominant language of narrative discourse, Algerian dialect the humorous linguistic subtext.

Slim also indulges in highly sophisticated games which, in a literary context, might be labeled a postmodern use of intertextuality and metastripology (from metafiction). After the frequently humorous evocation of a variety of shortages stands an entire register of blank frames and below them the words "shortage of ink" (*Zid I & II*, p. 16). In another story, a desperate Bouzid threatens suicide, but Slim enters as a character (represented by his own photograph) who argues with his hero about why he cannot let him die (fig. 10.14) (*Zid I & II*, p. 11).

10.14. *Slim enters his own strip to talk to his character.*

References to comic-strip heroes (or other mass-media icons) are frequent, and rarely politically innocent. In "Taoura!" killers hired by enemies of the revolution are after Bouzid. When he calls on the people to support him, one man objects: it's Bouzid they are after, and isn't he the hero of the strip? Another gives the politically correct answer, "One must not confuse Bouzid with SM 15," effectively satirizing the not-so-socialist romantic individualism implicit in that secret-agent narrative (*Zid 3*, p. 12).

Astérix the Gaul, hero of the French comic strip of that name, appears along with his sidekick Obélix. They are arguing with Bouzid, who, as head of the village, insists that they pay what they owe before they receive any more oil. Combining his identity as an ancient Gaul with a reference to the practices of French cultural imperialism, Astérix observes that it was easier to push the Algerians around when they thought that their ancestors were Gauls. And Obélix warns the Algerians that after they (the Gauls) leave, the sky will fall on the heads of the Algerians. Linked to the reference to a running joke in *Astérix* (the Gauls only fear one thing, that the sky will fall on their heads)[40] is a cut on the persistent French claim that the Algerians would not be able to survive the departure of their colonial masters. Thus do the feisty Gauls, good-natured symbols of French chauvinism, become caricatures of Gallic imperialism.

Most of the politics of the Bouzid stories comes directly from their plots. Of these, there are two basic sorts: threats to the revolution (the larger group) and threats to Bouzid's betrothed (and later wife) Zina. Even these can have a political component, as when the young woman is drugged by a corrupt member of the upper class who seeks to marry her (*Zid I & II*, pp. 7–13). The enemies of the revolution seek to get to it through its local leader, Bouzid. They try to kidnap and replace him with a double, to buy him off with candy (shades of the Tanâbila),[41] or to hire mercenaries (or even a metallic spaceman) to kill him. In one story an investigation of shortages ends with gunmen shooting at Bouzid and his urban ally, Amziane.

There is also a consistency in the villains. They are the corrupt bourgeois and crooked businessmen we have seen in other Algerian strips. They are qualified by names such as "Ben Trust" (*Zid I & II*, p. 28) and by a history. The "spiritual father" of a group of enemies of the people is called "the Bachagha Benilkelb" (*Zid 3*, pp. 23–24). The Bachaghas acted as agents of French colonization and were known for their corruption. The Bachagha Benilkelb, we are told, cut off the ears of those who opposed French imperialism. By linking his modern crooks to the class of corrupt traitors pilloried in historical strips like *La Ballade du proscrit*, Slim inserts his political satire into the anti-imperialist vision of the Algerian historical strips. And Benilkelb means Sons of the Dog, about as flattering in context as the English "son of a bitch."

The enemies of Algeria extend geographically as well as temporally. As Bouzid and Amziane search for the source of the widespread shortages afflicting their society they keep coming upon the name of a "Cheikh (*shaykh*) Parrain." *Parrain* means "godfather," but the allusion gets clearer when the two Algerians surprise a meeting of the leading "pénuristes." These "bloodsuckers" receive a message from their leader, the representative of ITT ("International Tiliphoune & Télégraph") who adjures them to defend "the free world" (*Zid I & II*, p. 28). The bad guys also make offhand references to the CIA, spelled out on one occasion as "Chabab Ittihad Athletic" (Athletic Youth Union). The irony of another version was sure to appeal to Arab leftists: "Copain Intime des Arabes" (Intimate Buddy of the Arabs) (*Zid I & II*, p. 18; *Zid 3*, p. 25). When Slim's Algerian bigwigs talk, their s's often turn into dollar signs (*Zid 3*, p. 24).

Clearly, as in *Soloeïs*, Uncle Sam is the ultimate villain (Bouzid even impersonates the symbol in a strip [*Zid I & II*, pp. 65–66]). Slim mixes cultural and political anti-imperialism when the local property owners, to kill Bouzid, hire seven mercenaries (a nod to *The Magnificent Seven* and through them to *Seven Samurai*). The hired guns think of Vietnam when they run into popular resistance. But the mercenaries have their own associations. One is the spitting image of Roger Moore as 007, another of Clint Eastwood from *A Fistful of Dollars*, while a third declares that he is Superman. As the Algerian hero, with the support of the people, defeats his Occidental counterparts, one of them exclaims in disbelief, "Some comic strip. Usually it is we who are the heroes" (*Zid 3*, pp. 6–14).

Many of Slim's plots thus seem to function as much as parodies of the revolution as of portrayals of it. The Bouzid strips also poke fun at the behavior of militants and the course of meetings (*Zid I & II*, p. 25). Does that mean that Bouzid satirizes the government's revolutionary projects? In effect, no. Criticisms, satire, and parodies are all recuperated by the official revolutionary project presented as the cure for the ills of Algerian society.

In the early 1970s, Boumedienne's government put through what it termed "the Agricultural Revolution," a set of agricultural reforms including the abolition of share-cropping, the creation of rural cooperatives, and some land redistribution.[42] This is the revolution celebrated in "Taoura! Taoura! Taoura!" When it comes to the positive aspects of the revolution, however, Slim eschews parody. Bouzid clearly explains the new reforms to his fellow villagers. He redistributes a herd of sheep to the shepherd who cares for them. All the clichés familiar to us from Communist regimes are present. Eager student volunteers arrive at the village by bus (the "volontariat"); the masses break out into triumphal demonstrations replete with appropriate banners (fig. 10.15) (*Zid I & II*, pp. 39, 87; *Zid 3*, pp. 7–8, 14).

10.15. *The triumph of the revolution as a feast of slogans.*

"Zid ya Bouzid" is an Algerian expression which means "go for it" or "on-ward," its political implications not unlike the "Avanti popolo" that our hero utters on one occasion (*Zid 3*, p. 14). With his peasant garb and popular leadership, Bouzid is the positive hero of Slim's socialist narratives.

Even apparently negative scenarios turn positive. "Une Loubia pour un marsien naïf" (A Bean Stew for a Naive Martian) (*Zid 3*, pp. 17–29) begins with a long sequence in which a stranded Martian plays the role of Montesquieu's Persians, exploring Algerian society as a mystified outsider. Searching for a retrorocket for his flying saucer, he discovers shortages, official stores with no products or services, and a thriving black market where everything is for sale. But social criticism turns to scapegoating when our Martian meets the exploiters who organize the shortages and who hire him to kill Bouzid. The latter, however, quickly turns the Martian around, who then explains that they had had the same problems on his planet until their successful revolution. "Au train où ça va pas" (At the rate things aren't going), with a French pun on *train* (*Zid I & II*, pp. 45–8), is a long, savage, yet funny indictment of the way Algerians trash their trains. It ends, however, with a patriotic appeal to Algerians to be vigilant and protect their collective property.

In the last analysis, behind all the exposure of the problems of Algerian society lies the assumption that all it will take is a bit more earnestness in following the official policies of the government and the FLN. This also applies to Slim's shorter, uniquely negative strips. One of these tells the story of a corrupt individual who uses his party membership to protect his ill-gotten gains—until the party wises up and throws him out (*L'Algérie*, p. 27).

Similarly, though the Bouzid series focuses on peasant life, no allusion is made (there or elsewhere in Slim's work) to the state-controlled agricultural sector which takes up the most productive land, where the peasants are effectively reduced to the status of workers, and where the reforms of the Agricultural Revolution do not apply.[43]

It is richly entertaining to imagine, as Slim does, an evil machine which immediately identifies any spot on the national territory where there are not people waiting in line—and then creates the line (*Zid 3*, p. 23). But this is a fantasy escape from the fact (verifiable across the region) that lines, shortages, and the black market are the regular consequences of state socialist systems of distribution (capitalism rations through price). This is the most important difference between Hijâzî and Slim. The Egyptian leftist locates the problems in his own society; his Algerian counterpart blames the internal enemy and his outside support.

Disarming Women

In "Taoura! Taoura! Taoura!" while the men talk politics, Zina has a thought balloon: "In all this revolution, there's not a little paragraph on women?" (*Zid 3*, p. 10). It is a good question. In his other strips, Slim speaks out eloquently against the traditional seclusion of women. A man builds a statue of himself (how symbolic!) which then falls on him. He calls out to his wife, Aïcha, but she cannot save him. For he locked her in the house and left the key in his clothing (*L'Algérie*, p. 13). And when Bouzid and Amziane plan their attack on the mercenaries of "Taoura! Taoura! Taoura!" the women demand their part; they pour hot liquids on the enemy from their windows. Zina is a strong-willed woman and her relationship with Bouzid plays a large role in the *Zid* series.

But this is a comic strip—and images often speak louder than words. Most visible on Zina is her outfit. She is completely veiled—face, hair and body—leaving, as her only visual distinction, a peak of polka-dotted material protruding below her gown (fig. 10.16). More bizarre, Zina has no arms—or at least none are normally visible in her visual portrayal. Almost like the arms and feet of Dalla and Finjân, Zina's arms reappear on a few occasions when the narrative situation demands it. Algerian (and some other North African) women frequently wear a white outer cloak that they wrap around the outside of their arms, holding it closed in the center with their hands or teeth. This is obviously what Slim's image seeks to represent. But Zina is as slender above the waist as below, no bulk being drawn to account for the arms.

10.16. *Zina, the armless woman.*

Such armlessness is not wholly unprecedented in the region. Little wooden dolls produced in Egypt paint in markings for the arms of men while omitting any indication of those of women, though both sexes wear the same galabias. Slim's armless females seem quite unusual in Arab comics, however, where even conservatively veiled women normally have all their limbs. Combined with the full veil, the almost constant occultation of the upper limbs of all traditionally clad females (the overwhelming majority in the Bouzid cycle) tends to increase the dimorphism between men and women while giving the latter an extra, comical, kind of gaucheness. Like the veil, the missing (or hidden) limbs suggest an inability to function in the modern world.

Slim almost seems aware that the traditional veil denudes its wearer of personality. The costume becomes the basis for games of multiple identity. Bouzid himself mistakes another woman for his Zina (*Zid I & II*, p. 62). More important, the veil is the major source of disguise throughout the Bouzid series. When the seven mercenaries seek to blend in with the Algerian landscape they dress not as men but as fully veiled women. Even the Martian disguises himself as a traditional woman, eliciting the erotic interest of the male Algerians who come into contact with him (*Zid 3*, pp. 11, 19, 22).

In his visual play, Slim also often materializes the notion of the woman as object. In "Il était une fois dans l'Oued," while the false Bouzid is a human impostor, the false Zina is an inflated plastic doll, like those sold in French sex-shops, except for her modesty (*Zid I & II*, pp. 34, 37) (fig. 10.17). In another story, Zina is kidnapped and Bouzid looks for her in the lost and found (in French, *objets trouvés*, found objects). There he finds not Zina but other women stashed around assorted objects (*Zid I & II*, p. 18) (fig. 10.18). Finally, without any apparent narrative relevance, Slim turns a veiled woman into the cuckoo of a clock (*Zid I & II*, p. 35) (fig. 10.19).

There is one issue concerning women's status to which Slim keeps returning: the question of whether a man has the right to beat his wife. According to the Sharî'a, the basis of traditional Islamic law, a husband has the right to use corporal punishment on his wife, insofar as this is necessary to enforce her obedience.[44] More to the point, this

10.17. *Zina as rubber doll.*

10.18. *Algerian women in
the lost and found.*

10.19. *Veiled woman as cuckoo.*

"right" has been traditionally used by husbands and others in authority in North Africa (and, of course, not only there).

When the false Bouzid (of "Il était une fois dans l'Oued") sees the false Zina (actually an inflated doll), his first reaction is to give her a solid punch. His handlers explain that Bouzid never hits his girl, a laudable attitude on the part of a positive hero. And it is contrasted with the general expectations of society. In the same story, Zina (the real one this time) gets cross with the false Bouzid, who has ceased supporting the revolution. The other women preach obedience to her: her husband has the right to make her miserable, "even to beat" her, a position the rebellious Zina rejects (*Zid I & II*, pp. 34, 38).

In yet another story, Slim links corporal punishment with an outmoded patriarchal authority. Zina's father, exasperated by shenanigans surrounding her engagement to be married, prepares to give her a spanking; when his wife objects, he threatens to punish her as well. Saying that she has awaited this moment during thirty-seven years of marriage, she turns the tables on her gray-bearded husband and gives him a solid spanking (*Zid I & II*, p. 55).

Yet the end of "Les Pénuristes" appears to contradict this. As a group of exploiters fire on Amziane and Bouzid, Zina comes riding to their rescue on a magic carpet, firing to cover their escape (she sprouts arms for the occasion). Once they are safe, Bouzid gives his Zina a spanking for having left the house; in the next frame she declares her love for him (*Zid I & II*, pp. 28–29). The French have an expression for this sort of erotic ambiguity: *qui aime bien châtie bien*.

Merely raising such a sensitive issue shows considerable courage on Slim's part. In no other country's strips, apparently, would this be possible. The often humorous treatment of the subject also clearly helps to make its discussion palatable. Nevertheless, the effective ambiguity in the strips reinforces the occasional objectification of Zina as veiled woman.

Having created a positive male hero in Bouzid, Slim has not made an equivalent female one of his companion. Part of this is Zina's very traditional veil, a reactionary outfit in the context of the secularist and socialist politics which dominate the rest of Slim's production. But does not Bouzid wear traditional peasant dress, and should not his "better half" do so as well? Yes and no. Veiling the face was never practiced among some rural populations, such as the Kabyles. Furthermore, it is general Muslim practice that a woman sheds her veil when she is in her own house, surrounded by her family. Neither Zina nor her mother ever do so. They remain almost icons, quaint and humorous. In the world of Slim, economic exploitation is condemned unambiguously, but the problem of women's status in the new socialist Algeria remains wrapped in equivocation.

Critique and Conformism

In many respects, Slim's strips only extend critiques of mercantile corruption adumbrated in other Algerian comics. On another level, the Algerian's social vision combines the attack on corruption that we saw in the work of the Egyptian Hijâzi with the anti-imperialism visible in the visual narratives of Syria, among other nations.[45]

Yet Hijâzi is more fundamentally subversive. His world is empty of justice. In Slim's world, justice has a location: in the programs of the government, in the ideals of the party, in the future of the revolution. In some respects, therefore, even the crypto-critical strips in a more heavily controlled environment like that of Syria are more subversive. But if Slim's political obeisances are typical in the Arab comic-strip context, the frankness of the social criticism more closely resembles European strips. Thus while the languages, the imagery, even many of the topics seem European, the mode of political integration remains essentially Arab.

11

Images in Exile:
Beur Comic Strips

Where there are Arabs, there are Arab strips. This is also true for the several million Arabs who live in France. North Africans, mostly Algerians but also Tunisians and Moroccans, they came to France first as immigrant labor in a process that began with the Algerian War and accelerated in the 1960s and early 1970s. By the mid-1970s, however, this Franco-Maghribian community had changed its nature. As the immigration of new workers slowed to a trickle, a change in French regulations encouraged the constitution of families. With women and children were created whole communities, with their neighborhoods, stores, Muslim butcher shops, and eventually mosques. For the children of these families, born in France and torn between two cultures, a new term was created in French slang —Beur. In the French slang called *verlan*, one reverses syllables: from *arabe*, *beur*. But Beurs (female: Beurettes) are a special kind of Arab, what we in the United States would call Frenchmen of Arab descent, the second generation. To be Beur is to be liminal: between two cultures, two societies, and often legally between two nationalities, since many Beurs can be considered French under French law and Algerian under Algerian law.[1]

Between the general lack of education of most North African workers and the de-Arabization of colonial Algeria (and to a lesser degree Tunisia and Morocco), few in the Maghribian community in France can read Arabic. Hence the circulation of Arabophone strips, like those from the Middle East, remains modest. Even the largely French strip production from Algeria receives a limited circulation. The truly Beur comic strip is a French production, written in the French language (though, as we shall see, a distinctive form of that language). The Beur strip, like much Beur culture, draws from at least three traditions. Its attachment to the French comic-strip tradition is the most obvious: in visual imagery, in tone, and to a considerable degree in subject matter. But as a French strip production centering on North Africans (in Algeria as well as France), it links itself to the Algerian Francophone strip. Behind this and despite the linguistic gap, Arab Muslim comic-strip and other cultural elements nourish Beur comic-strip production.

The Beur strip is primarily associated with the work of one artist and scenarist, Farid Boudjellal. A typical Beur, Boudjellal was born in the French port city of Toulon in 1953.[2] Active throughout the 1980s, Boudjellal published a three-volume series: *L'Oud* (The ʿUd) in 1983, *Le Gourbi: L'Oud II* (The Gourbi) in 1985, and *Ramadân: L'Oud III* (Ramadân) in 1988.[3] He published the very depressing *Les Soirées d'Abdulah: Ratonnade* in 1985, the cheerful *La Famille Slimani: Gags à l'Harissa* in 1989, and, with Larbi Mechkour, *Les Beurs* in 1985.[4]

Boudjellal's strips highlight the three major aspects of the North African immigrant experience in France. First comes the solitude and alienation of the lone worker in a culturally and socially foreign country sharpened by the French reaction of rejection so eloquently described in Tahar Ben Jelloun's *Hospitalité française*.[5] Then come the families, the joys and difficulties of living with wife and children in the new land. Third and finally comes the new generation, the Beurs who struggle for a place and an identity in a France which is at once their country and yet not their country. Each of the albums focuses on one of these aspects, without completely ignoring the others.

From Racism to Alienation

The tone for *Les Soirées d'Abdulah: Ratonnade* is set by its title. A *ratonnade* is an anti-Arab race riot (as practiced in colonial Algeria) or rat-hunt, from *raton*, little rat. The second, and shorter, of the two stories in this mini-album bears the title "Ratonnade".[6] While Abdulah narrates in the stripological equivalent of a voice-over, we see him as a pitiful figure, isolated in the city (Toulon), set upon and beaten mercilessly by a group of Frenchmen. The voice-over describes the scene as if it were a game, only adding to the cynical brutality of the images. After the bullies have beaten him senseless, they dump garbage on their victim, who sits like a piece of refuse surrounded by the debris of Occidental civilization: the local newspaper, a package of Omo (a leading soap product), and the head of Disney's Goofy (see fig. 11.1). The gap between the verbal and the visual narration suggests the occultation of such events in the French media. The juxtaposition created by the two discourses oscillates between a humorous (might we say black humorous?) bisociation and a strengthened sense of the pathetic. Fun and games and sadism are linked, as in the four-frame sequence at the end of the album. Answering an unseen interlocutor, who suggests to him that his stories make the fascists laugh, Abdulah responds that when the fascists amuse themselves they no longer beat up the Arabs.

But our Arab Everyman's relations with French culture transcend violence. *Les*

11.1. *After the beating: Abdulah in the refuse of Western culture.*

Soirées d'Abdulah brings together social impotence, sexual frustration, and the power of women over men in a story in which our hero struggles to get papers filled out for the Social Security Administration, in order to receive a disability pension from a work-related accident. The three opening frames introduce the thematic. All we see is the head of Abdulah in a polite nervous smile, in front of him a set of papers, and holding the papers a woman's fingers with long polished nails (fig. 11.2). The long-

11.2. *The power of polished nails: Abdulah and the French bureaucrat.*

nailed hands control the papers and thus his financial future. Their owner, a French bureaucrat, refuses to accept them because they are badly filled out. Appropriately, it is Abdulah's right hand which was injured in the work accident. Abdulah's landlady also refuses to fill out the papers, as does, effectively, the worker's former employer. It is a streetwalker (the whore-with-a-heart-of-gold) who bails him out. He offers to pay the regular price for her services if she will simply fill out the papers, but she does them gratis, explaining that this is not her profession.

Sexual solitude is made part of the immigrant's experience in a scene in which Abdulah masturbates while drinking a bottle of wine. A set of frames, rich with signification, brings together sex and alcohol (fig. 11.3). Abdulah masturbates holding the bottle

11.3. *Alienation: alcohol and pornography.*

in his hand (paralleling his organ in his other hand) while staring at a bikini-clad beauty on the bottle's label. Three closeups of the woman eliminate the bottle, merging sex object and wine bottle. Both, of course, function as signifiers of French culture. Again, an ironic voice-over adds its bisociation. While Abdulah releases his sexual tensions, the radio blares out a game in which listeners are invited to guess the amount of money in "the little pig." Through the radio we hear a French woman scream excitedly to her husband, Gérard, "We have won! We have won!" Greed replaces sex.

Beneath a discourse which is superficially modern, secular, and French in its brutal frankness, the artist has created a strikingly Islamic set of ideological juxtapositions. Alcohol and female sexual immodesty are topoi in the Islamic image of the West as land of perdition. From the fatal glass of beer in films such as *Abî fawq al-Shajara* to the pornographic trap of *ʿAntar Shâyil Sayfu,*[7] they are common in Arab popular culture. To these Boudjellal has added gambling (also forbidden by Islam) and the pig, the animal rejected with horror by all Muslim peoples. The resulting vision is similar to what one finds in the cautionary manuals, such as *Zâd al-Musâfirîn ilâ Ghayr Bilâd al-Muslimîn* by Muhammad al-Saʿûdî, put out by Islamic revivalist groups.[8] Not that a contemporary Muslim could express himself in such a way. Though Islamic cultures have generally been less puritanical in the discussion of sex than Christian ones, at least until very recently, Boudjellal's visual explicitness would be totally unacceptable in any visual medium produced in an Arab country. It is the underlying message, the lone Arab male exposed to the multiple sins of the West, that operates across boundaries.

Abdulah's solitude is also homelessness. Political graffiti mark the walls of the city. The first two, "Palestine for the Palestinians" and "Armenia for the Armenians," signify the quest for a homeland. The third, "France for the French" (*La France aux français*), becomes richly ironic in this context. Unlike Armenians and Palestinians, the French have a country; the slogan writer does not seek a home but rejects the Other, in this case our Abdulah.

The failure of effective integration is also the message of *L'Oud*, which chronicles the adventures of three representative North Africans: Aziz, the son of a rich Tunisian businessman, who has become a French citizen; Kader, who came to France from Algeria in 1961 as an immigrant laborer; and Nourredine the Beur, born in France. The three soon come in contact with Abdulah, a gentle ʿûd player whom we know from *Les Soirées d'Abdulah*. *L'Oud* revolves around the attempt to acquire a beautiful ʿûd, so that the three heroes can make money playing for weddings. When Abdulah buys the instrument at an auction, Aziz tries to steal it from him. Eventually the four come to an agreement: Abdulah will lend his new acquisition and play it at the wedding. The beautiful instrument is destroyed, however, in the course of a brawl at the group's first wedding. Their quest ends in failure. In a café, Kader says to Abdulah: "If I win the lottery, I'll bring my wife and my kids, or me, I'll leave." The other answers simply: "Inch Allah, Kader . . . Inch Allah" (God willing, Kader . . . God willing).

The ʿûd is an obvious symbol. "Beautiful . . . fit for a prince," it represents Middle Eastern culture, in its finest expression, trying to survive in France. After its destruction, French children fish its remains from the garbage and turn it into a toy sailboat.

Sexual tension and Mediterranean male jealousy are part of the problem. During the auction, Aziz distracts a rich North African merchant, whom the three fear will win the bidding, by claiming, in the crudest possible language, to be sleeping with the rich man's wife. The brawl at the wedding is started by the same Aziz, who becomes jealous when watching his French girlfriend dance with other guests.

North African–Islamic and French attitudes toward female modesty and especially the scopic activity associated with visual pornography are creatively displayed in the album. Recalling with Jean-Bruno Renard the importance of the cover of a comic-strip album,[9] we note that the cover of *L'Oud* shows Kader mournfully staring at a picture of his wife while eating a sandwich. This scene would merely suggest nostalgia were it not for the fact that the Algerian woman is veiled in black from head to toe and has her face covered by a *haïk*. Because of Islamic rules of modesty, the picture of her is not really a picture of her.

We saw this form for the first time through Kader's eyes as his train pulled away from his children and veiled wife (fig. 11.4). The frame chosen for the cover is part of a sequence (fig. 11.5) in which Kader, while eating a sandwich, reaches for a picture of his wife and draws it to him. In a stunning countershot, Kader is facing us and we see only the back of the picture in his hand. Instead, facing the reader on the wall behind Kader's head is a whole series of pornographic nudes. The veiled woman and the unveiled one: a better visual representation of these cultures' radically different attitudes toward the scopic possession of women can hardly be imagined. And it is Kader's

11.4. *Alienation: leaving the family behind.*

status as immigrant that brings the two together, reducing his relationship with his wife to the merely scopic.

As in *Ratonnade*, Boudjellal again plays ironically with the contrast between visual and verbal messages. As Kader leaves his family behind in the Algerian *bled*, his speech balloons are full of promises: he will send back a bag of gold, his wife can choose the best plot of land, "never again work, fatigue, hunger" (fig. 11.4). But while the balloons speak of hope, the pictures tell the real story: separation from home and family. And the falsehood continues. In the very next frame, Kader writes a letter to his wife in fractured French explaining that he lives in a beautiful house, while we see him sharing an overcrowded room with a group of men. In his thought balloon he curses Saïd, the Algerian who lied to him about conditions in France. What is said and the social reality of the immigrant experience are two different things, Boudjellal keeps reminding us.

Family Life

The connection between the two later volumes in this series (*Le Gourbi* and *Ramadân*) and the first is sometimes tenuous. In a subplot of *L'Oud*, Nourredine's sister, Nadia, disappears, leading the family to believe that she has followed a French boyfriend to Paris. In *Le Gourbi* and *Ramadân*, we meet the Slimani family, cousins of Nourredine with whom he stays while searching the capital for his lost sister. Nourredine's story becomes a small part of a larger narrative concerned essentially with the Slimani family. At the end of *Ramadân*, Nourredine finally finds his sister as

11.5. *East meets West: the veiled woman and the unveiled one.*

she is about to give birth to a child fathered by her French boyfriend. The two families are brought back together as Nourredine, his sister, and her child visit their family in Toulon. A rather artificial closure is created when the other original band members (Kader, Aziz, and Abdulah) appear out of nowhere to serenade the reunited family.

The two Parisian albums give us a soap-opera vision of a North African family. The storyline shifts back and forth among family members as they live out their lives in the French capital. Mr. Slimani is a barber; his portly wife assumes the duties of matriarch, making pastries while trying to keep after her brood of seven children. One daughter, Djamila (her name means "pretty" in Arabic), is a cashier in a super-market. Her sister, Ratiba, the family intellectual, is studying for her *bac*.[10] The happy-go-lucky teenage Mahmoud is a polio victim with an emaciated right leg.[11]

Gourbi is a word of North African origin referring to the overcrowded dwelling of a poor Arab. Effectively, the Slimani live in one. Their tiny two-room apartment is absurdly overcrowded with nine family members (and Nourredine makes a tenth). *Le*

Gourbi opens with a floor plan of the apartment and detailed descriptions of where everyone sleeps (the three youngest sleep on shelves in a closet). They have water, but the toilet is in the hall. The family has applied for low-rent public housing, or HLM,[12] but eight years later is still waiting. As Mr. Slimani puts it, the HLMs, "they're for the rich, now" (*Ramadân*, p. 12). Boudjellal makes his point clearly. The sense of crowding fills the album. Not only are the characters often straining to get out of each other's way, but the stripology itself is frequently claustrophobic. There are far more frames per page, far more characters and balloons per frame. Tower shots emphasize the cramped sleeping quarters (*Gourbi*, p. 21).

The problems of North Africans in France are, of course, regularly evoked. A French neighbor, driven crazy by the noise of the rambunctious Slimani household, curses the family and then turns to his wife with a cooler head and says, almost apologetically: "I think I am in the process of becoming a racist" (*Gourbi*, p. 27). European faces are so relatively rare in these two albums, however, that they stand out visually and become a minority. In general the French we do meet are not bad people. Several are friends of members of the Slimani family, and when conflicts develop it is generally not the "French" who are at fault.

The enormous gap between North African and French notions of female modesty, family honor, and appropriate sexual behavior appears frequently in the subplots of *Le Gourbi* and *Ramadân*, reflecting the very real problems these cultural cleavages pose for North African families in France. Nourredine is looking for his sister, partly because, as an Arab proverb says, a sister is the honor of her brother. A rather seedy young man whom Nourredine has befriended in Paris drives him to rage when he suggests a sexual jealousy behind the young man's obsessive concern with finding his sister (*Ramadân*, p. 7). In a quiet way, Boudjellal has evoked an issue central to the Arab psyche. The noted scholar Hasan El-Shamy has even suggested that brother-sister incestuous desire takes the place in the Arab family occupied by Oedipal feelings in the Western one.[13] In a far more familiar reaction, the Slimani patriarch has a fit when he discovers that his twenty-two-year-old daughter has been seeing a young man on the sly: "Did you think that I fed you for twenty-two years so that you could bring shame on me?" (*Gourbi*, p. 26). He beats his daughter, then takes her to the doctor to ascertain that she is still a virgin (*Gourbi*, pp. 26, 35). When the young man who has been courting her comes to the house, he seems the ideal catch, at least to the father: serious and hard-working, and he wants to move back with his bride to Algeria. Djamila, however, is put off when she discovers that he wishes to marry her and give her fifteen children (*Gourbi*, p. 37). Infuriated when he is unable to win her back, the young man resorts to physical violence, pulling her hair and slapping her around. In response, he is eventually beaten by her father and brother (*Ramadân*, pp. 1–2, 18–19).

On the wall, the Slimanis conserve a picture of their dead daughter, Latifa. Only later do we discover that she committed suicide at age fifteen because she was pregnant (*Gourbi*, pp. 18, 29, 35). "We had our children in France," her father laments, "and France takes them from us" (*Ramadân*, p. 33). Ratiba's love life is not really any happier: she is attracted to Nourredine, but he sees her only as a friend. In fact, the smoothest romantic relationships are between mixed couples: Mahmoud and his

French girlfriend, Nadia and her French boyfriend. Life may be difficult, but with patience eventual integration is possible.

Integrated Humor

Les Beurs is a collaborative work. Boudjellal did the scenario, Larbi Mechkour the art. Mechkour's visual style, rounder, more cheerful than Boudjellal's, combined with the use of color, sets the tone for the album. *Les Beurs* celebrates a moment in the history of the North African minority in France. The middle years of the last decade saw the flowering of what was effectively a Beur chic. The 1983 March for Equality and against Racism, popularly known as the March of the Beurs, kicked off a movement for Beur identity as a new youth-oriented Franco-Arab culture, part of a new multicultural France. As such, the Beur movement was leftist, hip, and largely secular. The importance of Islam among the North African community in France, while it was growing throughout the 1980s, became increasingly visible in the years that followed the Beur phenomenon and tended to function as an alternative pole of cultural definition.[14]

Boudjellal and Mechkour joyously play with a mixture of East and West. An artist is called Salvatore Ali, rock bands have names like Jambon-Beur and Captain Mohammed and His Mohamedettes. The first is a word play on a ham sandwich with butter, hardly a proper meal for a Muslim. The second plays with the name of the Prophet in a way that would be totally unacceptable in a proper Muslim context. The Islamic culture of North Africa becomes a colorful gimmick in a hip mass culture. While some of this is a reflection of the Beur cultural movement which produced bands with names like Mohammed Travolta and Babouch Rock,[15] Boudjellal and Mechkour have taken the process further, burlesquing a culture which was already a burlesque. These verbal games bear a great similarity to the Franco-Arabic puns so visible in French-language Algerian strips, especially those of Slim.[16] But Slim's games remain on the surface when compared to the bicultural implications of the Beur strips (including Islamic references).

Political issues associated with the coexistence of North Africans and European French, which appear fleetingly in *Le Gourbi* and *Ramadân*, take center stage in *Les Beurs*. One story chronicles the March of the Beurs. The march is shown in essentially heroic form with (besides the Beurs) a Catholic priest and a black, who explains that they are following the path of Martin Luther King. The visit of the Algerian president Chadli is treated as an associated triumph. Meanwhile, the strip pokes fun at the hostility of conservative Frenchmen. A working-class Frenchman is eating while listening to a report on the march on television. His comment: "Let them stay in their country," to which he adds, holding his plate out to his wife: "Here, serve me some more couscous, Régine," while the wine bottle on his table reads "Sidi Brahim, Algérie" (fig. 11.6). Another Frenchman, interviewed for the radio about the march, declares: "It's a good thing, while they're marching, they're not doing anything wrong." A Beur, his face covered with bruises, explains how he was beaten. The title of the story, "Marche ou Crève" (March or Croak), with its allusion to the French Foreign Legion, becomes

11.6. *French racist criticizes North Africans while asking for more couscous.*

doubly ironic in this instance: both an index of Frenchification and a warning of the potentially dire consequences of racism.

Another story title, "Journée Paisible à Dreux" (Peaceful Day at Dreux), also carries its measure of ironic antiphrasis, Dreux being the heavily immigrant town, replete with social problems, where the National Front of the French rightist Jean-Marie Le Pen had its first notable local electoral success.[17] On election day a group of North Africans note that they cannot vote. The right for resident aliens who are not French citizens to vote in local elections has been much discussed in France. Though promised by the Socialists, who have been in power since 1981, the measure has proved too controversial to be passed into law. A young Beur has his own idea: organize an informal polling of North Africans. This means stopping people in the street who look Arab. They stop a man with a typically North African face. He apologizes, and explains that his name is Henry Noël. Yes, he admits, he looks like an Arab, and boy does he get a hard time as a result (fig 11.7).

A more imaginative treatment of a more serious problem appears in "Cap'tain Samir." The early 1980s saw a rash of murderous attacks on North Africans and Beurs in France.[18] Often children were shot by Frenchmen firing down from the windows of apartment buildings, because the children were making too much noise. In our story, a group of children is fired on after one of them accidentally makes a noise. They decide to call in their hero, Cap'tain Samir. The young hero rides in on a motorcycle, blending French, American, and Arab mass-cultural elements. He wears a coonskin cap like Davy Crockett and signs with an "S" for Samir, like Zorro with his "Z" (both Zorro and Crockett have been popularized in France through the Disney television channel). In the Beurs' clubhouse, Samir tries (and fails) to draw faster than his shadow. This is the trademark of

11.7. *The Frenchman who looks like an Arab.*

the French comic-strip hero Lucky Luke, a fictional American cowboy. At the end of the episode, Samir whistles for his motorcycle, the way Lucky Luke does for his horse, Jolly Jumper (fig. 11.8)[19] Writing "Cap'tain" without the "i" strengthens the American connec-

11.8. *Cap'tain Samir whistles for his motorcycle.*

tion. But "Cap'tain Samir" has other reverberations. He is the hero of one of the most popular Egyptian comic-strip magazines, and he appears as such with his captain's hat on its cover.[20] The hero comes from the West—and the East. One of the Beurs asks to be admitted to the Order of Crimefighters. When Samir knights him, the young man shouts with glee: "I am baptized! I am baptized!" Multiple traditions are blended in this takeoff of a typical American TV serial.

The French villain is a caricature of working-class Aryanism: blond and blue-eyed, with a tee shirt over his protruding potbelly (fig. 11.9). When Samir challenges

11.9. *Cap'tain Samir faces down the blonde-haired bully.*

him, he answers with insults linked to North African food, which is, as in "Marche ou Crève," the point of cultural contact between racist Frenchmen and the Beurs: "Couscous Royal . . . He is sick or he has eaten too much harissa." When the blond-haired bully comes down from his apartment, Samir challenges him to a duel: "My colt against your twenty-two long rifle." Before Samir can count to three, the Frenchman has defecated in his pants from fear and must leave the street in humiliation.

There are winks at other comic-strip traditions throughout *Les Beurs*. A jinn (to whom we will return) makes a crack about "Nââdine Coke en Stock," evoking an album in the *Tintin* series by Hergé, probably the most famous series of comic strips in the French language.[21] Such allusions, combined with ethnic mixture, show up, though far more subtly, in the other Boudjellal albums. Casually foregrounded in a street scene in *Le Gourbi* are two Hasidic Jews. On closer inspection they look like a Hasidic version of Dupond and Dupont (the canes are a giveaway), the comic detectives from *Tintin*. Or better yet, the Dupond(t)s disguised as Hasidic Jews (itself an allusion to the comically obvious disguises of the detective pair).[22]

The social and political realities of being Beur are skillfully brought together in the humorous "Le Céfran qui voulait être Beur" (The Frenchman Who Wanted to Be a Beur). Philippe, a blond-haired, blue-eyed young Frenchman (if he were not blond, how would we know he could not be an Arab?), declares that he wants to be a Beur. An Arab gives the appropriate commentary: "Before taking on people, it would be necessary first that we have a country!" But Philippe insists, and the Beurs come up with three ordeals.[23] Their unspoken purpose is to introduce this European to the realities of Beur life. The first, similar to initiation rites used by French students, is to steal a policeman's billy club. Philippe is, of course, appropriately beaten. For the second ordeal, our would-be Beur must sit through a Le Pen rally. For the purposes of the strip, the French politician is renamed Jean-Marie Dedreux, which also means "from Dreux," the city whose connections to the Right we saw above. Boudjellal and Mechkour have a field day with their bête noire. The Front National (National Front) is renamed the Front de Nettoyage (Clean-Up Front), an accurate jab at Le Pen's rhetoric, which speaks often of cleaning up France. The humiliation of the rightist politician goes further, however, as his makeup man first decks him out as a clown with bright red nose. Nor are Le Pen's followers spared. One wears a swastika, one woman swoons with romantic admiration, and another bares her breasts in her enthusiasm: "I love you Jean-Marie! I love you!" The speech attributed to Dedreux is not far from Le Pen's rhetoric. Unemployment is blamed squarely on the immigrant workers: if they are sent home, France will take off again. But the speech swiftly turns to high comedy, as Dedreux/Le Pen disclaims being a racist: "A racist, me, who has called my dog Mohamed!!" The dog in question wears a German spiked helmet and receives a solid swat from his master (fig. 11.10). Philippe, at the end of his patience, cries "Enough," and Dedreux's goons very violently eject him from the rally. For the third ordeal, the Beurs, taking out their knives, explain to Philippe that they will baptize him by cutting off his foreskin. As one of them explains, "It's the only real difference between us," a mordant commentary on the cultivation of racial and ethnic difference.

Tradition as Fantasy

But there is more to *Les Beurs* than social realism (even mixed with satire) and more to the world of the text than contemporary French society. Tradition and the East are present, but refracted through the prism of fantasy. In one story, "La Djinna," a young man marries (and consummates his marriage with) a beautiful female jinn, whom only he can see. This is consistent with Arab folklore and popular culture in which sexual relations with beautiful female jinn are common.[24]

Relations with jinn are not always so positive, however. In another story, with a fairy-tale structure, a young Beur couple buys a drink for an old rug merchant. To reward them he reveals that he is a jinn and gives them a magic carpet which will fly upon the command "Chick Peas." The young Beurs and their friends take the carpet on a trip over Paris, but as one of them loses his grip, the rug unravels, dropping the whole group in the Seine. In the last scene we see them hitchhiking on a lonely road.

Beyond the obvious takeoff on *The Thousand and One Nights* and the good-

11.10. *Le Pen caricatured by the Beurs.*

natured *Schadenfreude* of the ending lies an unconscious commentary on the place of Arab tradition in the world of contemporary France. It enters essentially through the world of fantasy and comes unraveled in contact with the modern world. In the last frame the group is stranded on a modern highway. True, the crescent moon of Islam shines in the sky above. But the single road sign offers the young people only two destinations: Paris, the capital of France, and Poitiers, symbol of Occidental victory over invading Islam (fig. 11.11).

The Algerian Slim also introduced flying carpets into the modern world in his strips. In his case, however, they played no real role in the plot, functioning (like the

11.11. *After the magic carpet ride, only two choices, Paris or Poitiers.*

Algerian's multilingual puns) chiefly as humorous reminders of the layers of culture present in contemporary Algeria.[25] Only in Boudjellal and Mechkour's Beur creation does the carpet open the way to a frontal attack on tradition.

The fantasy–tradition nexus is blended with modern problems of identity and loyalty in Boudjellal and Mechkour's "Beur Blanc Rouge," a takeoff on "Bleu, Blanc, Rouge," the French equivalent of the Red, White, and Blue. Cap'tain Mohamed, a recurring character in this collection, announces that he has taken the French national identity card, in effect choosing French citizenship. This decision, whether to take the "French card," faces most Beurs, since the variations between French and Algerian law make them potential citizens of both countries. His colleagues tease him about this, a black observing: "It's a trick; I've been naturalized for five years and I still have a big nose and thick lips." Adding to the irony is the fact that Mohamed is the most Orientally dressed of the regular Beur characters. He wears a fez, baggy pants, and the *babouches* (slippers) with the upturned toes worn by an Ottoman gentleman or a character from a popular illustration of *The Thousand and One Nights*. The final argument of the other Beurs is that Mohamed has cut himself off from his home country; he will never be able to return to Algeria.

At this point, social commentary gives way to a standard folklore plot. Mohamed, another male, and a female friend are walking down the street at night when an old Arab, in traditional North African garb, asks them for charity. Despite their own poverty, the three are generous, and they start first by carrying the old man's belongings and then the old man himself (the young bearing the weight of tradition on their shoulders). The old beggar leads them to an office of the Caisse d'Epargne, the French national savings bank. When the three enter they are met by a large fierce squirrel (the squirrel is the symbol of the Caisse d'Epargne), who asks them what they want. Mohamed's two companions, frightened and caught unawares, say that they want nothing, and that is what they get. Mohamed gives the correct answer, "Everything," and he walks out with piles of banknotes, as the old man, clearly a jinn, disappears. But the treasure has a catch: the banknotes turn out to be not French francs but Algerian dinars, useless outside Algeria (the Algerian dinar is a nonconvertible currency). What about changing the money in Algeria, Mohamed asks, and his companion replies that he would get a pound of francs for a ton of dinars. Again, the magic from the East is impotent in the West. And the money is archetypically Arab. After Mohamed tosses his bills away we see one note peeking at us from the corner of a frame. On its face is a smiling camel, exotic—and useless.

But fantasy is also satire. Useless piles of dinars in Paris are not a rare occurrence. To hamper the black-market trade in dinars in France, otherwise so easy because of the large number of people going back and forth between that country and Algeria, the Algerian government periodically calls in its currency, replacing old notes with new. Those holding the old black-market dinars in France find themselves in the same position as our Mohamed. Cracks about the low value of the dinar also turn up in *Gags à l'Harissa* when the Slimani family goes to Algiers.

The major characters of *Les Beurs* are young people. Though some adults occasionally appear, an atmosphere of adolescent camaraderie and peer group solidarity prevails. This is not unrelated to the somewhat critical view of tradition embodied by older individuals. By the same token, despite Oriental touches in some other areas, the sexual mores seem largely contemporary French. The young Beurettes are dressed in all the provocative chic of French teenagers, with none of the concessions to Muslim standards of female modesty characteristic of the Slimani daughters.

The issues of adolescent coupling and tradition are most clearly foregrounded in "Love Story Beur" (in English in the original). Here again, Boudjellal and Mechkour begin with contemporary social realities only to slip into fantasy. Kamel and Naïma are teenagers madly in love. He takes her for rides on his motorcycle and serenades her outside her window at night. Naïma comes home late one day to find her father cross with her. A Mr. Djiouti has been waiting for her. A big square man, entering middle age, he offers her a set of real pearls (fig. 11.12), but she refuses his proposition of marriage, to the clear disappointment of her father. This much is banal, and the topos of the young woman proposed in marriage to the rich older man is common even in the Arab world.[26] But this Mr. Djiouti has other resources. He is a magician: he captures Kamel and imprisons him inside a hand-held video game. For the right to see Kamel again and a promise of his freedom, Naïma agrees first to marry the magician and eventually to sleep with him. Djiouti lives in a palace of extraordinary opulence that looks like a scene from *The Thousand and One Nights* or the palace of a Kuwaiti emir (fig. 11.13). The satisfied magician throws away the video game (with Kamel inside), and it eventually falls into the hands of a group of street children. One of them, "the King of the Handymen," hooks the video game up to a stereo system, allowing the young people to communicate with the trapped Kamel. Apprised of the situation, the young Beurs, led by Cap'tain Mohamed, set out to free their friend, but the magician turns their weapons into *merguez* (a popular sausage of North African origin). The final solution is to beat the magician at dominoes, and for this the young people find an idiotic-looking player with incredible luck. He defeats Djiouti, and Kamel is freed. Youth and love have triumphed over age, wealth, and tradition. The magician, as we have noted,[27] is not an unknown figure among North Africans, either in

11.12. *Love or money, M. Djiouti*
offers pearls.

11.13. *M. Djiouti's palace.*

their home countries or in France. In France such magicians (operating on the margins of official Islam) live by selling amulets, telling fortunes, and the like.[28] But with the triumph of modernity comes that of the new morality. As Kamel and Naïma ride off on his motorcycle, she remains sad, afraid that he will no longer love her, since she is no longer a virgin. "One kiss and we'll see if that's true," he answers, as they ride off surrounded by yelps of glee.

Integration, Islam, and France

The devaluation of religion is associated with a vision of Islam which is not exempt from humor. In "Beur Blanc Rouge" the old jinn indignantly refuses the offer of a ham sandwich: "Do you want me to eat pork and go to hell?" But he happily accepts a beer. "For that he is no Muslim," a Beurette comments with a laugh. During the magic carpet ride, the Beurs argue about where to go. One young man proposes

Mecca, and we see him praying on the moving carpet. But one of his colleagues is derisively kicking him in his rear (exposed by the gesture of prayer).

Islam is treated with more respect in *Le Gourbi* and *Ramadân*, the latter work clearly attempting to explain the procedures of a Muslim fast to a French audience. Some members of the family keep the fast, others, like Mahmoud, cheat at the first opportunity. Nevertheless, the one thing we do not see in this series is prayer, either individually or at a mosque. To some degree this is because two of the most important loci for mosques in France for many years, HLMs and factories, do not touch the lives of the Slimani family.

In *Gags à l'Harissa*, people pray. The father of the family demonstrates it to us, but without undue gravity. Part way through, he farts audibly, which leads him to explain that in such a case one has to begin the whole process over again, including the ablutions. While this vignette might seem particularly disrespectful, it is actually a form of humor well established even in classical Islamic civilization.[29]

Veiling and unveiling also come in for satire. During a trip to Algeria in *Gags à l'Harissa*, Djamila, short on clean clothes, goes out dressed as a traditional Algerian woman with long robes and face-veil, but with nothing on underneath. Mahmoud calls it "veiled nudism." Pandemonium breaks out when her robe falls off, exposing her completely. A wonderful little frame (fig. 11.14) shows a young Algerian man and woman dressed in the style of the Muslim revivalists. Her hands are around his eyes as she says (protecting his virtue) "Don't look, my brother," adopting a self-consciously Muslim form of address. He answers in the same vein (and protecting her virtue): "Remove your hands, my sister."

11.14. *Two Islamic revivalists protect each other's virtue.*

Islam is a part of Beur culture and as such is respectable—but only within limits. Its treatment in the work of Boudjellal never approaches what we regularly see in Muslim countries, whether in secular or in religious strips.[30] The contrast is clear with a small strip which we could call "Franco-Islamic," reproduced by Gilles Kepel in his excellent *Les Banlieues de l'Islam*.[31] The strip is similar to the Islamic poster strip discussed in chapter 6, in that it chronicles the day of a model Muslim child. The Franco-Islamic strip has two parts, however. The second is the countermodel: a day in the life of the bad boy. The good boy is called "the just," the bad boy "the false."[32] The pairing of such good and bad examples is, as we have seen, common enough in Middle Eastern Islamic strip materials, down to the physical injury sustained by the bad or foolish boy. What is distinctive here is that the good boy is an Arab. His name is Jamel and he is drawn with a Saudi-style headdress. The bad model is a Frenchman; his name is Luc, and he bears a striking physical similarity to the Francophone comic-strip hero Tintin. In the East, both good and bad boy belonged to the same community. What separated them was their behavior and the quality of their faith. In France, the division has been turned from a moral one into a social one, dividing ethnic and religious groups.[33]

Boudjellal's position contrasts sharply. In the final story of *Gags à l'Harissa*, Mahmoud and Ratiba Slimani attend a Christmas Eve *réveillon* with Mahmoud's French girlfriend. The last frame shows them at midnight mass singing the Christmas carol "Il est né le Divin Enfant," while Mahmoud sardonically adds: "After this, they can't say any more that we don't do anything to integrate ourselves."

The Lost Paradise

Arab tradition, of course, is more than Islam, and in Boudjellal it is more than a dead weight. One of the most consistent, though nonforegrounded, symbols of tradition in these strips is Umm Kulthûm. This Egyptian singer remains famous throughout the Arab world for her extended vocal performances on neoclassical texts. In the first frame of *Les Beurs*, the young people play dominoes, while Arabic music emerges from a jukebox. Uncharacteristically, the musical balloon contains Arabic characters (drawn by an unpracticed hand). The text refers to this as "folklore." The frontispiece of *L'Oud* is a one-page frame.[34] Again, young North Africans listen to Arabic music from a jukebox. This time, however, the figure of Umm Kulthûm emerges from the music machine like a genie from a magic lamp in *The Thousand and One Nights*. Her speech balloon is entirely in Arabic, translated into French in fine print at the bottom of the page. The translation is a bit loose. The Arabic reads: "O my heart do not ask where passion is . . . It was clear in my imagination but it has fallen away." The French, however, reads: "O my soul do not ask me where the *past* is . . . It was an edifice of dreams and it has tumbled down." The mistranslation is really a reinterpretation. It is not love which is gone but the past, an Arab culture which turns out to have been but a dream. This interpretation is strengthened by the title of the album from which the selection was taken and which is listed at the bottom of the frame: *al-Atlâl. Al-Atlâl* refers to the remains of a deserted encampment, a place one has left behind. But it is also, indeed primarily, part of the *nasîb*, or prologue, to the famous pre-Islamic Arabic ode, or *qasîda*. The poet comes upon the remains of a camp and nostalgically remembers old adventures, old loves. A sense of loss, of an unrecoverable past, is almost intrinsic.[35]

Like the *ʿûd* which cannot survive in France, like the jinn and magicians, Arab culture is of another place. The Beurs are in exile. Little wonder, then, that on the last page of *Ramadân* the family celebrating the *ʿîd*, or holiday, looks out across the Mediterranean toward Algeria. There, they say, is where the holiday is being truly celebrated.

12

Regional Highways, Regional Signs

In April 1988 the Beirut religious children's magazine, *Ahmad*, published a set of drawings from its readers, visual signs recirculated from the audience and selected and approved by the magazine (see fig. 12.1). They make a culturally disparate iconography. Below a calligraphy of the name of God, a bird chirps out "Allâhu Akbar." Other images: an aquatic scene, an Arab horseman with sword and sheath. Politics speak through the cartoon of the holy places of Jerusalem surrounded by barbed wire against the outline map of Palestine. This is a familiar image, much used in Arab political iconography, which Fischer and Abedi also found in Iran.[1] All this is reasonably Islamic, or Islamicized, as one would expect in a publication like *Ahmad*. Yet atop the two crescents that frame the double page stand drawings of, on the left, Disney's Grandma Duck and, on the right, Charles Schulz's Snoopy. Signs of the West nestle comfortably with those of Islam. Nor is such a juxtaposition atypical. On the streets of Cairo brightly colored billboards recently showed an attractive Minnie Mouse happily doing her laundry. But this rodent stand-in for the Egyptian housewife was peddling laundry soap for the Al-Rayyân company, one of the leading Islamic investment companies, and as such an institution dedicated to the exclusive use of Islamic business practices (fig. 12.2).

Hence it is not surprising that the Arab comic strip, even a religious one like *Ahmad*, acts as a locus for a potentially international circulation of signs. The religious symbols easily function regionally, and Palestine brings together religion and politics in what can be either an Arab regional or a broader Islamic context.

الوحيد الذي حصل على جائزة نوبل مرتين هو الكيميائي البريطاني فريدريك سانجر، فقد حصل عليها عامي ١٩٥٨ و ١٩٨٠ .

أطول مدة لتوقف قلب بشري هي ٣ ساعات و ٣٢ حدث هذا عام ١٩٧٧ للفتاة (جين جويون) وهي مدة قياسية حتى الآن .

استخدام قفازات الملاكمة يرجع إلى عام ١٥٢٠ أخذت عن أهل جزيرة ثيرا اليونانية .

أقدم نص مكتوب تم العثور عليه كان باللغة على ورقة بردية ، عثر عليها على بعد ١٣٫٧ كم بما يفلسطين ، ويرجع تاريخه إلى ٣٧٥ ـ ٣٣٥

حامد أبو زيد حسين
أسيوط ج . م . ع

الصورة
بسام جبير
١٠ سنوات

الصورة
علي حمداني
٨ سنوات

الصورة
هشام طليس

الصورة
خضر حيدر

وإن خيرت اخترتك أحد
دون شك سيظهر أو ندامه
أرقبها لأقرأها بشوق
كشوق الزارع كي تأتي الغيامه
سنبقى سميرتي دوماً لساعة
وإن أصبحت كهلاً ولست العامه

سلام شعيتو
الجنوب ـ لبنان

مخترع الديناميت هو الفرد نوبل .
مخترع التليفون هو جون ابراهام بل .
مخترع التليفون الآلي هو ادمون كولت .
مخترع الراديو هو ماركوني .
مخترع المسدس هو صامويل كولت .
مخترع رص الطرق هو جوماكوم .

كارولين هنا الخوري

المواكب الصاعدة

اخت مواكبهم في الطريق طروق بها الفرحة الغامره
كتبوا في سجل الزمان سطوراً منورة زاهره
أنت على الأفق راياتهم تعانقها البسمة العاطره
اح العدو فلا رجعة مع الحية المرة الخاسره
ست أشهد تلك الجموع وقد عبرت في خطأ صامده
مخذ الطريق وفي كفها مشاعل تباهة والده
ر السبيل وفي قوة تذيب خطأ الزمن الجاحده
ست مع النور في غيطة أحي مواكبنا الصاعده

إبراهيم عبدالله الفيشاوي ـ مصر

ـ تتم عملية الرؤية ؟
من الطبيعي أن عملية الرؤية لا يمكن أن الظلام الدامس ، فلا بد من وجود أشعة تخترق الحدقة،لتصل إلى الشبكة التي إشارات معينة لمركز الأبصار في المخ،فيرى إنسان كل ما هو أمامه .

معنى الحول ؟
إن كل إنسان لا بد له من ست عضلات في عين تساعده على تحريك عينه في كل اتجاه ، ربما يحدث أي خلل لأي من تلك لات .. وفي هذه الحالة تتحرك كل عين في اتجاه فيصير الشخص أحولاً .

شريف شهاب
ثانوية المقاصد ـ

١ ـ ما هو الشيء الذي لا يفكر ولا يتكلم ،
ولكن يقول الحقيقة ؟
٢ ـ أي شيء يولد بذنب ومن دون قوائم
وحين يموت . . . يموت بقوائم ومن دون ذنب ؟

ج ٨ ـ ١٢٣ ـ ٥
١ ـ ١٣٦٢
١٢٣

محمد إبراهيم بيضون ـ
الشهابية

القرش

مخلوق عجيب طالما أثار الرعب والخوف في قلوب الناس ، وهو ينتمي إلى فصيلة الأسماك ، ومنه ما هو متوحش وغير متوحش توجد منه عدة أنواع :

القرش ذو الذنب الطويل والقرش النمر والقرش الأبيض ، وهو أخطر الأنواع ، ويبلغ طوله ٦ ـ ٨ أمتار ، ويمتلك هذا القرش ، عند نهاية فتحة فمه ، صفاً من الأسنان المسطحة والمثلثة الجوانب والمسننة الأطراف ، بحيث يستطيع أن يبض ضحيته بعمق ، وله صف إضافي من الأسنان مخبأ تحت فكه العظمي وذلك للحالات الطارئة ، في وقت القنص العنيف .

وجلد القرش عامة غير مغطى بالحراشف بل بمادة معروفة بالأسنان الجلدية ، تشبه تركيبها الأسنان ، والقرش يحتاج عادة إلى كيس من الغاز داخل جسمه كي يبقى عائماً حتى وهو نائم ، فلا يغرق إلى قاع البحر ...

بسام شريم

من أقوال الرسول (ص)

قال رسول الله (ص) :

ومن خرج في سبيل الله مجاهداً فله بكل خطوة سيماها ألف حسنة ويمحى عنه سبعمائة ألف سيئة وترفع له سبعمائة ألف درجة ، وكان في ضمان الله ، بأي حتف مات ، كان شهيداً ، وإن رجع رجع مغفوراً له ، مستجاباً دعاؤه .

وقال (ص) : من اغتاب مسلماً أو مسلمة لم يقبل الله صلاة ولا صيامه أربعين يوماً وليلة

محمد حسين مهـ
بيروت ـ لـ

قوة الذاكرة

عرف عن العرب قوة الذاكرة ، ولولا ذلك لما استطاعوا حفظ القرآن الكريم .

وذات مرة استعاد الشاعر أبو العلاء المعري ، أمام أحد الولاة ، ما تكلم به رجل بلغة غريبة لا يفهمها .

واستطاع شخص من تركيا تسميع ٦٦٦٦ من القرآن الكريم في ٦ ساعات بحضور ٦ من الحفظة .

سعيد فضل الله

بأقلامنا

السيوف

السيف .. وهي الأدوات الأساسية للحرب قبل الإسلام وأثناءه وبعده . ولكن فنون الحرب تقدمت.

وتغيرت الأسلحة تغيراً كاملاً فلا تستعمل السيوف الآن . وقد بقيت لها أسماء بدل كل اسم على خاصية من خصائص السيف المسمى . ومن هذه الأسماء :

● الحاسم : وهو الذي يحسم المواقف الصعبة في الحرب .

● الصارم : وهو سيف يشتهر بصلابته ومتانته .

● ذو الفقار : وهو سيف يمتاز بأن له فقرات .

● الأبيض : وهو السيف الذي يشتهر ببياض لونه .

● المهند : وهو سيف منسوب إلى الهند .

● القاطع : وهو السيف الذي يستخدم في القطع .

محمد حسن عبد الحافظ
مصر ـ أسيوط

دعاء

يا رب يا غفار ، إملأ لي قلبي ،

اغفر لي ذنبي ، بالصدق والإيمان ،

يا رب يا غفار ، بالخير والإحسان ،

أنر لي دربي ، يا رب يا غفار ،

يا رب يا غفار ، اغفر لي ذنبي ،

محمد عمر موسى
طرابلس ـ لبنان

أحمد ـ ١٦ ـ

12.1. *Variety of visual symbols.*

12.2. *Minnie Mouse peddles for an Islamic
investment company.*

Cultural Spaces

The signs, and to a considerable degree the magazines which carry them, operate within a number of contexts which fit one into another in a chain of progressive
delocalization. They extend from that of the nation-state (which we can provisionally
call national) through the subregional and regional to the international.

The national is preeminently the domain of production. Even *Mâjid* with its crucial Egyptian contribution is essentially an Emirates magazine. Controlling production means that the individual Arab states are the principal loci of censorship. And it
is their leaders who are celebrated in the majority of publications.

The regional (and subregional) are the spaces of distribution. Most comic-strip
magazines are read in more than one Arab state. It is not just the Emirates' *Mâjid* that
travels well. Kuwaiti magazines are sold in the Gulf and in Egypt. Iraqi publications
are sold in Egypt and other countries. Syria keeps out the strips of most other countries, though Egyptian periodicals, such as *Mîkî*, show up in its bazaars. The range of
Lebanese periodicals has shrunk during the civil war, but Beirut magazines, and especially collections of back issues, reach as far as Morocco. Strips radiate from Tunis in
all directions, but preeminently westward, toward Algeria and Morocco. Algeria's
publications flow to France more than to any Arab country. Some comic-strip magazines sell copies in Britain and France to Arab exile communities in those countries,
but except for Algerian, and to a limited extent Tunisian, periodicals, this remains a
minor phenomenon. Finally, the Palestinians publish from their exile in Cyprus.[2]

The pattern outlines an old division, that between the Maghrib (the Arab West)
and the Mashriq (the Arab East). Traditionally, the East has been culturally supreme,
and it is not surprising that an Arabian periodical penetrates the entire Maghrib while

no Tunisian equivalent has such success in the Mashriq. If the subregional represents longstanding historico-cultural divisions, the regional pattern links culture and language. The Algerian case shows the crucial role of language. And the linguistic issue here is more absence than presence. If Algerian comic-strip life links better to France than to its Arab neighbors, it is because of the weakness of its Arabic, not the strength of its French. Tunisian intellectuals are almost as at home in the language of Corneille as are their Algerian counterparts. But their greater knowledge of written Arabic, combined with governmental encouragement of Arabic-language publication, has made Tunisian strips much like those of other Arab countries.

More than just a regional cement, the Arabic language also acts as a partial insulation against the international media. It is partly the differing linguistic environment which accounts for the sense of the virtual omnipotence of the international media in the discussion of Akbar S. Ahmed. Ahmed's examples are drawn preeminently from South Asian and British Muslim realities where English plays an enormous role.[3] The resulting situation has more in common with that of the Beurs in France or, to a lesser degree, that of Francophone Algerian media. Indeed, it is largely in Algerian Francophone comics that one finds the postmodern sense of intercultural and anachronistic play evidenced by Ahmed. Slim's "Abdelhimmler IV" is more postmodern than anything in Arabic language strips.

The Algerian-French connection, visible in distribution and intellectual influence and concretized in the existence of Beur comics, opens Arab strips to the international environment. Cultural currents flow in both directions. The French-born Boudjellal displays his hip secularism in the Algerian Francophone periodical, *Algérie-Actualité*, thus playing a role in the politico-cultural battle dividing the Algerian elite between largely Francophone secularists and heavily Arabophone Islamic revivalists. In the last few years, a Franco-Islamic comic strip production has emerged (alongside other religious-educational genres) that propagates the Islamic cultural message within Europe. At the same time, French technical collaboration was also crucial in both the biography of Nasser and the stripification of the Qur'ân. Yet equally important is the impact of American materials, especially Disney. The globalization of the American mouse threatens to swamp even France, with the recent implantation of Euro-Disneyland in Marne-la-Vallée. Nevertheless, the influence of Disney on Arab comic strips has been declining, as native production has expanded. Japanese comics, increasingly important in the United States, have yet to make significant inroads into the Middle East.[4] Their presence in France is also still modest. Yet, this French connection is opening a second path for the internationalization of Arab comic-strip materials. Farid Boudjellal has recently signed contracts to introduce the Franco-Arab Slimani family to Japanese (and who knows ultimately how many other international) audiences.[5]

The essentially regional reach of Arab strips is also manifest in the tendency of artists and scenarists to cross political boundaries. Algerians write and draw for Tunisian periodicals. Syrians use Egyptians and Palestinians, as do Iraqis. Comic-strip magazines from the Gulf publish artists and scenarists from Egypt, Syria, and Lebanon.

Of course, other media are also to some degree pan-Arab. But comic strips are unique in that they are usually a collaborative enterprise (unlike, for example, fiction) while far less expensive to create than, say, the cinema. Hence they are produced in a variety of countries by largely inter-Arab teams. They thus may well be the most pan-Arab of all modern forms of cultural expression. Newspapers are far more limited to their home countries in both authorship and circulation, perhaps at least partly because they are under tighter political control.[6]

These artists and writers who work from one end of the region to another are recreating an old pattern. In the classical Islamic world, scholars and artists of all sorts moved freely among the often rival states and empires. An individual could hail from Morocco, study in Egypt, and ply his trade from Syria to Central Asia. In our day, some frontiers are less passable. And as a space of circulation, the medieval Dâr al-Islâm has been replaced by a smaller Arab world, without Spain, Turkey, and Iran.

The frequent ineffectiveness of the Arab League and the political disunity of the Arab world, so cruelly exposed in the Gulf War, tend to obscure, from Western eyes, the essential cultural unity of the region. Comic strips remind us of it and show its dual bases, a common written language and a common cultural and historical heritage.

Individual national strips pay homage to this common heritage by negotiating links between regional and local identities. The most common strategy is the appeal to an original Arabian identity functioning at the same time as a substratum to modern existence and as an ultimate source of value.

Saddâm Husayn personified the Arab heritage of his country by linking modern Iraq to his bedouin ancestors. Though the officially Islamic *al-Firdaws* is miles apart ideologically from the Baath leader's secularism, it sets its moral tales in that same semimythical, implicitly valorizing space. A secularized Arabia delocalizes Iraqi politics just as an Islamic Arabia delocalizes Egyptian religious propaganda. Both also, of course, reflect nostalgia for a golden age, nobler, purer, and free of the oppressive bureaucratic state—a nostalgia Egyptianized in *Mîkî*'s Pharaonic strips. As we saw, the immensely successful *Mâjid* delocalizes in the other direction, but its camel hero, Sâbir, stands for both an Arabian specificity and a pan-Arab cult of origins. Tunisian strips effectively cultivate both an Arab regional and a Maghribian subregional identity, linking the two, for example, through the celebration of the Arab-Islamic conquest of North Africa.

Yet even when the focus is explicitly religious, the spaces of diffusion and textual reference rarely extend beyond the Arab countries to the larger unit of the Islamic world. It is not just that *Mâjid*, always respectful of Islam, treats non-Arab Muslim countries as purely exotic locales, ignoring their status as brother Muslim societies. References to non-Arab Muslim societies, even those in the Middle East, are rare. This is not to deny the influence of contemporary Islamic currents from non-Arab and even non–Middle Eastern societies on Arab Islam. Simply, when it is a matter of siting adventures, of giving origins to visitors from outside, other Muslim countries are ignored as much by Islamic as by more secular comic strips. Religion may be as important as or more important than language in defining the nature of group identity, but language takes precedence (again) in defining the geographical perimeters of that identity.

The most common of extra-Arab solidarities is not religion but politics: the Third

World and anti-imperialism, exploited from Algiers to Abu Dhabi. But the identification with non-Arab struggles tends to remain mediated, indirect. Far more concrete is the attention paid by virtually all Arab strips to the plight of the Palestinians, and the fact that Palestine is a consensus issue among non-Arab as well as Arab Muslims does not change its treatment in Arab strips as an Arab problem.

Indeed the anti-imperialist paradigm can as often be used for a narrower, local-national identification as for an international one. Both Syrian and Algerian strips have read the East versus West anticolonial model back in time to the Middle Ages or, more anachronistically, to the ancient world. Of such longitudinal focuses on "national" history, Egyptian Pharaonism is the best developed in both the country's comic strips and its sense of identity, partly, at least, because it is reinforced by the "international" Western culture's fascination with ancient Egypt.

Such interplay between local, regional, and international vectors shows the complications involved in the use of concepts like the transnational when speaking of cultural issues in the Arab world.[7] The term *transnational* was originally developed to discuss phenomena, such as international business and international organizations, which transcended the national state. Hence it is as much "trans-state" as it is "transnational."

Western influence—technical, cultural, or other—surely makes Arab strips a part of a transnational phenomenon, an emerging worldwide circulation of signs. But what about the far more intense circulation within the Arab world? To call this transnational would treat the state boundaries as cultural borders. As far as comic strips are concerned (and to a considerable degree other media), to speak of national cultures within each Arab state would be misleading. The Arab world functions as a cultural unit to a far greater extent (despite structural similarities) than do the worlds of Anglophonia or Francophonia. In this regional cultural system, local state forces function in tension with larger regional ones. Insofar as the concept of transnational implies an originally Western European model in which nation, state, and national culture coincide, its application to the non-Western world is problematic. And not only because of regional realities, like those of the Arab world. It is entirely possible that within many states, divisions between communities may be more culturally significant than common inclusion in a national community. But the minority cultures of the Arab world are absent from its strips. These are trans-statal within the region and transnational-international in their interactions with the essentially American and European cultural forces outside the region.

Elites, Masses, and Politics

Comic strips are an originally Western cultural product, imported and adapted in the region. Yet their place in the cultural world of the Arabs differs considerably from their position in the United States and Europe. In the United States, comics form part of what can be called either mass culture or popular culture depending on which aspects of the phenomenon one wishes to emphasize, its production and appeal to modern mass society or its nonelite audience and exploitation of themes that appeal to the common man.[8] In Europe a similar situation obtains, except that comics also appeal to a large section of the adult intellectual elite. They could almost be said to have both mass and elite audiences.[9]

Arab strips play neither the American nor the European role. Most visibly, and in distinction to both Western patterns, their creators are well integrated into the larger class of intellectuals. A significant percentage of the region's most prominent writers and scenarists enjoy established positions outside the comic-strip industry. These comic-strip creators fall into three groups: successful writers of serious fiction, successful artist painters, and well-placed editorial cartoonists. These last two groups often overlap. While in general the writers are responsible for scenarios and the artists and cartoonists for the drawings, many cartoonists (such as the Algerian Slim, the Egyptian Hijâzî, and the Syrian ʿAlî Farzât) or cartoonist-painters (such as the Egyptian Bahgory) are happy to provide their own scenarios. Hence Arab strips have one foot in the elite world of serious art and literature, the other in journalism.

One reason for these connections is the far greater links between branches of the intelligentsia in Arab countries than are found in the United States and even in Europe. Arab intellectuals are a self-conscious class functioning much as French intellectuals have done, but with even tighter links between branches of the arts and between the worlds of the creative arts, journalism, and the academy. At least from the viewpoint of the world of comic strips, the power of Arab intellectuals seems to have adapted well to the shift from intellectual and editorial power to the reign of the mass media (analyzed for France by Régis Debray).[10] The continuing influence of Arab intellectuals relates to the second major reason for their collaboration in comic-strip creation. This is the seriousness with which virtually everyone in Arab strips takes his or her product, whether it stems from concerns over the education and socialization of young people, on one hand, or the political implications of adult strips, on the other.

But even the Western concepts of high and low culture need to be modified in the Middle Eastern context. In the premodern Arab world the clearest boundary between what passed for high and low culture was language. High culture was created and transmitted (whether orally or in writing) in formal classical Arabic; low or popular culture was transmitted in dialect or a less literary form of written Arabic. Many of the elements and materials of the two cultures were held in common (from poetic topoi to stories, proverbs, and anecdotes).

With Westernization and modernization has come a new high culture, transmitted in a modern form of literary Arabic. The old high culture remains, largely confined to the more conservative sections of the religious elite. The old popular culture survives as a rapidly disappearing and largely rural folk culture which includes many folk religious practices. The popular culture of the cities, today, mixes surviving rural, folk-cultural elements and the new mass culture, of which comic strips form a part, along with cinema, television, popular music, the more popular press, etc.

This mass culture, associated with modern media, has been to a considerable degree either imported from the West or created locally in response to the challenge of Western mass culture. By and large the reception of Western culture has been the province (and to some degree also the legitimation) of the modern intellectual elite.

Hence it is they who are the chief purveyors of mass culture, and they quite naturally draw on their own modern high cultural references and resources.

This has also been, at least until recently, a secular culture. The problems in creating Islamic strips reflects this. Those who wanted to put the Qur'ân or the *Sîra* into strips often felt the need to turn to European technicians for aid. At the same time, propelled by the Islamic revival, a modern, mass-media-oriented Islamic culture is coming into being as a variant and challenge to the dominant secular high culture. Most Islamic children's magazines are a branch of this development.

The genesis of modern Arab mass culture from within secular elite culture is also reflected in the dominance of *fushâ*, the literary language, over dialect forms in strips. Here the trend has run contrary to that in television and cinema, where an earlier preference for formal language has increasingly given way to a preference for dialect. If strips, on balance, have gone in the other direction, it is perhaps an indication of the greater influence of literary groups in their preparation. It is certainly also a testimony to their pedagogical function, linked to official children's literature. The use of the more universal *fushâ*, in place of the local dialects, promotes regionwide distribution while permitting a multicentered production.

As a mass cultural product heavily influenced by Third World intellectuals, it is not surprising that Arab comics are so often political. But this does not mean that the intellectuals are the unreflective servants of state power. The recent books by Kanan Makiya on the politics and culture of contemporary Iraq[11] have reinforced a tendency to see such authoritarian Third World regimes as monolithic, to exaggerate the government's control over the realm of culture. For even in Saddâm Husayn's dictatorship (at least before the Gulf War), the people have access to a wide variety of materials, and talented figures from around the region participate in the national cultural life. Arab governments need the support of their intellectuals as reinforcements to their legitimacy. Provided that the writers and artists are willing to take certain risks (and most are willing to risk the milder forms of government disfavor), they have considerable room to maneuver vis-à-vis their governments. The cultural discourse of most Arab states results from a dialectical tension between the strategies of the governments who pay and censor and the artists who create.

Thus, far more visible than a contest between a high dominant and a subaltern or popular culture is the struggle between a state-sponsored propaganda culture and the expression of a semiautonomous intellectual class, itself articulating values (and bringing members) covering a social range from the petite bourgeoisie to remnants of the old aristocracy.

The tensions between the national-local and regional-Arab forces in comic-strip creation and distribution provide extra space for political nonconformism. Artists can work for a variety of governments. If their political line is out of favor in their home country, they can often make their living by selling to another state. Or they can turn to private companies in other jurisdictions. Thus Hijâzî, once he could no longer peddle his subversive Tanâbila series in the state-controlled *Samîr*, turned to the Beirut-based Dâr al-Fatâ al-ʿArabî to publish further installments, which then found their way back into Egypt. Ideological competition between Arab states also strengthens the hands of the intelligentsia. Artists can (and often do) embarrass their own governments by writing for, or moving to, rival states, as the Nasserite Ahmad ʿUmar did when he set up shop in Abu Dhabi.

Individual state governments handle censorship and generally insist on the more or less direct praise of their own leaders and often on the promotion as well of their state ideologies. Yet the comics are often read outside the jurisdiction of the leaders they praise. When a child or young person in one Arab state sees the praise of the leader of another, or better yet of several others, the plurality of objects virtually obliges a certain skepticism on his or her part. While one cannot poll Arabs to determine their attitudes to their political leaders, there is considerable reason (reinforced, for example, by popular political jokes) to believe that the audiences for comic strips treat the cults of personality to which they are exposed the same way most of their fellow citizens react to the ubiquitous pictures of their leaders. That is, they see them as road signs; they tell the individual who the leader of his country is. They instill a kind of legitimacy, that of de facto power.

The types of messages much more likely to durably influence the attitudes of their young readers are those more general ideological positions (ideology here including both politics and religion) that are substantially common across the strips of different Arab states: Arab solidarity, anti-imperialism and anti-Zionism, the glory of the Arab heritage, and respect for Islam as heritage and as continuing moral basis for social life. These are also, of course, to a considerable degree, consensus values throughout the region. Such positions can effectively be made to fit, with some slight differences in emphasis, both the secular and the Islamist approaches to contemporary Arab culture. Between them and the more obvious forms of political conformism lies a considerable realm for political and social debate. One subject, hotly contested in the Arab world as it is in the United States, is the question of appropriate roles for women. Slightly less directly, other issues, from corruption to the roles of the state and the media and forms of economic organization, also frequently color the world of Arab comic strips. It is these debates, carried on in a regionwide discourse, that give Arab strips much of their raison d'être. And it is they, as much as the desire to maintain and forge a distinctive identity, that suggest that Arab strips will remain as a vital alternative to the international mass media.

But is the culture of Arab strips a viable alternative to Western products? Abdallah Laroui could be talking about much of the material in Arab strips when he argues that

> . . . there are two types of alienation. . . . Westernization indeed signifies an alienation. . . . But there exists another form of alienation in Modern Arab society . . . this is the exaggerated medievalization obtained through quasi-magical identification with the great period of classical Arabian culture. The cultural policy of all the Arab states combats the alienation of Westernization by two means: the sanctification of Arabic in its archaic form and the vulgarization of classic texts (the resurrection of the cultural legacy).[12]

We believe that contemporary Arab comic strips show that it is possible to evoke national identity and tradition without abandoning the modern world. The treatment of the *turâth* in *Mâjid* and in the children's magazines of Tunisia reveals how old stories and events can be the basis for the evocation of modern problems. They can also be creative rereadings of traditional materials by artists who have something to say to both the adults and the children of their societies. And the success of literary Arabic, of *fushâ*, in a pan-Arab periodical such as *Mâjid* shows that this is far from being an archaic form of the language. Read avidly by the children of the region, it is the linguistic future of the Arab world.

But the liveliest force sweeping the Middle East today is not the secular, more-or-less socialist nationalism that nurtured most Arab strips. It is the Islamic revival, whose penetration is extending into previous bastions of secular culture such as literature. Will an Islamist intolerance of visual propaganda make the 1980s into a bygone golden age of Arab strips? We have already seen that some Islamist groups, at least, are more than willing to adopt this language of iconography and word. Iran is a model of limited value here, because the Twelver Shî'ism of that country has long used iconographic propaganda. Nevertheless, the general tendency of postrevolutionary Iranian production has been the Islamicization of existing high cultural forms (such as the novel and cinema), not their elimination. Besides, future Islamist ministers of culture will find themselves faced with the same challenges as their predecessors. If they do not want to be overwhelmed by the international production with its often alien values, they must make their own native pictures, balloons, and heroes.

Notes

1. Introduction

1. Walt Kelly, *Pluperfect Pogo*, ed. Mrs. Walt Kelly and Bill Crouch, Jr. (New York: Simon & Schuster, 1987), p. 210.

2. Ariel Dorfman and Armand Mattelart, *How to Read Donald Duck: Imperialist Ideology in the Disney Comic*, trans. David Kunzle (New York: International General, 1975); Ariel Dorfman, *The Empire's Old Clothes*, trans. Clark Hansen (New York: Pantheon, 1983).

3. See, for example, Pierre Fresnault-Deruelle, *Récits et discours par la bande: Essais sur les comics* (Paris: Librairie Hachette, 1977); Alain Rey, *Les Spectres de la bande: Essai sur la B.D.* (Paris: Les Editions de Minuit, 1978); Philippe Souchet et al., *Le Message politique et social de la bande dessinée* (Toulouse: Privat, 1975); and the articles in *Communications* 24 (1976). An example of recent American scholarship is the critically sophisticated Joseph Witek, *Comic Books as History: The Narrative Art of Jack Jackson, Art Spiegelman, and Harvey Pekar* (Jackson: University Press of Mississippi, 1989).

4. Allen Douglas and Fedwa Malti-Douglas, *L'Idéologie par la bande: Héros politiques de France et d'Egypte au miroir de la BD* (Cairo: CEDEJ, 1987); Bertrand Millet, *Samir, Mickey, Sindbad et les autres: Histoire de la presse enfantine en Egypte* (Cairo: CEDEJ, 1987); Bertrand Millet, "Egypte: Cent ans de bande dessinée," in *Langues et cultures populaires dans l'aire arabo-musulmane* (Paris: Association Française des Arabisants, 1988), pp. 53–67; Abdelhamid Helali, "La Littérature enfantine extra-scolaire dans le monde arabe: Analyse formelle et thématique des revues pour enfants," Thèse d'Etat, Université de Paris V, 1986; Allen Douglas and Fedwa Malti-Douglas, "Le Peuple d'Egypte et son chef: Tensions iconographiques dans un strip nassérien," in *Images d'Egypte de la fresque à la bande dessinée* (Cairo: CEDEJ, 1991), pp. 77–87.

5. Mohamed Aziza, *L'Image et l'Islam* (Paris: Albin Michel, 1978); Frantz Fanon, *Peau noire masques blancs* (Paris: Editions du Seuil, 1975), pp. 119-21.

6. See, for example, the articles in *Middle East Report*, special issue, "Popular Culture," no. 159 (1989). See also Chapter 12, note 9, below.

7. For a fuller discussion, see Fedwa Malti-Douglas, "Sign Conceptions in the Islamic World," in *Semiotics: A Handbook on the Sign-Theoretic Foundations of Nature and Culture*, ed. Roland Posner, Klaus Robering, and Thomas E. Sebeok (Berlin and New York: Walter de Gruyter, forthcoming).

8. See, for example, Ibn Dâniyâl, *Khayâl al-Zill wa-Tamthîliyyât Ibn Dâniyâl*, ed. Ibrâhîm Hamâda (Cairo: al-Mu'assasa al Misriyya al-ʿAmma lil-Ta'lîf wal-Tarjama wal-Tibâʿa wal-Nashr, 1961).

9. On manuscript miniatures, see, for example, Aziza, *L'Image*, pp. 54–58; Thomas W. Arnold, *Painting in Islam* (New York: Dover, 1965), pp. 79–81; Katharina Otto-Dorn, *L'Art de l'Islam*, trans. Jean-Pierre Simon (Paris: Editions Albin Michel, 1967), pp. 222–33.

10. See, for example, Maurice Horn, ed., *The World Encyclopedia of Comics* (New York: Avon, 1977), p. 47.

11. See chap. 3.

12. The term *sequential art*, which covers materials from photonovels to Hogarth, is too broad for our purpose. See, for example, Witek, *Comic Books*, pp. 5–10; Pierre Fresnault-Desruelle, "Aspects de la Bande Dessinée," in Alphons Silbermann and H. D. Dyroff, eds., *Comics and Visual Culture* (Munich: K. G. Saur, 1986), pp. 63–66.

13. Fanon, *Peau noire*, pp. 119–21; Akbar S. Ahmed, *Postmodernism and Islam: Predicament and Promise* (London: Routledge, 1992), pp. 222–65.

14. For example, Muhyî al-Dîn al-Labbâd, *Nazar* (Cairo: al-ʿArabî lil-Nashr wal-Tawzîʿ, 1987), pp. 20–21; Muhyî al-Dîn al-Labbâd, personal interview, Paris, June 23, 1988.

15. See, for example, Millet, "Egypte," and *Samîr*, pp. 26–89; Helali, "La Littérature enfantine," pp. 3–13; Muʿtaz Sawwaf, "La B.D. arabe," in *Histoire mondiale de la bande dessinée*, ed. Claude Moliterni (Paris: Pierre Horay, 1989), pp. 274–75.

16. See chap. 9.

17. Nutayla Râshid (known as Mâmâ Lubnâ), personal interview, Cairo, Mar. 1, 1988; Millet, *Samîr*, p. 59.

18. The Iraqi periodical *Majallatî* adopts the intermediate solution of using partly vocalized Arabic.

19. Horn, *Encyclopedia*, pp. 745–47; Jean-Bruno Renard, *Bandes dessinées et croyances du siècle* (Paris: Presses Universitaires de France, 1986), p. 5.

20. Khadîja Safwat, personal interview, Cairo, Mar. 5, 1988. See also Witek, *Comic Books*, pp. 96-98. Witek's other major examples, Harvey Pekar and Jack Jackson, characteristically embody highly critical views of U.S. history and society.

21. Horn, *Encyclopedia*, pp. 26–27.

22. Art Spiegelman, *Maus* (New York: Pantheon, 1986), and *Maus II* (New York: Pantheon, 1991), which won a Pulitzer prize.

23. Beyond the question of relative social permissiveness, we have seen no evidence of any influence by U.S. underground comics on Arab production. Witek argues convincingly for the importance of the underground tradition in the rise of American fact-based comics, while in the Arab world fact-based comics have often developed in the context of official education and propaganda. See Witek, *Comic Books*, pp. 58–61.

24. Samir al-Khalil, *The Monument: Art, Vulgarity, and Responsibility in Iraq* (Berkeley: University of California Press, 1991), p. 3. There is, of course, another element here (which al-Khalil does not mention), and that is an insistence on authenticity in an environment where mendacious propaganda is common. For another example of this kind of device, see chap. 9.

2. Mickey in Cairo, Ramsîs in Paris

1. An earlier version of this chapter appeared in Douglas and Malti-Douglas, *L'Idéologie*, pp. 18–55. Some of the elements from this earlier version were later taken up by Bertrand Millet in "Cent ans."

2. See chap. 8.

3. Dorfman and Mattelart, *How to Read Donald Duck*.

4. Since all of the examples discussed are taken from the 1972 series of *Mîkî*, they will be identified exclusively by the issue number.

5. See A. J. Wensinck and G. Vajda, "Firʿawn," *EI²*.

6. Of course, Mickey *Mouse* and Red *Cat* are technically already animals. This and later complications herein created (i.e., turning Red Cat and his group into cats) testify to the relative lack of sophistication with which the Egyptian strip deals with the common comic situation of characters who can possess either human or animal qualities, as in the quack of Donald Duck or the deliberately ambiguous behavior of Pogo characters.

7. Jean Vercoutter, *L'Egypte ancienne* (Paris: Presses Universitaires de France, 1973), p. 78.

8. Since most of the speech in the strip is written in Cairene and not in literary Arabic, it has been transliterated with the appropriate dialectical pronunciation.

9. An attempt to identify folkloric elements in comic strips has been made by Rolf Wilhelm Brednich, "Comic Strips as a Subject of Folk Narrative Research," in *Folklore Today*, ed. Linda Dégh et al. (Bloomington: Indiana University Research Center for Language and Semiotic Studies, 1976), pp. 45–55.

10. Dorfman and Mattelart, *How to Read Donald Duck*, pp. 42–43.

11. Roland Barthes, *Mythologies* (Paris: Editions du Seuil, 1970), pp. 44–46.

12. Dorfman and Mattelart, *How to Read Donald Duck*, pp. 55–57.

13. Georges Sadoul, *al-Sînamâ fî al-Buldân al-ʿArabiyya* (Beirut: Markaz al-Tansîq al-ʿArabî lil-Sînamâ wal-Tilifizyûn, n.d.), p. 285.

14. Lionel Balout, *La momie de Ramsès II* (Paris: Musée de l'Homme, 1985).

15. This can be seen, for example, in Najîb Mahfûz, *Zuqâq al-Midaqq* (Beirut: Dâr al-Qalam, 1972).

16. Bernard Lewis, *The Middle East and the West* (New York: Harper & Row, 1964), p. 67; Kate Millett, *Going to Iran* (New York: Coward, McCann & Geoghegan, 1982), p. 57.

17. Vicky du Fontbaré and Philippe Sohet, "Codes culturels et logique de classe dans la bande dessinée," *Communications* 24 (1976), pp. 70–73.

18. Ramsîs, of course, is a figure who alternates between giant and normal size. One could easily see this, following Bruno Bettelheim, as a focusing on the difficult transition from childhood to adulthood, since giants in fairy tales often represent the world of adults. Some such evocation may be present here. Its general applicability to "The Adventures of Ramsîs" is limited, however. Ramsîs ends as a giant. But it would be a mistake to see this giant status as a successfully achieved adulthood, since it represents, instead, a return to the point of origin. See Bruno Bettelheim, *The Uses of Enchantment: The Meaning and Importance of Fairy Tales* (New York: Vintage, 1977), p. 27.

19. In its day, this was the most successful commercial film in the history of the Egyptian cinema. See ʿAbd al-Munʿim Saʿd, *Mûjaz Ta'rîkh al-Sînamâ al-Misriyya* (Cairo: Matâbiʿ al-Ahrâm al-Tijâriyya, 1976 [?]), p. 52.

20. The comparison of Nasser with Ramsîs II was reported to the authors by Cairenes; and Sadat, in interviews on U.S. television, argued that he had acted like Ramsîs II, who made peace with the Hittites after the victorious battle of Carchemish.

3. Nasser, or the Hero in Strips

1. On the continuum between fictional comic strips and political, nonfiction strips as well as the symbiosis between comic-strip hero and historical figure suggested by the comic treatment of history or politics, see Pierre Fresnault-Deruelle, *La Chambre à bulles: Essai sur l'image du quotidien dans la bande dessinée* (Paris: Union Générale d'Editions, 1977), pp. 63–81, 187–91.

2. Muhammad Nuʿmân al-Dhâkirî et al., *Jamâl ʿAbd al-Nâsir* (Paris: Manshûrât al-Sihâfa al-Ifrîqiyya al-Mushtaraka, 1973). In his *Comment on raconte l'histoire aux enfants* (Paris: Payot, 1986), pp. 93–96, Marc Ferro discusses this strip but most likely did not read the text in the original. That may be the explanation of several inexactitudes. Ferro insists, for example, that "the name of the State of Israel is not even mentioned" (p. 96) when the word *Israel* is used to indicate the Jewish state throughout the strip. Further, Ruffieux is cited under the form "Riviou," evidently in transcription from the Arabic, when his name is written clearly in Roman characters several times in the text (*Jamâl ʿAbd al-Nâsir*, pp. 12, 18, 20, etc.). Ferro's analysis is limited essentially to a summary of the strip (not always accurate) and a list of the points allegedly omitted from the biography.

3. For a fuller discussion of this point, see Allen Douglas, "Al-Muʾarrikh, al-Nass, wal-Nâqid al-Adabî," trans. F. Kâmil, *Fusûl* 4, no. 1 (1983), pp. 95–105.

4. Hayden White, *Metahistory: The Historical Imagination in Nineteenth-Century Europe* (Baltimore: Johns Hopkins University Press, 1973). See also Douglas, "al-Muʾarrikh," p. 100.

5. See chap. 2.

6. See Witek's similar discussions of this problem in his analyses of historical comics from the United States. It is noteworthy that the phenomenon of double narrative also appears despite the fact that most of Witek's texts select the more adventure-oriented, fictionlike parts of the historical record. See Witek, *Comic Books*, pp. 22, 38–39, 43, 65, 79–90.

7. Xavier Musquera and André Bérélowitch, "L'Aventure coloniale," in *Histoire de France en bandes dessinées: De la révolution de 1848 à la IIIᵉ République* (Paris: Larousse, 1978), pp. 964–65.

8. Gino Nebiolo, Introduction to *The People's Comic Book*, trans. Endymion Wilkinson (Garden City: Doubleday, 1973). It is worthy of note that the Chinese authors have chosen this technique even though the relatively fictional character of their narratives would have made their adaptation to the use of balloons less difficult.

9. See, for example, Agnès Richomme, *Sainte Marguerite-Marie et le message du Coeur de Jésus* (Paris: Editions Fleurus, 1965).

10. Michel Roquebert and Gérald Forton, *Aymeric et les cathares* (Toulouse: Loubatières, 1978).

11. See, for example, Roquebert and Forton, *Aymeric*, pp. 4–7, 18.

12. Hu Chi-Hsi and Dupuis, *La Longue marche: Mao Tse-Toung* (Neuilly-sur-Seine: Dargaud, 1981).

13. This album forms the subject of chap. 4. An intermediate solution has been adopted in the comic-strip biographies of Indian heroes (both historical and mythological) in the Amar Chitra Katha series. Though the amount of parallel historical narrative is kept to a minimum and the more traditional narrative aspects of the story are emphasized, historical-political considerations are included and considerable use is made of the explanatory material in the strip. See, for example, Pushpa Bharati and C. M. Vitankar, *Jayaprakash Narayan* (Bombay: India Book House Education Trust, n.d.).

14. G. Buzzelli, Fernando Tacconi, and Robert Bielot, "Chronique de l'entre-deux-guerres" and "Sur tous les fronts," in *Histoire de France en bandes dessinées: De la Grande Guerre à la Vᵉ République*, pp. 1059, 1081.

15. Victor de la Fuente and Maurice Delotte, *Charles de Gaulle: Les Français et le gaullisme* (Salon de Provence: Service de l'Homme, 1977).

16. For a full discussion of this album, see Douglas and Malti-Douglas, *L'Idéologie*, pp. 68–123.

17. Yûsuf Shâhîn, *al-ᶜUsfûr* (1973).

18. On this adaptation of this originally cinematic concept to the analysis of strip compositions, see Annie Baron-Carvais, *La Bande dessinée* (Paris: Presses Universitaires de France, 1985), pp. 59–61, and Michel Pierre, *La Bande dessinée* (Paris: Librairie Larousse, 1976), pp. 142–45.

19. Baron-Carvais notes that one can superimpose a closeup on a long shot "pour donner une impression de relief" (*La Bande dessinée*, pp. 60–61). In the pages under discussion, however, we not only have cases of closeups superimposed over long shots but also of smaller scenes done as long shots superimposed over larger scenes portrayed from the same distance. As we will show later, the effect of these superimpositions is not simply to foreground but also to create narrative synchrony.

20. See Buzzelli et al., "Chronique," p. 1081; Witek, *Comic Books*, pp. 87–90.

21. It is true, as Paul Ricoeur notes, that all narratives, including fictional ones, must combine synchronic elements with the more dominant diachronic ones (in Ricoeur's terms, chronological and nonchronological elements). Nevertheless, history, by its nature, demands larger and more frequent doses of synchrony. That is why Ricoeur, while arguing for the absence of a clear structural distinction in this matter, can go no further than the idea of a "continuity" between story and history. See his *Hermeneutics and the Human Sciences*, ed. and trans. John B. Thompson (Cambridge: Cambridge University Press, 1981), pp. 277–80.

22. Organization of the comic text by pages (instead of a purely syntagmatic ordering of frames) can extend from the relatively common adaptation of one page to one episode (or not even one true narrative episode when the break is a literal or metaphorical "cliffhanger") to purely formal balancings of color or shape. Less often, this has permitted the juxtaposition of arrangements of frames that must be read "simultaneously" and recomposed by the reader. It is these last, of course, that are closest to our examples. See Fresnault-Deruelle, *Récits et discours*, pp. 41–71; Witek, *Comic Books*, pp. 20, 87–90.

23. On this distinction, see Roland Barthes, "Eléments de sémiologie," *Communications* 4 (1964), p. 105.

24. Fresnault-Deruelle, *Récits et discours*, p. 54.

25. Shâdî ʿAbd al-Salâm used this technique, for example, in his film about the 1973 War, *Juyûsh al-Shams* (1974).

26. Jean Lacouture, *Nasser* (Paris: Editions du Seuil, 1971), p. 268.

27. Lacouture, *Nasser*, pp. 147–51.

28. See Fresnault-Deruelle, *Récits et discours*, pp. 185–99.

29. For a fuller discussion of this topic, see Douglas and Malti-Douglas, "Le Peuple d'Egypte," pp. 77–87. For a comparative discussion of the leader-people nexus in charismatic politics, see Jean C. Robinson, "Institutionalizing Charisma," *Polity* 28, no. 2 (1985), pp. 181–203.

30. The best treatment of this question, with a refutation of the idea of Nasserism as fascist, is in Stanley Payne, *Fascism: Comparison and Definition* (Madison: University of Wisconsin Press, 1980), p. 207.

31. Buzzelli et al., "Chronique," p. 1081.

32. See chap. 2.

33. We will see another attempt at this same pretended transcendance of sign and referent in chap. 9.

4. Machismo and Arabism

1. See chap. 3.

2. See, for example, Majid Khadduri, *Socialist Iraq* (Washington, D.C.: Middle East Institute, 1978), pp. 36–41.

3. The government has, for example, produced a series of heroic war stories for children under the title *Hikâyât min Qâdisiyyat Saddâm* (Baghdad: Dâr Thaqâfat al-Atfâl). Though the stories do not concern Saddâm Husayn, the Iraqi leader's portrait is placed in cameo on every cover.

4. The biography of Nasser discussed in chap. 3 was Franco-Arabic, and strip biographies of Qadhdhâfî and Hassan II were both written in French and later translated into Arabic.

5. ʿAbd al-Amîr Muʿalla, *al-Ayyâm al-Tawîla*, 3 vols. (Baghdad: Dâr al-Hurriyya lil-Tibâʿa, 1978).

6. Adîb Makkî, *al-Ayyâm al-Tawîla* (Baghdad: Dâr Thaqâfat al-Atfâl, 1981).

7. It is this closure which permits its analysis as a self-contained work.

8. Gérard Genette, *Figures III* (Paris: Seuil, 1972), pp. 82–114.

9. One could, of course, qualify the story of the hero as biography and thus as a form of history, but a historical biography is one that integrates the life into history, not separating it as is the case here.

10. See, for example, Fresnault-Deruelle, *La chambre à bulles*, pp. 142 and 148, and du Fontbaré and Sohet, "Codes culturels," p. 66.

11. Muʿalla, *al-Ayyâm*, vol. 1, pp. 161–90.

12. Bernard Lewis, *The Political Language of Islam* (Chicago: University of Chicago Press, 1988), pp. 21–22. This politically reversed use of shadow, by linking Qâsim's rule with traditional Islamic sovereignties, potentially redefines these last in negative terms. (And the implication is stronger when we remember that the ʿAbbâsid capital was the same city of Baghdad.) Such a view would not be inconsistent with the evocation of Jâhilî ideals. Such ideals stand in marked contrast to the traditions of medieval Islamic bureaucratic states which drew more from Byzantine and Persian than from pre-Islamic Arab traditions. It should be noted that shadow (or shade) survives as a positive connotation in other modern contexts, like the work of Sayyid Qutb, *Fî Zilâl al-Qurʾân* (In the Shade of the Qurʾân), (Beirut: Dâr al-Shurûq, 1992).

13. See, for example, Marion Farouk-Sluglett and Peter Sluglett, *Iraq since 1958* (London: KPI, 1987), pp. 205–13.

14. R. A. Nicholson, *A Literary History of the Arabs* (Cambridge: Cambridge University Press, 1969), p. 55.

15. See, for example, Ignaz Goldziher, *Muslim Studies*, ed. and trans. S. M. Stern (Chicago: Aldine, 1967), vol. 1, pp. 11–44.

16. Al-Dhâkirî et al., *Jamâl ʿAbd al-Nâsir*, p. 7.

17. Muʿalla, *al-Ayyâm*, vol. 1, p. 40.

18. Muʿalla, *al-Ayyâm*, vol. 1, p. 69. The corresponding location in the strip narrative is p. 34.

19. Characteristic of this identification is the elimination from the album of material in the novel which distinguishes the hero from his bedouin environment. See, for example, Muʿalla, *al-Ayyâm*, vol. 1, pp. 183–86.

20. See chap. 9.

21. See chap. 9.

22. Of course, the idea of rite of passage in no way conflicts with the evocation of bedouin ideals. See, for example, Suzanne Stetkevych, "The Suʿlûk and His Poem: A Paradigm of *Passage Manqué*," *Journal of the American Oriental Society* 104 (1984), pp. 661–68.

23. The association of dreams with political legitimization and even predictions of future rule was quite common in the Arabo-Islamic oneiric tradition. Nevertheless, both the types of dreams and the ways in which they are used are generally quite different from our case here. See, for example, Jacob Lassner, *The Shaping of ʿAbbâsid Rule* (Princeton: Princeton University Press, 1980), pp. 25–26.

24. On the implications of color choices, see, for example, Baron-Carvais, *La Bande desinée*, p. 59.

25. Myth is being used here not in the sense of falsehood but of stories carrying collective values.

26. See, for example, Charles Saint-Prot, *Saddam Hussein* (Paris: Albin Michel, 1987), p. 41. The parallels between the lives of Saddâm Husayn and the Prophet Muhammad were developed in a museum display underneath a later monument. See al-Khalil, *The Monument*, p. 15. The Islamicization of the regime's propaganda represents a later development than the secular Baathism of our strip.

27. For example, none of the politically descriptive frames, even that of the revolution, has the least Islamic referent, whether architectural or linguistic (pp. 10, 11, 12). This careful omission of Islamic referents was certainly not followed in *Jamâl ʿAbd al-Nâsir* and is hardly reflective of the texture of life in even modern Arab cities. In these terms, *The Long Days* parallels the most leftist of European comic strips, avoiding, however, any obvious anticlericalism. See Renard, *Bandes dessinées*, pp. 50–91.

28. See, for example, A. J. Greimas and J. Courtès, *Sémiotique: Dictionnaire raisonné de la théorie du langage* (Paris: Hachette, 1979), p. 222.

5. Radicalism in Strips

1. See, for example, Jean-Luc Chalumeau, drawings by Agathe, *Le Capitalisme en bandes dessinées* (Paris: Hachette, 1979), pp. 38–43.

2. Sometimes his name is given as Faysal ibn Muhammad.

3. See chaps. 7 and 9.

4. See, for example, "Sî Juhâ" in *Le Maghreb*, March–May 1988. On the image of Juhâ, see, for example, ʿAbbâs Mahmûd al-ʿAqqâd, *Juhâ al-Dâhik al-Mudhik* (Cairo: Dâr al-Hilâl, n.d.).

5. The political nature of some of Hijâzî's strips was noted by Millet, "Cent ans," pp. 60–62.

6. The comic strips of the well-known Algerian artist Slim, aimed largely at an adult audience, are, despite certain critical positions, essentially conformist in the Algerian political context. See chap. 10.

7. Ahmad Hijâzî, personal interview, Cairo, Mar. 11, 1988. A recent series published by the government-controlled Dâr al-Hilâl publishing house is more politically conformist than Hijâzî's earlier work. See Hijâzî, *Yâ Halâwatak Yâ Jamâlak* (Cairo: Dâr al-Hilâl, 1989).

8. See, for example, *al-Intifâda bil-Kârîkâtîr* (Tunis: al-Ahâlî lil-Tibâʿa wal-Nashr wal-Tawzîʿ, 1988).

9. The biographical information was provided by Ahmad Hijâzî, personal interview, Cairo, Mar. 11, 1988.

10. Nutayla Râshid, personal interview, Cairo, Mar. 1, 1988.

11. See chap. 9.

12. Ahmad Hijâzî, numerous conversations, February through June 1988. Such positions

are not unique in the Arab world, since they are close to those effectively propagated by other cartoonists, most notably the prize-winning Syrian ʿAlî Farzât.

13. See, for example, Hijâzî, the cartoon strip *al-Ahâlî*, no. 285, Mar. 25, 1987, p. 3.

14. Hijâzî, "Teacher Nazîha's Program," *al-Ahâlî*, no. 318, Nov. 11, 1987, p. 3.

15. Hijâzî, *al-Ahâlî*, no. 285, Mar. 25, 1987, p. 1.

16. Hijâzî prepared three other Tanâbilas. One, the *Qaryat al-Tanâbila* (Village of the Tanâbila), was lost in the mail and never completed. It paints a picture of larceny and corruption in an Egyptian village. The second, *Tanâbilat al-Sibyân wal-Nisr al-Mashûr* (The Tanâbilat al-Sibyân and the Magic Eagle), was unavailable to us. Neither the creator nor the publisher had conserved copies. Ahmad Hijâzî, personal interview, Cairo, Mar. 11, 1988. Cf. Millet, "Cent ans," pp. 60–63. The third and most recent, *Yâ Halâwatak Yâ Jamâlak* (1989), is a pale reflection of his earlier efforts. In it, the Tanâbila, now children, organize a burglary ring and escape the country as the police are closing in on them. It is most noteworthy for a significant increase in Islamic referents, an apparent reflection of recent changes in the Egyptian environment.

17. We are taking the *Tanâbilat al-Khirfân* from the reprint of the series in booklet form: Ahmad Hijâzî, *Tanâbilat al-Sibyân wa-Tanâbilat al-Khirfân* (Cairo: Dâr al-Hilâl, n.d.).

18. Actually, the names appear for the first time in the movie sequence toward the end of *Tanâbilat al-Sibyân*, but they never play a real role in that series. Instead, people speak of the Tanâbila or of one or another of the Tanâbila.

19. See Ulrich Marzolph, *Der Weise Narr Buhlûl*, Abhandlungen für die Kunde des Morgenlandes 46, no. 4 (Wiesbaden: Franz Steiner, 1983).

20. This current Arabic term is derived from the English *luncheon meat* and usually describes a product similar to Spam. The pronunciation of this term can vary. Hijâzî has written it *lânshû*.

21. As its name suggests, *bluebeef* is normally made from beef. But there seems to be nothing more behind this than Hijâzî's sense of play.

22. The last part of this quote was corrected from the printed version, on our copy, by the author's hand. The original read: "and while eating *bluebeef* I think of *bluebeef*."

23. Tambûl is apparently the speaker. But because of the visual identity of the three Tanâbila and the occasional either absence or nonrealist use of color, it is not always possible to distinguish them in the text.

24. See, for example, Fedwa Malti-Douglas, "Yûsuf al-Qaʿîd wal-Riwâya al-Jadîda," *Fusûl* 4, no. 3 (1984), pp. 190–202, and Afterword to trans. of *War in the Land of Egypt* by Yusuf al-Qaʿîd (London: al-Saqi Books, 1986), pp. 185–92; James Monroe, *The Art of Badîʿ al-Zamân al-Hamadhânî as Picaresque Narrative* (Beirut: American University of Beirut, 1983).

25. Yûsuf al-Qaʿîd, *al-Harb fî Barr Misr* (Beirut: Dâr Ibn Rushd lil-Tibâʿa wal-Nashr, 1978), and *Yahduth fî Misr al-An* (Cairo: Dâr Usâma lil-Tabʿ wal-Nashr, 1977); Malti-Douglas, "Yûsuf al-Qaʿîd," and Afterword.

26. Millet, "Cent ans," p. 65.

27. Ahmad Hijâzî, *Tambûl al-Awwal* (Beirut: Dâr al-Fatâ al-ʿArabî, 1981).

28. A popular Egyptian vegetable, somewhat resembling spinach.

29. A European-style white bread, distinct from the bread eaten by the average Egyptian.

30. All the items in this list are well-known Oriental pastries.

31. Al-Qaʿîd, *al-Harb*, pp. 62, 72–73. Food references are used similarly in the verses of the popular leftist poet, Ahmad Fuʾâd Nigm. See Kamal Abdel-Malek, *A Study of the Vernacular Poetry of Ahmad Fuʾâd Nigm* (Leiden: E. J. Brill, 1990).

32. Ahmad Hijâzî, *Tahrîk al-ʿAql*, *al-Ahâlî*, no. 293, May 20, 1987, p. 12.

33. Since all the frames are numbered and on one large page, we are citing them by frame numbers.

34. A sly swipe at the Camp David peace accords between Egypt and Israel.

35. This was expressed to us over and over in conversations with Egyptian leftist intellectuals.

6. Sacred Images

1. See chap. 2.

2. See chap. 9.

3. Dr. Bahâ' al-Dîn, personal interview, Cairo, Mar. 6, 1988. *Al-Firdaws* describes itself as "The Magazine of the Muslim Child."

4. In its prehistory, *al-Muslim al-Saghîr* appeared as a supplement to *Majallat al-Shubbân al-Muslimîn* and briefly in reduced format before achieving its current form in 1984. Asked about financial support, Hilâl insisted that his costs were covered completely by advertisements. Given the circulation and the small amount of space devoted to advertisements, this would seem difficult, unless the advertising rates are pitched uneconomically high, which would make them equivalent to subventions. Marzûq Hilâl, personal interviews, Cairo, Feb. 18, Mar. 2, and Mar. 4, 1988.

5. See, for example, *Zam Zam*, no. 3, Ramadân/April 1988, pp. 1, 23.

6. *Zam Zam*, no. 3, Ramadân/April 1988, p. 23.

7. Al-Mukhtâr al-Islâmî, magazine and publishing house, also promotes anti-Nasserite pro-Muslim Brothers literature. See, for example, *al-Mukhtâr al-Islâmî*, no. 64, Shawwâl/May 1988.

8. A similar amorality can be found in an Ashʿab anecdote made into a strip in *Barâʿim al-Imân* (1988, no. 158). Ashʿab is a traditional trickster figure, and this moral system, which privileges cleverness over justice or Islamic morality (though not absolutely), is typical of *adab* anecdotal literature. See Franz Rosenthal, *Humor in Early Islam* (Leiden: E. J. Brill, 1956), and Fedwa Malti-Douglas, "Classical Arabic Crime Narratives: Thieves and Thievery in *Adab* Literature," *Journal of Arabic Literature* 19, no. 2 (1988), pp. 121–27.

9. Marzûq Hilâl, personal interviews, Cairo, Feb. 18, Mar. 2, and Mar. 4, 1988.

10. See, for example, *Mâjid*, 1988, no. 482; on this journal, see chap. 9.

11. We will be dealing with this pattern later in this chapter in a detailed examination of *al-Firdaws* moral tales.

12. Since the real periodicity of the publication is in Muslim months, though every issue is also labeled in Western months, it sometimes happens that two issues appear within one Western month.

13. A. J. Wensinck, "al-Khadir (al-Khidr)," *EI²*.

14. Cairo: Safîr, (Iʿlâm, Diʿâya, Nashr, 1988). The booklet version is in Wahdat Thaqâfat al-Tifl bi-Shirkat Safîr, *Kitâb al-Muslim al-Saghîr 2* (Cairo: Safîr—Iʿlâm, Diʿâya, Nashr, 1988), pp. 25–32. Despite a similarity in title, this series is not a product of the magazine *al-Muslim al-Saghîr*, discussed above.

15. Michael Riffaterre, "Intertextual Scrambling," *Romanic Review* 68 (1977), p. 197.

16. Muslim, *Sahîh Muslim bi-Sharh al-Nawawî* (Beirut: Dâr Ihyâ' al-Turâth al-ʿArabî, n.d.), vol. 16, p. 214. For the *hadîth*, see also Ibn Mâja, *Sunan*, ed. Muhammad Fu'âd ʿAbd al-Bâqî (Beirut: al-Maktaba al-ʿIlmiyya, n.d.), vol. 1, p. 31, and vol. 2, p. 1395.

17. Several variants of this *hadîth* exist, but in all of them the argument is the same. See, for example, al-Bukhârî, *Sahîh al-Bukhârî bi-Sharh al-Kirmânî* (Beirut: Dâr Ihyâ' al-Turâth al-ʿArabî, 1981), vol. 11, p. 18, and vol. 14, p. 42; al-Tirmidhî, *al-Jâmiʿ al-Sahîh—Sunan al-Tirmidhî*, ed. Kamâl Yûsuf al-Hût (Beirut: Dâr al-Kutub al-ʿIlmiyya, 1987), vol. 4, p. 453; al-Dârimî, *Sunan al-Dârimî* (Beirut: Dâr Ihyâ' al-Sunna al-Nabawiyya, n.d.), vol. 2, p. 311.

18. See chap. 4.

19. See chap. 9.

20. ʿAliyya Tawfîq and Kamâl Darwîsh, *Hikâyât ʿArabiyya wa-Islâmiyya: Al-Qâdî al-ʿAdil wa-Hikâyât Ukhrâ* (Cairo: Matâbiʿ al-Ahrâm al-Tijâriyya, 1986).

21. ʿAliyya Tawfîq and Kamâl Darwîsh, *Hikâyât ʿArabiyya wa-Islâmiyya: Sâlim wal-Asîr wa-Hikâyât Ukhrâ* (Cairo: Matâbiʿ al-Ahrâm al-Tijâriyya, 1986).

22. Marzûq Hilâl, personal interview, Cairo, Mar. 2, 1988.

23. Sayyid Qutb, *Maʿrikatunâ maʿa . . . al-Yahûd* (Cairo: Dâr al-Shurûq, 1988), pp. 20–38. The Moroccan series by Muhammad Binmasʿûd and ʿAbd al-ʿAzîz Ishbâbû, *Silsilat Ta'rîkh al-Islâm* (Mohamedia: Manshûrât Dâr al-Afâq al-Jadîda, 1988-), displays a similarly anachronistic (and uncharacteristic) anti-Judaism that even slides into anti-Semitic caricature (4/6). References in this series are identified by volume and page number.

24. See, for example, al-Baydâwî, *Tafsîr al-Baydâwî*, (Beirut: Dâr al-Kutub al-ʿIlmiyya, 1988), vol. 1, pp. 344–47, and 459–62; al-Thaʿlabî, *Qisas al-Anbiyâ'—ʿArâ'is al-Majâlis* (Beirut: Dâr al-Qalam, n.d.), pp. 61–72.

25. Ibn Hishâm, *al-Sîra al-Nabawiyya*, ed. Mustafâ al-Saqâ, Ibrâhîm al-Abyârî, and ʿAbd al-Hafîz Shalabî (Beirut: Dâr al-Qalam, n.d.), pp. 171–73.

26. Cf. Iva Hoth and Andre LeBlanc, *The Picture Bible* (Elgin: David C. Cook, 1979), pp. 524–35, whose Virgin Mary is slightly more modest than *al-Firdaws*'s Halîma.

27. To point out such similarities is not necessarily to imply direct influence. Complicating the matter is the existence of similar Ottoman iconography. See, for example, Zeren Tanindi, *Siyer-I Nebî, Islâm Tasvir Sanatinda Hz. Muhammed'in Hayati* (Istanbul: Hürriyet Vakvi Yayinlari, 1984), vol. 1, p. 225a. We owe this reference to Professor Spellberg. See also Denise A. Spellberg, "Marriages Made in Heaven and Illustrated on Earth: A Note on the Disjunction between Verbal and Visual Images in an Ottoman Manuscript," *Harvard University Bulletin of the Center for the Study of World Religions* 16 (1989–90), pp. 126–27. Thus contemporary Arab artists are willy-nilly influenced by an enormous range of iconography, on both a conscious and an unconscious level. As regards the representation of Christianity itself, in general, Arab comic strips avoid dealing directly with religious or ethnic minorities and pay no attention to religions other than Islam.

28. These are *al-Qâdî* and *Sâlim* (cited in nn. 20 and 21).

29. Bernard Lewis, *Race and Slavery in the Middle East* (New York: Oxford University Press, 1990), pp. 87, 96.

30. See chap. 4.

31. See, for example, *al-Rajul al-Sâlih wal-Kalb* (Cairo: Safîr—Iʿlâm, Diʿâya, Nashr, 1987).

32. See, for example, al-Bukhârî, *Sahîh*, vol. 21, pp. 170–71.

33. See, for example, al-Jâhiz, *Kitâb al-Bursân wal-ʿUrjân wal-ʿUmyân wal-Hûlân*, ed. ʿAbd al-Salâm Muhammad Hârûn (Baghdad: Dâr al-Rashîd lil-Nashr, 1982), pp. 539–47.

34. In one story (*Qâdî*, pp. 48–50), a judge does render a judgment, though it is justice and not law which is foregrounded.

35. Denise Spellberg, "Nizâm al-Mulk's Manipulation of Tradition: ʿA'isha and the Role of Women in the Islamic Government," *Muslim World* 78 (1988), pp. 111–17; Fedwa Malti-Douglas, *Woman's Body, Woman's Word: Gender and Discourse in Arabo-Islamic Writing* (Princeton: Princeton University Press, 1991), pp. 51–52.

36. Renard, *Bandes dessinées*, p. 196.

37. The Arabic original, published by al-Maʿrifa in 1983, is unavailable to us. The French text is *L'Avènement de l'Islam*, trans. Dalal Khoury (Paris: Robert Laffont/Al Marifa, 1985). This work should be distinguished from Mohamed Kada, Omar Bencheikh, and Abdel Majid Turki, *L'Avènement de l'Islam* (Paris: ACR Edition Internationale, 1987). The latter is a biography of the Prophet, with text on the left side of the page and, on the right, illustrations without text, whose division and sequencing into frames apes that of comic strips. The work, however, cannot be considered a comic strip.

38. W. Montgomery Watt, "Ibn Hishâm," *EI²*.

39. See chap. 2.

40. Later volumes by their subject matter may have dealt with issues like the Prophet's Night Journey (*miʿrâj*) in which there is an iconographic tradition.

41. Mohammad Arkoun, "Islam, Thought and Literature," public lecture, Austin, Tex., Sept. 18, 1989.

42. See chap. 8.

43. Youssef Seddik, Philippe Teulat, and Philippe Jouan, *Si le Coran m'était conté: Peuples Maudits*, Arabic title: *Hûd, Sâlih, Yûnus* (Geneva and Tunis: Editions Alif, 1989); Youssef Seddik and Benoît de Pelloux, *Si le Coran m'était conté: Abraham*, Arabic title: *Ibrâhîm* (Geneva and Tunis: Editions Alif, 1989); Youssef Seddik and Gioux, *Si le Coran m'était conté: Les Hommes de l'Eléphant*, Arabic title: *Ashâb al-Fîl* (Geneva and Tunis: Editions Alif, 1989).

44. Jean-Pierre Péroncel-Hugoz, "Le Coran en bandes dessinées," *Le Monde*, Jan. 7–8, 1990, pp. 1, 9; Djeynab Hane, "A travers l'Afrique: Non au Coran en bandes dessinées," *Jeune Afrique*, Jan. 29, 1990, p. 31; "Islam's Satanic Comics," *Newsweek*, Feb. 5, 1990, p. 36.

45. Youssef Seddik, "Avertissement," in *Peuples Maudits*, p. 4. Cf., however, *Hûd, Sâlih, Yûnus*, pp. 4–5.

46. This *sûra* has not yet been covered in any of the available albums.

47. Seddik, "Avertissement,", p. 3; *Hûd, Sâlih, Yûnus*, p. 6.

48. Peter J. Awn, *Satan's Tragedy and Redemption: Iblîs in Sufi Psychology* (Leiden: E. J. Brill, 1983), pp. 26–30.

49. Renard, *Bandes dessinées*, pp. 45–46.

50. Al-Qurtubî, *al-Jâmiʿ li-Ahkâm al-Qur'ân* (Cairo: Dâr al-Kutub al Misriyya, n.d.), vol. 9, p. 60.

51. We cannot see this contradiction as the work of the Western illustrator because the aging is also in a speech balloon and Seddik indicates in the Arabic introduction that he checked and approved all of the illustrations.

52. Sûrat al-Anbiyâ', verse 69; A. J. Arberry, *The Koran Interpreted* (New York: Macmillan, 1974), vol. 2, p. 22.

53. "Islam's Satanic Comics," *Newsweek*, Feb. 5, 1990, p. 36.

7. Syria

1. For example, Syrian television runs Soviet cartoons.

2. Names for the followers are derived either as a *nisba* from the plural name of the group (*talâ'i'î*), which is then sometimes pluralized; as a *nisba* from the singular noun (*talî'î*), itself used in singular or plural; or from the plural noun itself. For the interchangeability of these forms, see, for example, 1987, no. 10, pp. 42–43.

3. Yâsîn Zuhdî, personal interview, Damascus, Feb. 18, 1988; Dalâl Hâtim, personal interview, Damascus, Feb. 18, 1988.

4. The numbering begins at one in the middle of each calendar year after one year of publication.

5. D. Sourdel, "Bayt al-Hikma," *EI²*.

6. This imagery may also derive partly from the example of Soviet productivism.

7. The Arabic title has *nuhâsiyya*, derived from *nuhâs*, which is normally "copper," while *nuhâs asfar* is "brass." In the context of this story, however, and *The Thousand and One Nights* tale on which it is based, brass is normally understood.

8. *Alf Layla wa-Layla* (Cairo: Matba'at Bûlâq, n.d.), vol. 2, pp. 37–52; Richard Burton, *The Book of a Thousand Nights and a Night* (Burton Club Edition), vol. 6, pp. 83–122.

9. On the spiritual aspect of the tale, see, for example, Andras Hamori, *On the Art of Medieval Arabic Literature* (Princeton: Princeton University Press, 1974), pp. 145–63; David Pinault, *Story-Telling Techniques in the Arabian Nights* (Leiden: E. J. Brill, 1992), pp. 231–37.

10. Dalâl Hâtim, personal interview, Damascus, Feb. 18, 1988.

11. Usâma ibn Munqidh, *Kitâb al-I'tibâr*, ed. Philip Hitti (Beirut: al-Dâr al-Muttahida, 1981), trans. Philip K. Hitti as *Memoirs of an Arab-Syrian Gentleman* (Beirut: Khayats, 1964).

12. Zakariyyâ Tâmir, personal interview by telephone, Oxford, England, July 30, 1991.

13. Dalâl Hâtim, personal interview, Damascus, Feb. 18, 1988.

14. Zakariyyâ Tâmir and Ahmad Hijâzî, *al-Jarâd fî al-Madîna* (Beirut: Dâr al-Fatâ al-'Arabî lil-Nashr wal-Tawzî', 1975).

15. Zakariyyâ Tâmir, personal interview by telephone, Oxford, England, July 30, 1991.

16. Ibn Battûta, *Rihlat Ibn Battûta*, ed. Talâl Harb (Beirut: Dâr al-Kutub al-'Ilmiyya, 1987).

17. Fâtima Ba'labakkî, Nabîl Qaddûh, and Sarmad Junayd, *Rihlât Ibn Battûta*, 2 vols. (Beirut: Mu'assasat Bisât al-Rîh, n.d.); Muhammad 'Amir and Jum'a, "Rihlât Ibn Battûta," *Mâjid*, 1981, nos. 116–20. On *Mâjid*, see chap. 9.

18. See chap. 2.

19. Zakariyyâ Tâmir, personal interview by telephone, Oxford, England, July 30, 1991.

20. See chap. 9.

21. See chap. 6.

22. Ibn Shaddâd, *The Life of Saladin*, trans. C. W. Wilson and Lt.-Col. Conder (London: Palestine Exploration Fund, 1897), pp. 205–6. The incident is also evoked by the Palestinian author Emile Habiby in his most recent novel, *Khurâfiyya (Sarâyâ Bint al-Ghûl)* (Haifa: Arabesque, 1991), p. 45. Habiby has deliberately misspelled the word *khurâfiyya* by putting a *shadda* on the "r."

23. See chap. 6.

24. On Ash'ab, see Rosenthal, *Humor in Early Islam*. On *tufaylîs*, see Fedwa Malti-Douglas, "Structure and Organization in a Monographic *Adab* Work: *al-Tatfîl* of al-Khatîb al-Baghdâdî," *Journal of Near Eastern Studies* 40 (1981), pp. 227–45.

25. Al-Jâhiz, *al-Bukhalâ'*, ed. Tâhâ al-Hâjirî (Cairo: Dâr al-Ma'ârif, 1971); Fedwa Malti-Douglas, *Structures of Avarice: The Bukhalâ' in Medieval Arabic Literature* (Leiden: E. J. Brill, 1985).

26. The *kunya* is a name element meaning "father (or mother) of so-and so"; it can signify real parenthood or a metaphorical relation with an object or concept.

27. Al-Jâhiz, *al-Bukhalâ'*, p. 18.

28. Al-Jâhiz, *al-Bukhalâ'*, pp. 18, 131–32, 139–40.

29. *The Book of Misers* of al-Jâhiz has sometimes been seen as an anti-Persian work in these terms, but the reality is considerably more complex. See Malti-Douglas, *Structures of Avarice*, pp. 152–58.

30. Malti-Douglas, *Structures of Avarice*, pp. 72–78, 94–96, 144.

31. See chap. 4.

32. Malti-Douglas, *Structures of Avarice*, p. 30.

33. See chap. 6.

8. Tradition Viewed from the Maghrib

1. For the Algerian comic strip, see chap. 10.

2. Moroccan production has been extremely limited and has only become quantitatively significant in the last few years. See, for example, Zoubida Chahi, "La production des livres pour enfants au Maroc (1947–1991)," Mémoire for Diplôme, Ecole des Sciences de l'Information, Morocco, 1992, pp. 69–74. For some Tunisian materials which sit on the border between the editorial cartoon and the comic strip, see chap. 5.

3. This is the case, for example, in *'Irfân*. An ephemeral children's magazine which appeared in the late 1980s, *al-Jadwal*, is virtually bilingual French and Arabic. See, for example, *al-Jadwal*, 1988, no. 9.

4. Bilkhâmisa al-Shâdhilî and al-Tayyib al-Tirîkî, personal interviews, Tunis, Mar. 23, 1988; Farîd al-Shamlî, personal interview, Tunis, Mar. 24, 1988; Kamâl al-'Askarî, personal interview, Tunis, Mar. 31, 1988; 'Abd al-Hamîd al-Qusantînî, personal interviews, Tunis, Apr. 1, 1988, and May 24, 1988.

5. Farîd al-Shamlî, personal interview, Tunis, Mar. 24, 1988; 'Abd al-Hamîd al-Qusantînî, personal interviews, Tunis, Apr. 1, 1988, and May 24, 1988.

6. As of this writing, and despite some formal gestures, Tunisia is still a nondemocratic state whose other parties have no real access to power.

7. Kamâl al-'Askarî, personal interview, Tunis, Mar. 31, 1988.

8. *Bû* is the common North African form for *Abû* (father of), often used in onomastic constructions that link an individual with an attribute or object.

9. See chaps. 7 and 9.

10. The title of the magazine given to the girl varies from *'Irfân* in earlier years to *Shahlûl* after the creation of that periodical.

11. Farîd al-Shamlî, personal interview, Tunis, Mar. 24, 1988.

12. Bilkhâmisa al-Shâdhilî and al-Tayyib al-Tirîkî, personal interviews, Tunis, Mar. 23, 1988.

13. Kamâl al-'Askarî, personal interview, Tunis, Mar. 31, 1988.

14. Bilkhâmisa al-Shâdhilî, *Jâbir wal-Samak al-'Ajîb* (Tunis: Manshûrât Tûnis Qartâj, n.d.).

15. See Muhsin Mahdi, "Exemplary tales in the *1001 Nights*," in *The 1001 Nights: Critical Essays and Annotated Bibliography*, special issue of *Mundus Arabicus* 3 (1983), pp. 1–24.

16. *Alf Layla wa-Layla*, ed. Muhsin Mahdi (Leiden: E. J. Brill, 1984), vol. 1, pp. 86–126; *The Arabian Nights*, trans. Husain Haddawy (New York: Norton, 1990), pp. 30–66.

17. Richard Corben and Jan Strnad, *The Last Voyage of Sindbad* (New York: Catalan Communications, 1988).

18. See chap. 2.

19. See chap. 7.

20. Samîr 'Abd al-Bâqî and Abû 'Alâ', "Al-Sayyâd wal-Mârid al-Sharîr" *Mâjid*, 1987, no. 450.

21. Malti-Douglas, *Woman's Body*, pp. 11–28.

22. See, for example, the studies in Lawrence I. Conrad, ed., *The World of Ibn Tufayl: Interdisciplinary Perspectives on Hayy ibn Yaqzân* (forthcoming).

23. See the three texts of *Hayy ibn Yaqzân*, by Ibn Sînâ, Ibn Tufayl, and al-Suhrawardî, ed.

Ahmad Amîn (Cairo: Dâr al-Maʿârif, 1952). See also Malti-Douglas, *Woman's Body*, pp. 67–84, 96–110.

24. A fuller version of the discussion which follows can be found in Malti-Douglas, *Woman's Body*, pp. 67–84.

25. Riffaterre, "Intertextual Scrambling," p. 197.

26. Léon Gauthier, *Ibn Thofaïl, sa vie, ses oeuvres* (Paris: E. Leroux, 1909), p. 65.

27. Al-Waqwâq is the most common form of the name of this island. Many others exist in the geographical literature. The comic strip uses Wâq al-Wâq. See Malti-Douglas, *Woman's Body*, pp. 85–96.

28. See Malti-Douglas, *Woman's Body*, pp. 85–96.

29. See Ibn al-Jawzî, *Akhbâr al-Adhkiyâ'*, ed. Muhammad Mursî al-Khawlî (Cairo: Matâbiʿ al-Ahrâm al-Tijâriyya, 1969).

30. See the interview with Jamîla Bouhayrid translated in Elizabeth W. Fernea and Basima Qattan Bezirgan, eds., *Middle Eastern Muslim Women Speak* (Austin: University of Texas Press, 1987), p. 255.

31. See chap. 7.

32. Leila Khaled, *Mon peuple vivra*, trans. Michel Pagnier (Paris: Gallimard, 1973).

33. Assia Djebar, *Femmes d'Alger dans leur apartement* (Paris: Des Femmes, 1980), p. 60.

34. See, for example, Ibn al-Jawzî, *Ahkâm al-Nisâ'* (Beirut: Dâr al-Kutub al-ʿIlmiyya, 1985), pp. 49, 96; al-Suyûtî, *al-Ashbâh wal-Nazâ'ir fî Qawâʿid wa-Furûʿ Fiqh al-Shâfiʿiyya* (Cairo: ʿIsâ al-Bâbî al-Halabî, n.d.), p. 262. For the highly controversial cases of women's participation in warfare in the early history of Islam, see Leila Ahmed, *Women and Gender in Islam* (New Haven: Yale University Press, 1992), pp. 53, 61, 69–72.

35. The word *jihâd* has another, larger meaning than "holy war": any effort undertaken in the way of religion, like the struggle that one makes against one's own bad impulses. Nevertheless, the context (one is in a real war) indicates the military signification. In addition, Jamîla has just been identified as an artisan, which is already, in this context, an effort for religion.

36. René Chateaubriand, *Atala, René, les aventures du dernier Abencérage* (Paris: Editions Garnier Frères, 1962), p. 254.

37. See, for example, al-Tirmidhî, *Sahîh al-Tirmidhî*, vol. 5 (Cairo: al-Matbaʿa al-Misriyya bil-Azhar, 1931), pp. 120–21, and vol. 9 (Cairo: Matbaʿat al-Sâwî, 1934), pp. 8–10. For a contemporary example, see Yûsuf Idrîs, "al-ʿAmaliyya al-Kubrâ," in Yûsuf Idrîs, *al-Naddâha* (Cairo: Dâr Misr lil-Tibâʿa, n.d.), p. 120.

9. Arabian Success Story

1. Ahmad ʿUmar, personal interview, Abu Dhabi, Feb. 22, 1988.

2. For a brief description of *Mâjid*, see ʿAbd Allâh al-Nuways, *Wasâ'il al-Iʿlâm fî Dawlat al-Imârât al-ʿArabiyya al-Muttahida* (Abu Dhabi: Shirkat Abû Zabî lil-Tibâʿa wal Nashr, 1982[?]), pp. 101–20.

3. See chap. 5.

4. Muhyî al-Dîn al-Labbâd, *Nazar*; Bahjat [ʿUthmân], *al-Diktâtûriyya lil-Mubtadi'în: Bahjâtûs, Ra'îs Bahjâtiyâ al-ʿUzmâ* (Cairo: Misriyya lil-Nashr wal-Tawzîʿ, 1989); Jûrj al-Bahjûrî, *Bahjar fî al-Mahjar* (London: Riad El-Rayyes, 1989).

5. Ahmad ʿUmar, personal interview, Abu Dhabi, Feb. 22, 1988; S. Maqbul Ahmad, "Ibn Mâdjid," *EI²*.

6. Ahmad ʿUmar, personal interview, Abu Dhabi, Feb. 22, 1988; Muhammad al-Minsî Qindîl, personal interview , Cairo, Mar. 6, 1988. These crime narratives were collected and reprinted as Anwar Badr and Muhammad Bayram, *al-Naqîb Khalfân wal-Musâʿid Fahmân wal-Khârijûn ʿalâ al-Qânûn* (Abu Dhabi: Mu'assasat al-Ittihâd lil-Sihâfa wal-Nashr wal-Tawzîʿ, n.d.).

7. Collected and reprinted as Jamâl Salîm and Hijâzî, *ʿIsâbat al-Khamsa wal-Maharâjâ* (Abu Dhabi: Matâbiʿ Mu'assasat al-Ittihâd lil-Sihâfa wal-Nashr, n.d.).

8. See chap. 8.

9. The implication is more clearly drawn in the Disney company's recent animated version of *Beauty and the Beast*.

10. The story is taken with slight variations from Ibn al-Jawzî, *Akhbâr al-Adhkiyâ'*, pp. 55–56.

11. Lefebvre argues that the hero is an oasis dweller and probably not a peasant. See Gustave Lefebvre, *Romans et contes égyptiens de l'Epoque Pharaonique* (Paris: Adrien-Maisonneuve, 1949), p. 41. Nevertheless, the title "Eloquent Peasant" has become well established and is the one adopted by all modern Egyptians when referring to this text. For translations, see Lefebvre, *Romans*, pp. 47–69, and Miriam Lichteim, *Ancient Egyptian Literature*, vol. 1: *The Old and Middle Kingdoms* (Berkeley: University of California Press, 1975), pp. 170–82.

12. See, for example, Fathî Sa'îd, *al-Fallâh al-Fasîh* (Cairo: al-Hay'a al-Misriyya al-'Amma lil-Kitâb, 1982); Muhammad Mahrân al-Sayyid, *Hikâya . . . min Wâdî al-Milh* (Cairo: Mu'assasat 'Inân lil-Tibâ'a, 1984); 'Alî Ahmad Bâkathîr, *al-Fallâh al-Fasîh* (Cairo: Maktabat Misr, 1985). See also Allen Douglas and Fedwa Malti-Douglas, "'al-'Adl wal-Fann fî 'al-Fallâh al-Fasîh,' " in *Shâdî 'Abd al-Salâm wal-Fallâh al-Fasîh*, ed. Salâh Mar'î et al. (Cairo: al-Ha'ya al-Misriyya al-'Amma lil-Kitâb, forthcoming).

13. See chap. 5.

14. See chap. 8.

15. See chap. 6.

16. Ahmad 'Umar, personal interview, Abu Dhabi, Feb. 22, 1988.

17. The "Zakiyya al-Dhakiyya" strips have been reprinted in Ahmad 'Umar and Hijâzî, *Dâ'irat Ma'ârif Zakiyya al-Dhakiyya* (Abu Dhabi: Maktabat Mâjid, n.d.). References are to volumes and pages in this reprint.

18. Ahmad 'Umar, personal interview, Abu Dhabi, Feb. 22, 1988.

19. See, for example, the discussion in Fedwa Malti-Douglas, *Blindness and Autobiography: al-Ayyâm of Tâhâ Husayn* (Princeton: Princeton University Press, 1985), pp. 75–77.

20. Ahmad 'Umar, personal interview, Abu Dhabi, Feb. 22, 1988.

21. Ahmad 'Umar, personal interview, Abu Dhabi, Feb. 22, 1988.

22. De la Fuente and Delotte, *Charles de Gaulle*, pp. 21, 39.

23. Zakiyya's photographs, with their protest authenticity and attempt to occult the process of representation, are similar to Saddâm Husayn's decision to cast his own arms in his Baghdad monument, or the decision to copy real soldiers in his statues to the martyrs in Basra. See al-Khalil, *The Monument*, pp. 5–9, 29–31.

24. See chap. 6.

25. Edward Said, *Orientalism* (New York: Pantheon, 1978). See also the excellent work by Thierry Mentsch, *L'Orient imaginaire: La Vision politique occidentale de l'Est méditerranéen* (Paris: Les Editions de Minuit, 1988). In this school, see also Denise Brahimi, *Arabes des Lumières et Bédouins romantiques* (Paris: Le Sycamore, 1982); J. P. Charnay, *Les Contre-Orients ou Comment penser l'Autre selon soi* (Paris: Sindbad, 1980); Hichem Djaït, *L'Europe et l'Islam* (Paris: Editions du Seuil, 1978); Claudine Grossir, *L'Islam des romantiques 1811–1840* (Paris: Maisonneuve & Larose, 1984); Kathryn Tidrick, *Heart-Beguiling Araby* (Cambridge: Cambridge University Press, 1981). Closer to our subject are studies of U.S. mass culture, such as Jack G. Shaheen, *The TV Arab* (Bowling Green: Bowling Green State University Popular Press, 1984).

26. Claude Michel Cluny, *Dictionnaire des nouveaux cinémas arabes* (Paris: Sindbad, 1978), p. 285.

27. Cf. the similar dynamics in "The Adventures of Ramsîs in Paris," in chap. 2.

28. This series is reprinted in Ahmad 'Umar and Mustafâ Rahma, *Kaslân Jiddan Hawl al-'Alam wa-Qisas Ukhrâ* (Abu Dhabi: Maktabat Mâjid, 1984), pp. 6–27. Page references in the text are to this edition.

29. See, for example, Hergé, *Le lotus bleu* (Tournai: Casterman, 1946), p. 45.

30. Cf. Hergé's coming to awareness of this situation, in Numa Sadoul, *Tintin et moi: Entretiens avec Hergé* (Tournai: Casterman, 1975), p. 36.

10. Bilingual Politics

1. See, for example, B. Masmûdî and Ahmâd Bû Hilâl, *al-Amîr 'Abd al-Qâdir*, part I (Algiers: Entreprise Nationale du Livre, 1985), p. 31; Bû 'Allâm Bil-Sâ'ih, Bin 'Umar Bakhîtî, and B.

Masmûdî, *Malhamat al-Shaykh Bû ʿImâma*, part I (Algiers: Entreprise Nationale du Livre, 1986), p. 21.

2. In standard Arabic transcription, the word is *mujâhid*. Since this term is commonly used in Algerian political discourse, even when speaking or writing in French, we have conserved the Algerian French transcription.

3. Helali, "La littérature," p. 9.

4. Bibliographies of leading comic-strip artists are available in the catalogue of the Festival International de la Bande Dessinée et de la Caricature, July 1987 (Réghaïa: Entreprise Nationale des Arts Graphiques, 1987). See also, for example, Abdelhakim Meziani, quoted in Mustapha Tenani, *Le Fusil chargé* (Algiers: Entreprise Nationale du Livre, 1986), p. 6.

5. Ramzi Rafik, *SM 15: Halte au "Plan" Terreur* (Algiers: Entreprise Nationale du Livre, 1983), p. 21.

6. See, for example, Hergé, *Le lotus bleu*, pp. 5–6.

7. The pun is also exploited in Slim, *Réédition de Zid Ya Bouzid I & II!* (Algiers: Entreprise Nationale du Livre, 1986), p. 91.

8. Malek, *La Route du Sel* (Algiers: Entreprise Nationale du Livre, 1984).

9. Mahfoud Aïder, *Histoires pour rire* (Algiers: Entreprise Nationale du Livre, 1984).

10. ʿAbd al-Halîm Riyâd, *Mukhâtarât Muhtâl*, Arabic version with the assistance of Muhammad Dahw and ʿAlî Hakkâr (Algiers: al-Muʾassasa al-Wataniyya lil-Kitâb, 1986).

11. See chap. 5.

12. Lob, Gotlib, and Alexis, *Superdupont* (Paris: J'ai Lu, 1987).

13. Slim, *L'Algérie de Slim* (Paris and St-Martin-D'Hères: Editions l'Harmattan and Revue "Grand Maghreb," 1983), p. 38.

14. Slim, *Zid Ya Bouzid 3* (Algiers: Entreprise Nationale du Livre, 1986), p. 37.

15. Mustapha Tenani, *Les Hommes du Djebel* (Algiers: Entreprise Nationale du Livre, 1985). The title refers to the mountains (Djebel) where FLN fighters held out against the French more effectively than in the plains.

16. Garawî and ʿAbbâs, *Abnâʾ al-Hurriyya* (Algiers: al-Muʾassasa al-Wataniyya lil-Kitâb, 1986).

17. See, for example, ʿUmar and Hijâzî, *Dâʾirat Maʿârif*, vol. I, pp. 78–79.

18. The figure of one million is reasonable (and even then it is probably excessive) only if one includes Algerians killed by the French and those killed by the FLN, as well as deaths in the European population; see Bernard Droz and Evelyne Lever, *Histoire de le guerre d'Algérie* (Paris: Editions du Seuil, 1984), p. 343.

19. See, for example, Garawî and ʿAbbâs, *Abnâʾ al-Hurriyya*, p. 15; Tenani, *Les Hommes du Djebel*, pp. 9, 10.

20. See chap. 9.

21. See chaps. 7 and 8.

22. Tenani, *Le Fusil chargé*; Masmûdî, *al-Amîr ʿAbd al-Qâdir*; Bil-Sâʾih, *Bû ʿImâma*; M. Bouslah, *La Ballade du proscrit* (Algiers: Entreprise Nationale du Livre, 1984).

23. See also chap. 3. The U.S. comic artist Jack Jackson makes similar use of documentary references; see Witek, *Comic Books*, p. 75.

24. Laurent Achache and Anissa Abderrahim et al., *Juba II: Roi des Maures* (Meknes: Enseignement Français au Maroc, Le Lycée Paul Valéry, 1991).

25. Mohamed Hankour, *Soloeïs: L'Ile du Grand Ordo* (Algiers: Entreprise Nationale du Livre, 1985).

26. Cluny, *Dictionnaire*, pp. 228–32.

27. Kenza and Christiane Achour, "La B.D., l'histoire, les femmes: Formation par la lecture," *Présence de Femmes* (1987), pp. 50–60.

28. Mansûr ʿAmmûrî and Ahmâd Bû Hilâl, *al-Durûb al-Waʿra* (Algiers: al-Muʾassasa al-Wataniyya lil-Kitâb, 1984).

29. Achour and Achour, "La B.D.," pp. 58–59.

30. Achour and Achour, "La B.D.," p. 60.

31. See, for example, Frantz Fanon, *A Dying Colonialism*, trans. Haakon Chevalier (New York: Grove Press, 1967), pp. 35–67, 99–120.

32. Kaci, *Bas les voiles* (Paris: Les Editions Rochevignes, 1984), inside cover.

33. Of course, there is nothing sociologically unique or even particularly Islamic in this development. It is well known that after the Second World War in the United States, women who had entered the work force were eased back into more domestic roles.

34. Algiers: Entreprise Nationale du Livre, 1983 and 1985.

35. See, for example, Gérard de Villiers, *KGB contre KGB* (Paris [?]: Editions Gérard de Villiers, 1992).

36. See, for example, Fatima Mernissi, *Beyond the Veil: Male-Female Dynamics in a Modern Muslim Society* (New York: Schenkman, 1975), pp. 3ff, and Malti-Douglas, *Woman's Body*, p. 43.

37. Menouar Merabtene (Slim), personal interview by telephone, Algiers, Jan. 19, 1993. Slim, *L'Algérie de Slim*; Slim, *Zid Ya Bouzid 3*, pp. 31–52. Susan Slyomovics includes a discussion of a recent Slim cartoon in her "Algeria Caricatures the Gulf War," *Public Culture* 4, no. 2 (1992), p. 95.

38. The first two volumes have been reprinted as Slim, *Réédition de Zid Ya Bouzid I & II!*

39. Roger Manvell et al., *The International Encyclopedia of Film* (New York: Bonanza Books, 1975), p. 196.

40. See, for example, Goscinny and Uderzo, *Le Devin* (Paris: Dargaud, 1972), pp. 4–5.

41. See chap. 5.

42. John P. Entelis, *Algeria: The Revolution Institutionalized* (Boulder: Westview Press, 1986), pp. 140–47.

43. Entelis, *Algeria*, pp. 140–48.

44. See, for example, Ghassan Ascha, *Du Statut inférieur de la femme en Islam* (Paris: L'Harmattan, 1989), pp. 103–14.

45. See chaps. 5 and 7.

11. Images in Exile

1. See Alain Gillette and Abdelmalek Sayad, *L'Immigration algérienne en France* (Paris: Editions Etienne, 1984); Gilles Kepel, *Les Banlieues de l'Islam: Naissance d'une religion en France* (Paris: Editions du Seuil, 1987).

2. Farid Boudjellal, personal interview by telephone, Paris, France, January 10, 1993.

3. Farid Boudjellal, *L'Oud* (Paris: Futuropolis, 1983), *Le Gourbi: L'Oud II* (Paris: Futuropolis, 1985), and *Ramadân: L'Oud III* (Paris: Futuropolis, 1988). The ʿūd is the Middle Eastern stringed instrument which is the ancestor of the lute.

4. Farid Boudjellal, *Les Soirées d'Abdulah: Ratonnade* (Paris: Futuropolis, 1985), and *La Famille Slimani: Gags à l'Harissa* (Paris: Editions Humanos, 1989); Farid Boudjellal and Larbi Mechkour, *Les Beurs* (Paris: L'Echo des Savanes/Albin Michel, 1985).

5. Tahar Ben Jelloun, *Hospitalité française: Racisme et immigration maghrébine* (Paris: Editions du Seuil, 1984).

6. Since most of these albums consist of unnumbered pages, we will attempt no page references where pages are not numbered.

7. Both are popular Egyptian films.

8. Muhammad al-Saʿûdî, *Zâd al-Musâfirîn ilâ Ghayr Bilâd al-Muslimîn* (Cairo and Riyad: Dâr al-Sahwa and Dâr al-Fitya, 1988).

9. Renard, *Bandes dessinées*, p. 196. See also chaps. 4 and 6.

10. The *bac*, or baccalaureate, is the French degree which provides admission to the university.

11. In *Le Gourbi* his name is spelled Marhmoud (apparently to help transcribe the Arabic pronunciation) and in *Ramadân*, the more normal Mahmoud.

12. HLM stands for Habitation à Loyer Modéré.

13. See Hasan El-Shamy, "The Brother-Sister Syndrome in Arab Family Life, Socio-Cultural Factors in Arab Psychiatry: A Critical Review," *International Journal of Sociology of the Family* 11 (1981), pp. 313–23, and *Brother and Sister Type 872*: A Cognitive Behavioristic Analysis of a Middle Eastern Oikotype* (Bloomington: Folklore Publications Group, 1979); Malti-Douglas, *Woman's Body*, pp. 74–75.

14. Kepel, *Les Banlieues*, pp. 14–15.

15. See, for example, Annie Krieger-Krynicki, *Les Musulmans en France* (Paris: Maisonneuve & Larose, 1985), pp. 110–11.

16. See chap. 10.

17. Allen Douglas, "Le Pen, Jean-Marie," in *Historical Dictionary of the French Fourth and Fifth Republics, 1946–1991*, ed. Wayne Northcutt (New York: Greenwood Press, 1992), pp. 262–64.

18. See the eloquent list in Ben Jelloun, *Hospitalité*, pp. 27–32.

19. See, for example, Morris and Goscinny, *Lucky Luke: Le Cavalier blanc* (Paris: Dargaud, 1975), p. 29.

20. See chap. 5.

21. Hergé, *Coke en Stock* (Tournai: Casterman, 1958).

22. See chap. 9.

23. When the subject first comes up, one of the Beurs speaks of four ordeals, but in the story there are only three.

24. D. B. MacDonald and H. Massé, "Djinn," *EI²*.

25. See chap. 10.

26. One finds it, for example, in many Farîd al-Atrash films and in *Case Number 68* by Salâh Abû Sayf.

27. See chap. 10.

28. Kepel, *Les Banlieues*, pp. 104–5.

29. See, for example, al-Râghib al-Isfahânî, *Muhâdarât al-Udabâ' wa-Muhâwarât al-Shu'arâ' wal-Bulaghâ'*, (Beirut: Dâr Maktabat al-Hayât, n.d.), vol. 3, pp. 275–76.

30. See chap. 6.

31. Kepel, *Les Banlieues*, pp. 269–74.

32. This false antinomy is apparently the result of an attempt to translate the pair, well-known in Islamic discourse, *al-haqq wal-bâtil*.

33. In his perceptive discussion, Kepel points out that the French "nonbeliever" is described as appearing to be a serious boy but really is not. The French scholar associates this with both a polemical resentment and the idea of the bad boy as "false." Undoubtedly, but the notion of "false" probably echoes the *al-haqq wal-bâtil* noted above.

34. Apparently not by Boudjellal, it is signed Golo.

35. On the evolution of the *nasîb*, see Jaroslav Stetkevych, "Spaces of Delight: A Symbolic Topoanalysis of the Classical Arabic Nasîb," in *Critical Pilgrimages: Studies in the Arabic Literary Tradition*, ed. Fedwa Malti-Douglas, *Literature East and West* 25 (1989), pp. 5–28. See also Jaroslav Stetkevych, *The Zephyrs of Najd: The Poetics of Nostalgia in the Classical Arabic Nasîb* (Chicago: University of Chicago Press, 1993).

12. Regional Highways, Regional Signs

1. Michael M. J. Fischer and Mehdi Abedi, *Debating Muslims: Cultural Dialogues in Postmodernity and Tradition* (Madison: University of Wisconsin Press, 1990), pp. 364–65.

2. These patterns are based on observations during the 1970s and the mid-to-late 1980s.

3. See Ahmed, *Postmodernism*.

4. The importance of Japanese strips can be shown by the ready availability in U.S. stores of English translations produced by the collaboration of the Japanese publishing giant Kodansha International and Epic Comics. See, for example, Katsihiro Utomo, *Akira Book 4* (New York: Epic Comics, 1992).

5. Farid Boudjellal, personal interviews, Paris, May 14, and May 21, 1993. For the Franco-Islamic production some of which exists also in Arabic, see, for example, Jaafar Al-kange, Gabriel Garcia, and Mohammed Baina, *L'Encyclopédie de l'Histoire Islamique en Bandes Dessinées* (Paris: Editions La BBD, 1990-); Mohamed Kada and H. ben Hafsi, *Histoire de l'Islam en Bandes Dessinées* (Paris: Magma-Média, 1989-).

6. There are also, of course, a number of newspapers and other periodicals published in Europe and frequently read in more than one Arab country.

7. For an early explanation of transnational phenomena, see, for example, Robert O. Keohane and Joseph S. Nye, Jr., *Transnational Relations and World Politics* (Cambridge: Harvard University Press, 1972). The journal *Public Culture* has more recently specialized in transnational cultural issues.

8. On the concepts of mass and popular culture, see James Naremore and Patrick Brantlinger, "Introduction: Six Artistic Cultures," in Naremore and Brantlinger, eds., *Modernity and Mass Culture* (Bloomington: Indiana University Press, 1991), pp. 1–23.

9. See, for example Fresnault-Deruelle, "Aspects," p. 78. It will be clear from the following discussion how our approach differs from the schemata in *Mass Culture, Popular Culture, and Social Life in the Middle East*, ed. Georg Stauth and Sami Zubaida (Frankfurt am Main and Boulder: Campus Verlag and Westview Press, 1987). See, for example, Georg Stauth and Sami Zubaida, "Introduction," pp. 13–14; Amr Ibrahim, "Consommation et décalages culturels en Egypte," pp. 85–133; Nicholas S. Hopkins, "Popular Culture and State Power," pp. 225–41; Ahmed A. Zayed, "Popular Culture and Consumerism in Underdeveloped Urban Areas: A Study of the Cairene Quarter of Al-Sharrabiyya," pp. 287–89. On the whole, the essays in this collection concern themselves with the dynamics of social interaction, occasionally the vectors of cultural transmission, but not really with the analysis of the content of the cultural products themselves.

10. Régis Debray, *Le Pouvoir intellectuel en France* (Paris: Editions Ramsay, 1979).

11. These books were written under the pen name Samir al-Khalil: *Republic of Fear: The Politics of Modern Iraq* (Berkeley: University of California Press, 1989) and *The Monument*.

12. Abdallah Laroui, *The Crisis of the Arab Intellectual: Traditionalism or Historicism?*, trans. Diarmid Cammell (Berkeley: University of California Press, 1976), p. 156.

Sources

Interviews

al-ʿAskarî, Kamâl.
Dr. Bahâʾ al-Dîn.
Boudjellal, Farid.
Hâtim, Dalâl.
Hijâzî, Ahmad.
Hilâl, Marzûq, al-Hâjj.
al-Labbâd, Muhyî al-Dîn.
Merabtene, Menouar (Slim).
Qindîl, Muhammad al-Mansî.
al-Qusantînî, ʿAbd al-Hamîd.
Râshid, Nutayla (Mâmâ Lubnâ).
Safwat, Khadîja.
al-Shâdhilî, Bilkhâmisa.
al-Shamlî, Farîd.
Tâmir, Zakariyyâ.
al-Tirîkî, al-Tayyib.
ʿUmar, Ahmad.
Zuhdî, Yâsîn.

Periodicals with Comic Strips

al-Ahâlî. Egypt.
Ahmad/al-Malâk Ahmad. Lebanon.
al-ʿArabî al-Saghîr. Kuwait.
al-Ashbâl. Cyprus.
Barâʿim al-Imân. Kuwait.
Bâsim. Egypt.
Bisât al-Rîh. Lebanon.
Djeha. Algeria.
al-Firdaws. Egypt.

'Irfân. Tunisia.
al-Jadwal. Tunisia.
Jeunesse-Action. Algeria.
Le Maghreb/al-Maghrib al-'Arabî. Tunisia.
Majallatî. Iraq.
Mâjid. Abu Dhabi.
M'Cid. Algeria.
Mîkî. Egypt.
Misha. USSR.
al-Mizmâr. Iraq.
M'Quidèch. Algeria.
al-Muslim al-Saghîr. Egypt.
Qaws Quzah. Tunisia.
al-Riyâd. Tunisia.
Riyâd/Rayyâd. Algeria.
Samîr. Egypt.
Sandûq al-Dunyâ. Egypt.
Shahlûl. Tunisia.
al-Talî'î. Syria.
Tarik. Algeria.
Usâma. Syria.
Zam Zam. Egypt.

Comic Strip Albums and Collections

'Abd al-'Azîz, Ahmad. "A Day in the Life of the Muslim Child." Cairo: Safîr (I'lâm, Di'âya, Nashr, 1988).

Abou Ghoudda, Abdel Satar, and Clave Florencio. *L'Avènement de l'Islam.* Trans. Dalal Khoury. Paris: Robert Laffont/Al Marifa, 1985.

Achache, Laurent, and Anissa Abderrahim, et al. *Juba II: Roi des Maures.* Meknes: Enseignement Français au Maroc, Le Lycée Paul Valéry, 1991.

Aïder, Mahfoud. *Histoires pour rire.* Algiers: Entreprise Nationale du Livre, 1984.

Alkange, Jaafar, Gabriel Garcia, and Mohammed Baina. *L'Encyclopédie de l'Histoire Islamique en Bandes Dessinées.* Paris: Editions La BBD, 1990–.

'Ammûrî, Mansûr, and Ahmâd Bû Hilâl. *Al-Durûb al-Wa'ra.* Algiers: al-Mu'assasa al-Wataniyya lil-Kitâb, 1984.

Ba'labakkî, Fâtima, Nabîl Qaddûh, and Sarmad Junayd. *Rihlât Ibn Battûta.* 2 vols. Beirut: Mu'assasat Bisât al-Rûh, n.d.

Badr, Anwar, and Muhammad Bayram. *Al-Naqîb Khalfân wal-Musâ'id Fahmân wal-Khârijûn 'alâ al-Qânûn.* Abu Dhabi: Mu'assasat al-Ittihâd lil-Sihâfa wal-Nashr wal-Tawzi', n.d.

Bahjat ['Uthmân]. *Al-Diktâtûriyya lil-Mubtadi'în: Bahjâtûs, Ra'îs Bahjâtiyâ al-'Uzmâ.* Cairo: Misriyya lil-Nashr wal-Tawzî', 1989.

Bharati, Pushpa, and C. M. Vitankar. *Jayaprakash Narayan.* Bombay: India Book House Education Trust, n.d.

Bil-Sâ'ih, Bû 'Allâm, Bin 'Umar Bakhîtî, and B. Masmûdî. *Malhamat al-Shaykh Bû 'Imâma.* Part I. Algiers: Entreprise Nationale du Livre, 1986.

Binmas'ûd, Muhammad and 'Abd al-'Azîz Ishbâbû. *Silsilat Ta'rîkh al-Islâm.* Mohamedia: Manshûrât Dâr al-Afâq al-Jadîda, 1988-.

Boudjellal, Farid. *L'Oud.* Paris: Futuropolis, 1983.

_____ . *La Famille Slimani: Gags à l'Harissa.* Paris: Editions Humanos, 1989.

_____ . *Le Gourbi: L'Oud II.* Paris: Futuropolis, 1985.

_____ . *Les Soirées d'Abdulah: Ratonnade.* Paris: Futuropolis, 1985.

_____ . *Ramadân: L'Oud III.* Paris: Futuropolis, 1988.

Boudjellal, Farid, and Larbi Mechkour. *Les Beurs.* Paris: L'Echo des Savanes/Albin Michel, 1985.

Bouslah, M. *La Ballade du proscrit.* Algiers: Entreprise Nationale du Livre, 1984.

Chalumeau, Jean-Luc, drawings by Agathe. *Le Capitalisme en bandes dessinées*. Paris: Hachette, 1979.

Corben, Richard, and Jan Strnad. *The Last Voyage of Sindbad*. New York: Catalan Communications, 1988.

De la Fuente, Victor, and Maurice Delotte. *Charles de Gaulle: Les Français et le gaullisme*. Salon de Provence: Service de l'Homme, 1977.

al-Dhâkirî, Muhammad Nu'mân, et al. *Jamâl 'Abd al-Nâsir*. Paris: Manshûrât al-Sihâfa al-Ifrîqiyya al-Mushtaraka, 1973.

Garawî and 'Abbâs. *Abnâ' al-Hurriyya*. Algiers: al-Mu'assasa al-Wataniyya lil-Kitâb, 1986.

Goscinny and Uderzo. *Le Devin*. Paris: Dargaud, 1972.

Hankour, Mohamed. *Soloeïs: L'Ile du Grand Ordo*. Algiers: Entreprise Nationale du Livre, 1985.

Hergé. *Coke en Stock*. Tournai: Casterman, 1958.

———. *Le Lotus bleu*. Tournai: Casterman, 1946.

Hijâzî, Ahmad. *Tambûl al-Awwal*. Beirut: Dâr al-Fatâ al-'Arabî, 1981.

———. *Tanâbilat al-Sibyân wa-Tanâbilat al-Khirfân*. Cairo: Dâr al-Hilâl, n.d.

———. *Yâ Halâwatak Ya Jamâlak*. Cairo: Dâr al-Hilâl, 1989.

Histoire de France en bandes dessinées. Paris: Larousse, 1978.

Hoth, Iva, and Andre LeBlanc. *The Picture Bible*. Elgin: David C. Cook, 1979.

Hu Chi-hsi and Dupuis. *La Longue marche: Mao Tse-toung*. Neuilly-sur-Seine: Dargaud, 1981.

Kaci, *Bas les voiles*. Paris: Les Editions Rochevignes, 1984.

Kada, Mohamed, Omar Bencheikh, and Abdel Majid Turki. *L'Avènement de l'Islam*. Paris: ACR Edition Internationale, 1987.

Kada, Mohamed, and H. ben Hafsi. *Histoire de l'Islam en Bandes Dessinées*. Paris: Magma-Média, 1989–.

Kelly, Walt. *Pluperfect Pogo*. Ed. Mrs. Walt Kelly and Bill Crouch, Jr. New York: Simon & Schuster, 1987.

Lob, Gotlib, and Alexis. *Superdupont*. Paris: J'ai Lu, 1987.

Makkî, Adîb. *Al-Ayyâm al-Tawîla*. Baghdad: Dâr Thaqâfat al-Atfâl, 1981.

Malek. *La Route du Sel*. Algiers: Entreprise Nationale du Livre, 1984.

Masmûdî, B., and Ahmâd Bû Hilâl. *Al-Amîr 'Abd al-Qâdir*. Part I. Algiers: Entreprise Nationale du Livre, 1985.

Morris and Goscinny. *Lucky Luke: Le Cavalier blanc*. Paris: Dargaud, 1975.

The People's Comic Book. Trans. Endymion Wilkinson. Garden City: Doubleday, 1973.

Rafik, Ramzi. *SM 15: Echec au "Plan Terreur."* Algiers: Entreprise Nationale du Livre, 1985.

———. *SM 15: Halte au "Plan" Terreur*. Algiers: Entreprise Nationale du Livre, 1983.

Richomme, Agnès. *Sainte Marguerite-Marie et le message du Coeur de Jésus*. Paris: Editions Fleurus, 1965.

Riyâd, 'Abd al-Halîm. *Mukhâtarât Muhtâl*. Arabic version with the assistance of Muhammad Dahw and 'Alî Hakkâr. Algiers: al-Mu'assasa al-Wataniyya lil-Kitâb, 1986.

Roquebert, Michel, and Gérald Forton. *Aymeric et les cathares*. Toulouse: Loubatières, 1978.

Salîm, Jamâl, and Hijâzî. *'Isâbat al-Khamsa wal-Maharâjâ*. Abu Dhabi: Matâbi' Mu'assasat al-Ittihâd lil-Sihâfa wal-Nashr, n.d.

Seddik, Youssef, and Gioux. *Si le Coran m'était conté: Les Hommes de l'Eléphant*. Arabic title: *Ashâb al-Fîl*. Geneva and Tunis: Editions Alif, 1989.

Seddik, Youssef, and Benoît de Pelloux. *Si le Coran m'était conté: Abraham*. Arabic title: *Ibrâhîm*. Geneva and Tunis: Editions Alif, 1989.

Seddik, Youssef, Philippe Teulat, and Philippe Jouan. *Si le Coran m'était conté: Peuples maudits*. Arabic title: *Hûd, Sâlih, Yûnus*. Geneva and Tunis: Editions Alif, 1989.

al-Shâdhilî, Bilkhâmisa. *Jâbir wal-Samak al-'Ajîb*. Tunis: Manshûrât Tûnis Qartâj, n.d.

Slim. *L'Algérie de Slim*. Paris and St-Martin-D'Hères: Editions l'Harmattan and Revue "Grand Maghreb," 1983.

———. *Réédition de Zid Ya Bouzid I & II!* Algiers: Entreprise Nationale du Livre, 1986.

———. *Zid Ya Bouzid 3*. Algiers: Entreprise Nationale du Livre, 1986.

Spiegelman, Art. *Maus*. New York: Pantheon, 1986.

———. *Maus II*. New York: Pantheon, 1991.

Tawfîq, 'Aliyya, and Kamâl Darwîsh. *Hikâyât 'Arabiyya wa-Islâmiyya: Al-Qâdi al-'Adil wa-Hikâyât Ukhrâ*. Cairo: Matâbi' al-Ahrâm al-Tijâriyya, 1986.

———. *Hikâyât 'Arabiyya wa-Islâmiyya: Sâlim wal-Asîr wa-Hikâyât Ukhrâ*. Cairo: Matâbi' al-Ahrâm al-Tijâriyya, 1986.

Tenani, Mustapha. *Le Fusil chargé*. Algiers: Entreprise Nationale du Livre, 1986.

―――― . *Les Hommes du Djebel*. Algiers: Entreprise Nationale du Livre, 1985.

ʿUmar, Ahmad, and Hijâzî. *Dâ'irat Maʿârif Zakiyya al-Dhakiyya*. Abu Dhabi: Maktabat Mâjid, n.d.

ʿUmar, Ahmad, and Mustafâ Rahma. *Kaslân Jiddan Hawl al-ʿAlam wa-Qisas Ukhrâ*. Abu Dhabi: Maktabat Mâjid, 1984.

Utomo, Katsihiro. *Akira Book 4*. New York: Epic Comics, 1992.

Wahdat Thaqâfat al-Tifl bi-Shirkat Safîr. *Kitâb al-Muslim al-Saghîr 2*. Cairo: Safîr―Iʿlâm, Diʿâya, Nashr, 1988.

Other Sources

ʿAbd al-Salâm, Shâdî. *Juyûsh al-Shams* (1974).

Abdel-Malek, Kamal. *A Study of the Vernacular Poetry of Ahmad Fu'âd Nigm*. Leiden: E. J. Brill, 1990.

Achour, Kenza, and Christiane Achour. "La B.D., l'histoire, les femmes: Formation par la lecture." *Présence de femmes* (1987): 50-60.

Ahmed, Akbar S. *Postmodernism and Islam: Predicament and Promise*. London: Routledge, 1992.

Ahmed, Leila. *Women and Gender in Islam*. New Haven: Yale University Press, 1992.

Alf Layla wa-Layla. Ed. Muhsin Mahdi. 2 vols. Leiden: E. J. Brill, 1984.

Alf Layla wa-Layla. 2 vols. Cairo: Matbaʿat Bûlâq, n.d.

al-ʿAqqâd, ʿAbbâs Mahmûd. *Juhâ al-Dâhik al-Mudhik*. Cairo: Dâr al-Hilâl, n.d.

The Arabian Nights. Trans. Husain Haddawy. New York: Norton, 1990.

Arberry, A. J. *The Koran Interpreted*. 2 vols. in 1. New York: Macmillan, 1974.

Arkoun, Mohammed. "Islam, Thought and Literature." Public lecture, Austin, Texas. Sept. 18, 1989.

Arnold, Thomas W. *Painting in Islam*. New York: Dover, 1965.

Ascha, Ghassan. *Du Statut inférieur de la femme en Islam*. Paris: L'Harmattan, 1989.

Awn, Peter J. *Satan's Tragedy and Redemption: Iblîs in Sufi Psychology*. Leiden: E. J. Brill, 1983.

Aziza, Mohamed. *L'Image et l'Islam*. Paris: Albin Michel, 1978.

al-Bahjûrî, Jûrj. *Bahjar fî al-Mahjar*. London: Riad El-Rayyes, 1989.

Bâkathîr, ʿAlî Ahmad. *Al-Fallâh al-Fasîh*. Cairo: Maktabat Misr, 1985.

Balout, Lionel. *La momie de Ramsès II*. Paris: Musée de l'Homme, 1985.

Baron-Carvais, Annie. *La Bande dessinée*. Paris: Presses Universitaires de France, 1985.

Barthes, Roland. "Eléments de sémiologie." *Communications* 4 (1964): 91-144.

―――― . *Mythologies*. Paris: Editions du Seuil, 1970.

al-Baydâwî. *Tafsîr al-Baydâwî*. 2 vols. Beirut: Dâr al-Kutub al-ʿIlmiyya, 1988.

Ben Jelloun, Tahar. *Hospitalité française: Racisme et immigration maghrébine*. Paris: Editions du Seuil, 1984.

Bettelheim, Bruno. *The Uses of Enchantment: The Meaning and Importance of Fairy Tales*. New York: Vintage, 1977.

Brahimi, Denise. *Arabes des Lumières et Bédouins romantiques*. Paris: Le Sycamore, 1982.

Brednich, Rolf Wilhelm. "Comic Strips as a Subject of Folk Narrative Research." In *Folklore Today*, ed. Linda Dégh et al., pp. 45-55. Bloomington: Indiana University Research Center for Language and Semiotic Studies, 1976.

al-Bukhârî. *Sahîh al-Bukhârî bi-Sharh al-Kirmânî*. 25 vols. in 9. Beirut: Dâr Ihyâ' al-Turâth al-ʿArabî, 1981.

Burton, Richard. *The Book of a Thousand Nights and a Night*. 10 vols. Burton Club Edition.

Catalogue. Festival International de la Bande Dessinée et de la Caricature. July 1987. Réghaïa: Entreprise Nationale des Arts Graphiques, 1987.

Chahi, Zoubida. "La production des livres pour enfants au Maroc (1947-1991)." Mémoire for Diplôme, Ecole des Sciences de l'Information. Morocco, 1992.

Charnay, J. P. *Les Contre-Orients ou Comment penser l'Autre selon soi*. Paris: Sindbad, 1980.

Chateaubriand, René. *Atala, René, les aventures du dernier Abencérage*. Paris: Editions Garnier Frères, 1962.

Cluny, Claude Michel. *Dictionnaire des nouveaux cinémas arabes*. Paris: Sindbad, 1978.

Communications 24 (1976).

Conrad, Lawrence I, ed. *The World of Ibn Tufayl: Interdisciplinary Perspectives on Hayy ibn Yaqzân* (forthcoming).

al-Dârimî. *Sunan al-Dârimî*. 2 vols. Beirut: Dâr Ihyâ' al-Sunna al-Nabawiyya, n.d.

Debray, Régis. *Le Pouvoir intellectuel en France*. Paris: Editions Ramsay, 1979.

De Villiers, Gérard. *KGB contre KGB*. Paris[?]: Editions Gérard de Villiers, 1992.

Djaït, Hichem. *L'Europe et l'Islam*. Paris: Editions du Seuil, 1978.

Djebar, Assia. *Femmes d'Alger dans leur apartement*. Paris: Des Femmes, 1980.

Dorfman, Ariel. *The Empire's Old Clothes*. Trans. Clark Hansen. New York: Pantheon, 1983.

Dorfman, Ariel, and Armand Mattelart. *How to Read Donald Duck: Imperialist Ideology in the Disney Comic*. Trans. David Kunzle. New York: International General, 1975.

Douglas, Allen. "Le Pen, Jean-Marie." In *Historical Dictionary of the French Fourth and Fifth Republics, 1946-1991*, ed. Wayne Northcutt, pp. 262-64. New York: Greenwood Press, 1992.

_____ . "Al-Mu'arrikh, al-Nass, wal-Nâqid al-Adabî." Trans. F. Kâmil. *Fusûl* 4, no. 1 (1983): 95-105.

Douglas, Allen, and Fedwa Malti-Douglas. "Al-ʿAdl wal-Fann fî 'al-Fallâh al-Fasîh.' " In *Shâdî ʿAbd al-Salâm wal-Fallâh al-Fasîh*, ed. Salâh Marʿî et al. Cairo: al-Haʿya al-Misriyya al-ʿAmma lil-Kitâb (forthcoming).

_____ . "Le Peuple d'Egypte et son chef: Tensions iconographiques dans un strip nassérien." In *Images d'Egypte de la fresque à la bande dessinée*, pp. 77-87. Cairo: CEDEJ, 1991.

_____ . *L'Idéologie par la bande: Héros politiques de France et d'Egypte au miroir de la BD*. Cairo: CEDEJ, 1987.

Droz, Bernard, and Evelyne Lever. *Histoire de la guerre d'Algérie*. Paris: Editions du Seuil, 1984.

Du Fontbaré, Vicky, and Philippe Sohet. "Codes culturels et logique de classe dans la bande dessinée." *Communications* 24 (1976): 70-73.

El-Shamy, Hasan. *Brother and Sister Type 872*: A Cognitive Behavioristic Analysis of a Middle Eastern Oikotype*. Bloomington: Folklore Publications Group, 1979.

_____ . "The Brother-Sister Syndrome in Arab Family Life, Socio-Cultural Factors in Arab Psychiatry: A Critical Review." *International Journal of Sociology of the Family* 11 (1981): 313-23.

The Encyclopaedia of Islam. 2d ed. Ed. H. A. R. Gibb et al. Leiden: E. J. Brill, 1960–.

Entelis, John P. *Algeria: The Revolution Institutionalized*. Boulder: Westview Press, 1986.

Fanon, Frantz. *A Dying Colonialism*. Trans. Haakon Chevalier. New York: Grove Press, 1967.

_____ . *Peau noire masques blancs*. Paris: Editions du Seuil, 1975.

Farouk-Sluglett, Marion, and Peter Sluglett. *Iraq since 1958*. London: KPI, 1987.

Fernea, Elizabeth W., and Basima Qattan Bezirgan, ed. *Middle Eastern Muslim Women Speak*. Austin: University of Texas Press, 1987.

Ferro, Marc. *Comment on raconte l'histoire aux enfants*. Paris: Payot, 1986.

Fischer, Michael M. J., and Mehdi Abedi. *Debating Muslims: Cultural Dialogues in Postmodernity and Tradition*. Madison: University of Wisconsin Press, 1990.

Fresnault-Deruelle, Pierre. *La Chambre à bulles: Essai sur l'image du quotidien dans la bande dessinée*. Paris: Union Générale d'Editions, 1977.

_____ . "Aspects de la Bande Dessinée." In *Comics and Visual Culture*, ed. Alphons Silbermann and H. D. Dyroff, pp. 62-78. Munich: K. G. Saur, 1986.

_____ . *Récits et discours par la bande: Essais sur les comics*. Paris: Librairie Hachette, 1977.

Gauthier, Léon. *Ibn Thofaïl, sa vie, ses oeuvres*. Paris: E. Leroux, 1909.

Genette, Gérard. *Figures III*. Paris: Seuil, 1972.

Gillette, Alain, and Abdelmalek Sayad. *L'Immigration algérienne en France*. Paris: Editions Etienne, 1984.

Goldziher, Ignaz. *Muslim Studies*. Ed. and trans. S. M. Stern. 2 vols. Chicago: Aldine, 1967.

Greimas, A. J., and J. Courtès. *Sémiotique: Dictionnaire raisonné de la théorie du langage*. Paris: Hachette, 1979.

Grossir, Claudine. *L'Islam des romantiques 1811-1840*. Paris: Maisonneuve & Larose, 1984.

Habiby, Emile. *Khurrâfiyya (Sarâyâ Bint al-Ghûl)*. Haifa: Arabesque, 1991.

Hamori, Andras. *On the Art of Medieval Arabic Literature*. Princeton: Princeton University Press, 1974.

Hane, Djeynab. "A travers l'Afrique: Non au Coran en bandes dessinées." *Jeune Afrique* (Jan. 29, 1990): 31.

Helali, Abdelhamid. "La Littérature enfantine extra-scolaire dans le monde arabe: Analyse formelle et thématique des revues pour enfants." Thèse d'Etat. Université de Paris V, 1986.

Hikâyât min Qâdisiyyat Saddâm. Baghdad: Dâr Thaqâfat al-Atfâl.

Horn, Maurice, ed. *The World Encyclopedia of Comics*. New York: Avon, 1977.

Ibn Battûta. *Rihlat Ibn Battûta*. Ed. Talâl Harb. Beirut: Dâr al-Kutub al-ʿIlmiyya, 1987.

Ibn Dâniyâl. *Khayâl al-Zill wa-Tamthîliyyât Ibn Dâniyâl*. Ed. Ibrâhîm Hamâda. Cairo: al-Muʾassasa al-Misriyya al-ʿAmma lil-Taʾlîf wal-Tarjama wal-Tibâʿa wal-Nashr, 1961.

Ibn Hishâm. *Al-Sîra al-Nabawiyya*. Ed. Mustafâ al-Saqâ, Ibrâhîm al-Abyârî, and ʿAbd al-Hafîz Shalabî. 4 vols. Beirut: Dâr al-Qalam, n.d.

Ibn al-Jawzî. *Ahkâm al-Nisâʾ*. Beirut: Dâr al-Kutub al-ʿIlmiyya, 1985.

_____ . *Akhbâr al-Adhkiyâʾ*. Ed. Muhammad Mursî al-Khawlî. Cairo: Matâbiʿ al-Ahrâm al-Tijâriyya, 1969.

Ibn Mâja. *Sunan*. Ed. with commentary by Muhammad Fuʾâd ʿAbd al-Bâqî. 2 vols. Beirut: al-Maktaba al-ʿIlmiyya, n.d.

Ibn Shaddâd. *The Life of Saladin*. Trans. C. W. Wilson and Lt.-Col. Conder. London: Palestine Exploration Fund, 1897.

Ibn Sînâ. *Hayy ibn Yaqzân*. In *Hayy ibn Yaqzân*, ed. Ahmad Amîn. Cairo: Dâr al-Maʿârif, 1952.

Ibn Tufayl. *Hayy ibn Yaqzân*. In *Hayy ibn Yaqzân*, ed. Ahmad Amîn. Cairo: Dâr al-Maʿârif, 1952.

Idrîs, Yûsuf. "Al-ʿAmaliyya al-Kubrâ." In Yûsuf Idrîs, *al-Naddâha*, pp. 113-37. Cairo: Dâr Misr lil-Tibâʿa, n.d.

al-Intifâda bil-Kârîkâtîr. Tunis: al-Ahâlî lil-Tibâʿa wal-Nashr wal-Tawzîʿ, 1988.

"Islam's Satanic Comics." *Newsweek* (Feb. 5, 1990): 36.

al-Jâhiz. *Al-Bukhalâʾ*. Ed. Tâhâ al-Hâjirî. Cairo: Dâr al-Maʿârif, 1971.

_____ . *Kitâb al-Bursân wal-ʿUrjân wal-ʿUmyân wal-Hûlân*. Ed. ʿAbd al-Salâm Muhammad Hârûn. Baghdad: Dâr al-Rashîd lil-Nashr, 1982.

Keohane, Robert O., and Joseph S. Nye, Jr. *Transnational Relations and World Politics*. Cambridge: Harvard University Press, 1972.

Kepel, Gilles. *Les Banlieues de l'Islam: Naissance d'une religion en France*. Paris: Editions du Seuil, 1987.

Khadduri, Majid. *Socialist Iraq*. Washington, D.C.: Middle East Institute, 1978.

Khaled, Leila. *Mon peuple vivra*. Trans. Michel Pagnier. Paris: Gallimard, 1973.

al-Khalil, Samir. *The Monument: Art, Vulgarity, and Responsibility in Iraq*. Berkeley: University of California Press, 1991.

_____ . *Republic of Fear: The Politics of Modern Iraq*. Berkeley: University of California Press, 1989.

Krieger-Krynicki, Annie. *Les Musulmans en France*. Paris: Maisonneuve & Larose, 1985.

al-Labbâd, Muhyî al-Dîn. *Nazar*. Cairo: al-ʿArabî lil-Nashr wal-Tawzîʿ, 1987.

Lacouture, Jean. *Nasser*. Paris: Editions du Seuil, 1971.

Laroui, Abdallah. *The Crisis of the Arab Intellectual: Traditionalism or Historicism?* Trans. Diarmid Cammell. Berkeley: University of California Press, 1976.

Lassner, Jacob. *The Shaping of ʿAbbâsid Rule*. Princeton: Princeton University Press, 1980.

Lefebvre, Gustave. *Romans et contes égyptiens de l'Epoque Pharaonique*. Paris: Adrien-Maisonneuve, 1949.

Lewis, Bernard. *The Middle East and the West*. New York: Harper & Row, 1964.

_____ . *The Political Language of Islam*. Chicago: University of Chicago Press, 1988.

_____ . *Race and Slavery in the Middle East*. New York: Oxford University Press, 1990.

Lichteim, Miriam. *Ancient Egyptian Literature*. Vol. 1: *The Old and Middle Kingdoms*. Berkeley: University of California Press, 1975.

Mahdi, Muhsin. "Exemplary Tales in the *1001 Nights*." In *The 1001 Nights: Critical Essays and Annotated Bibliography*. Special issue of *Mundus Arabicus* 3 (1983): 1-24.

Mahfûz, Najîb. *Zuqâq al-Midaqq*. Beirut: Dâr al-Qalam, 1972.

Majallat al-Mukhtâr al-Islâmî. Cairo: Maktabat al-Mukhtâr al-Islâmî.

Malti-Douglas, Fedwa. Afterword to trans. of *War in the Land of Egypt* by Yusuf al-Qaʾid, pp. 185-192. London: al-Saqi Books, 1986.

_____ . *Blindness and Autobiography: al-Ayyâm of Tâhâ Husayn*. Princeton: Princeton University Press, 1985.

_____ . "Classical Arabic Crime Narratives: Thieves and Thievery in *Adab* Literature." *Journal of Arabic Literature* 19, no. 2 (1988): 121-27.

_____ . "Sign Conceptions in the Islamic World." In *Semiotics: A Handbook on the Sign-Theoretic Foundations of Nature and Culture*, ed. Roland Posner, Klaus Robering, and Thomas E. Sebeok. Berlin and New York: Walter de Gruyter (forthcoming).

_____ . "Structure and Organization in a Monographic *Adab* Work: *al-Tatfîl* of al-Khatîb al-Baghdâdî." *Journal of Near Eastern Studies* 40 (1981): 227-45.

_____ . *Structures of Avarice: The Bukhalâ' in Medieval Arabic Literature.* Leiden: E. J. Brill, 1985.

_____ . *Woman's Body, Woman's Word: Gender and Discourse in Arabo-Islamic Writing.* Princeton: Princeton University Press, 1991.

_____ . "Yûsuf al-Qaʿîd wal-Riwâya al-Jadîda." *Fusûl* 4, no. 3 (1984): 190-202.

Manvell, Roger, et al. *The International Encyclopedia of Film.* New York: Bonanza Books, 1975.

Marzolph, Ulrich. *Der Weise Narr Buhlûl.* Abhandlungen für die Kunde des Morgenlandes 46, no. 4. Wiesbaden: Franz Steiner, 1983.

Mentsch, Thierry. *L'Orient imaginaire: La Vision politique occidentale de l'Est méditerranéen.* Paris: Les Editions de Minuit, 1988.

Mernissi, Fatima. *Beyond the Veil: Male-Female Dynamics in a Modern Muslim Society.* New York: Schenkman, 1975.

Middle East Report, no. 159 (1989). Special issue, "Popular Culture."

Millet, Bertrand. "Egypte: Cent ans de bande dessinée." In *Langues et cultures populaires dans l'aire arabo-musulmane*, pp. 53-67. Paris: Association Française des Arabisants, 1988.

_____ . *Samir, Mickey, Sindbad et les autres: Histoire de la presse enfantine en Egypte.* Cairo: CEDEJ, 1987.

Millett, Kate. *Going to Iran.* New York: Coward, McCann & Geoghegan, 1982.

Monroe, James. *The Art of Badîʿ al-Zamân al-Hamadhânî as Picaresque Narrative.* Beirut: American University of Beirut, 1983.

Muʿalla, ʿAbd al-Amîr. *Al-Ayyâm al-Tawîla.* 3 vols. Baghdad: Dâr al-Hurriyya lil-Tibâʿa, 1978.

Muslim. *Sahîh Muslim bi-Sharh al-Nawawî.* 18 vols. in 9. Beirut: Dâr Ihyâ' al-Turâth al-ʿArabî, n.d.

Naremore, James, and Patrick Brantlinger, eds. *Modernity and Mass Culture.* Bloomington: Indiana University Press, 1991.

Nicholson, R. A. *A Literary History of the Arabs.* Cambridge: Cambridge University Press, 1969.

al-Nuways, ʿAbd Allâh. *Wasâ'il al-Iʿlâm fî Dawlat al-Imârât al-ʿArabiyya al-Muttahida.* Abu Dhabi: Shirkat Abû Zabî lil-Tibâʿa wal-Nashr, 1982[?].

Otto-Dorn, Katharina. *L'Art de l'Islam.* Trans. Jean-Pierre Simon. Paris: Editions Albin Michel, 1967.

Payne, Stanley. *Fascism: Comparison and Definition.* Madison: University of Wisconsin Press, 1980.

Péroncel-Hugoz, Jean-Pierre. "Le Coran en bandes dessinées." *Le Monde* (Jan. 7-8, 1990): 1, 9.

Pierre, Michel. *La Bande dessinée.* Paris: Librairie Larousse, 1976.

Pinault, David. *Story-Telling Techniques in the Arabian Nights.* Leiden: E. J. Brill, 1992.

Public Culture.

al-Qaʿîd, Yûsuf. *Al-Harb fî Barr Misr.* Beirut: Dâr Ibn Rushd lil-Tibâʿa wal-Nashr, 1978.

_____ . *Yahduth fî Misr al-An.* Cairo: Dâr Usâma lil-Tabʿ wal-Nashr, 1977.

al-Qur'ân. Cairo: Mustafâ al-Bâbî al-Halabî, 1966.

al-Qurtubî. *Al-Jâmiʿ li-Ahkâm al-Qur'ân.* 20 vols. in 10. Cairo: Dâr al-Kutub al-Misriyya, n.d.

Qutb, Sayyid. *Fî Zilâl al-Qur'ân.* 6 vols. Beirut: Dâr al-Shurûq, 1992.

_____ . *Maʿrikatunâ maʿa . . . al-Yahûd.* Cairo: Dâr al-Shurûq, 1988.

al-Râghib al-Isfahânî. *Muhâdarât al-Udabâ' wa-Muhâwarât al-Shuʿarâ' wal-Bulaghâ'.* 4 vols. in 2. Beirut: Dâr Maktabat al-Hayât, n.d.

al-Rajul al-Sâlih wal-Kalb. Cairo: Safîr–Iʿlâm, Diʿâya, Nashr, 1987.

Renard, Jean-Bruno. *Bandes dessinées et croyances du siècle.* Paris: Presses Universitaires de France, 1986.

Rey, Alain. *Les Spectres de la bande: Essai sur la B.D.* Paris: Les Editions de Minuit, 1978.

Ricoeur, Paul. *Hermeneutics and the Human Sciences.* Ed. and trans. John B. Thompson. Cambridge: Cambridge University Press, 1981.

Riffaterre, Michael. "Intertextual Scrambling." *Romanic Review* 68 (1977): 197-206.

Robinson, Jean C. "Institutionalizing Charisma." *Polity* 28, no. 2 (1985): 181-202.

Rosenthal, Franz. *Humor in Early Islam.* Leiden: E. J. Brill, 1956.

Saʿd, ʿAbd al-Munʿim. *Mûjaz Ta'rîkh al-Sînamâ al-Misriyya.* Cairo: Matâbiʿ al-Ahrâm al-Tijâriyya, 1976[?].

Saʿîd, Fathî. *Al-Fallâh al-Fasîh.* Cairo: al-Hayʾa al-Misriyya al-ʿAmma lil-Kitâb, 1982.

Sadoul, Georges. *Al-Sînamâ fî al-Buldân al-ʿArabiyya.* Beirut: Markaz al-Tansîq al-ʿArabî lil-Sînamâ wal-Tilifizyûn, n.d.

Sadoul, Numa. *Tintin et moi: Entretiens avec Hergé.* Tournai: Casterman, 1975.

Said, Edward. *Orientalism.* New York: Pantheon, 1978.

Saint-Prot, Charles. *Saddam Hussein.* Paris: Albin Michel, 1987.

al-Saʿûdî, Muhammad. *Zâd al-Musâfirîn ilâ Ghayr Bilâd al-Muslimîn.* Cairo and Riyad: Dâr al-Sahwa and Dâr al-Fitya, 1988.

Sawwaf, Muʾtaz. "La B.D. arabe." In *Histoire mondiale de la bande dessinée,* ed. Claude Moliterni, pp. 274-75. Paris: Pierre Horay, 1989.

al-Sayyid, Muhammad Mahrân. *Hikâya . . . min Wâdî al-Milh.* Cairo: Muʾassasat ʿInân lil-Tibâʿa, 1984.

Shaheen, Jack G. *The TV Arab.* Bowling Green: Bowling Green State University Popular Press, 1984.

Shâhîn, Yûsuf. *Al-ʿUsfûr* (1973).

Slyomovics, Susan. "Algeria Caricatures the Gulf War." *Public Culture* 4, no. 2 (1992): 93-96.

Souchet, Philippe, et al. *Le Message politique et social de la bande dessinée.* Toulouse: Privat, 1975.

Spellberg, Denise. "Marriages Made in Heaven and Illustrated on Earth: A Note on the Disjunction between Verbal and Visual Images in an Ottoman Manuscript." *Harvard University Bulletin of the Center for the Study of World Religions* 16 (1989-90): 126-27.

———. "Nizâm al-Mulk'sʾManipulation of Tradition: ʿAʾisha and the Role of Women in the Islamic Government." *Muslim World* 78 (1988): 111-17.

Stetkevych, Jaroslav. "Spaces of Delight: A Symbolic Topoanalysis of the Classical Arabic Nasîb." In *Critical Pilgrimages: Studies in the Arabic Literary Tradition,* ed. Fedwa Malti-Douglas. *Literature East and West* 25 (1989): 5-28.

———. *The Zephyrs of Najd: The Poetics of Nostalgia in the Classical Arabic Nasîb.* Chicago: University of Chicago Press, 1993.

Stetkevych, Suzanne. "The Suʿlûk and His Poem: A Paradigm of Passage Manqué." *Journal of the American Oriental Society* 104 (1984): 661-68.

Stauth, Georg, and Sami Zubaida, eds. *Mass Culture, Popular Culture, and Social Life in the Middle East.* Frankfurt am Main and Boulder: Campus Verlag and Westview Press, 1987.

al-Suhrawardî. *Hayy ibn Yaqzân.* In *Hayy ibn Yaqzân,* ed. Ahmad Amîn. Cairo: Dâr al-Maʿârif, 1952.

al-Suyûtî. *Al-Ashbâh wal-Nazâʾir fî Qawâʿid wa-Furûʿ Fiqh al-Shâfiʿiyya.* Cairo: ʿIsâ al-Bâbî al-Halabî, n.d.

Tâmir, Zakariyyâ, and Ahmad Hijâzî. *Al-Jarâd fî al-Madîna.* Beirut: Dâr al-Fatâ al-ʿArabî lil-Nashr wal-Tawzîʿ, 1975.

Tanindi, Zeren. *Siyer-I Nebî, Islâm Tasvir Sanatinda Hz. Muhammed'in Hayati.* 6 vols. Istanbul: Hürriyet Vakvi Yayinlari, 1984.

al-Thaʿlabî. *Qisas al-Anbiyâʾ—ʿArâʾis al-Majâlis.* Beirut: Dâr al-Qalam, n.d.

Tidrick, Kathryn. *Heart-Beguiling Araby.* Cambridge: Cambridge University Press, 1981.

al-Tirmidhî. *Al-Jâmiʿ al-Sahîh—Sunan al-Tirmidhî.* Ed. Ahmad Muhammad Shâkir, Muhammad Fuʾâd ʿAbd al-Bâqî, et al. 5 vols. Beirut: Dâr al-Kutub al-ʿIlmiyya, 1987.

al-Tirmidhî. *Sahîh al-Tirmidhî.* Cairo: al-Matbaʿa al-Misriyya bil-Azhar and Matbaʿat al-Sâwî, 1931-34.

Usâma ibn Munqidh. *Kitâb al-Iʿtibâr.* Ed. Philip K. Hitti. Beirut: al-Dâr al-Muttahida, 1981.

Usâma ibn Munqidh. *Memoirs of an Arab-Syrian Gentleman.* Trans. Philip K. Hitti. Beirut: Khayats, 1964.

Vercoutter, Jean. *L'Egypte ancienne.* Paris: Presses Universitaires de France, 1973.

White, Hayden. *Metahistory: The Historical Imagination in Nineteenth-Century Europe.* Baltimore: Johns Hopkins University Press, 1973.

Witek, Joseph. *Comic Books as History: The Narrative Art of Jack Jackson, Art Spiegelman, and Harvey Pekar.* Jackson: University Press of Mississippi, 1989.

Index

Allen Douglas is Associate Professor of History and Semiotics at Indiana University. His most recent book is *From Fascism to Libertarian Communism: Georges Valois against the Third Republic*.

Fedwa Malti-Douglas is Professor of Arabic, Women's Studies, and Semiotics and Chair of the Department of Near Eastern Languages and Cultures at Indiana University. Her most recent book is *Woman's Body, Woman's Word: Gender and Discourse in Arabo-Islamic Writing*.